CCH PREPARING FRS 105
ACCOUNTS FOR MICRO-ENTITIES

CCH PREPARING FRS 105 ACCOUNTS FOR MICRO-ENTITIES

James Lole FCA

© 2015 Wolters Kluwer (UK) Ltd

Wolters Kluwer (UK) Limited
145 London Road
Kingston upon Thames
KT2 6SR
Tel: 0844 561 8166
Fax: 0208 547 2638
E-mail: cch@wolterskluwer.co.uk
www.cch.co.uk

© Financial Reporting Council (FRC). Financial Reporting Council material is adapted and reproduced with the kind permission of the Financial Reporting Council. All rights reserved. For further information, please visit www.frc.org.uk or call +44 (0)20 7492 2300.

ISBN: 978-1-78540-216-6

British Library Cataloguing-in-Publication Data

A catalogue record for this book is available from the British Library.

Typeset by Innodata Inc., India.
Printed by Sowa Sp. z o.o. Warsaw, Poland, 2015

Contents

Contents

Chapter 1   Introduction

1.1   The micro-entities' regime

In November 2013, the UK Government passed regulations that introduced an optional simpler reporting regime for very small companies ('micro-entities') preparing Companies Act individual accounts. The regulations were part of Directive 2013/34/EU of the European Parliament and regulations exempted those eligible companies from certain financial reporting requirements.

In response to this and in accordance with the changes to the revision of financial reporting standards in the UK and Ireland, the Financial Reporting Council (FRC) developed FRS 105 *The Financial Reporting Standard applicable to the Micro-entities Regime* as an accounting standard intended for accounts of companies which qualify for the micro-entities' regime.

FRS 105 is effective for periods commencing on or after 1 January 2016, although earlier adoption is permitted. Prior to the issue of FRS 105, micro-entities were required to apply the *Financial Reporting Standards for Smaller Entities (effective January 2015)* (FRSSE 2015) which is now withdrawn from the effective date of FRS 105.

1.2   Key accounting differences

Chapter 8 summarises the accounting requirements of FRS 105, however, the key differences for micro-entities who are likely to be transitioning from the FRSSE 2015 are:

- no revaluations of tangible or intangible fixed assets or investment properties is permitted;
- development expenditure must be written off as incurred;
- borrowing costs must be written off as incurred;
- no requirement to account for equity settled share-based payments prior to the issue of the shares;
- grants received must be recognised on the performance basis;
- purchased goodwill is amortised over its useful life with a maximum, where that life cannot be determined, of ten years;
- a contracted rate/forward rate (if applicable) for a foreign currency transaction must be used to translate the transaction;
- derivative contracts are recognised at cost (which is often zero);
- simplified debt/equity distinction rules;
- investments in ordinary or preference shares are measured at cost less impairment with no option to recognise at fair value;
- no deferred tax is recognised;
- contributions for the year for defined benefit schemes should be recognised together with any liability for contributions to reduce a deficit set out in a schedule;
- no related party transaction disclosure is required;
- biological assets are measured at the lower of cost and estimated selling price less costs to complete and sell (i.e. NRV).

1.3   Note on scope of this book

Preparing FRS 105 Accounts for Micro-entities is concerned solely with the accounts of micro-entities as defined by the CA 2006 under the micro-entities' regime for financial years beginning on or after 1 January 2016. The subject matter will principally be of interest to those companies applying or looking to apply FRS 105 *The Financial Reporting Standard applicable to the Micro-entities Regime* which meet the definition of 'micro-entities'.

Although the legislation refers to micro 'entities', the scope of the regime is restricted (at the time of writing this book) exclusively to companies incorporated under the Companies Act (excluding charitable companies).

Those preparing accounts for earlier periods seeking to apply FRSSE 2015 should seek out *Preparing Company Accounts for FRSSE and Micros 2015*.

Statutory references are to the *Companies Act* 2006 (CA 2006) itself, as amended from time to time or to regulations made under the Act, unless otherwise indicated.

This is an ever changing landscape and changes to legislation and to accounting standards issued up to 31 July 2015 have been considered in the writing of *Preparing FRS 105 Accounts for Micro-entities*.

Chapter 2   Companies Act 2006

Basic approach

The *Companies Act* 2006 received Royal Assent on 8 November 2006. Running to 701 pages of primary legislation together with 59 pages of index and comprising 47 Parts, 1,300 sections and 16 Schedules, it was the longest Act ever. It consolidated virtually all existing companies legislation, introduced many reforms and company law was re-written and re-presented to make it easier to understand and more flexible – especially for smaller companies.

Working on the 'think small first' approach, company law is presented on a basis that clearly recognises each of the following categories of company or group (CA 2006, s. 380):

- small companies (including the micro-entities sub-category);
- larger private companies;
- public companies (other than quoted companies);
- quoted public companies;
- all companies.

Different provisions apply to different kinds of company; the main distinctions are between:

- companies subject to the 'small companies' regime' (CA 2006, s. 381) and companies that are not subject to that regime; and
- quoted companies (CA 2006, s. 385) and companies that are not quoted.

Provisions applying to companies subject to the small companies' regime appear in the legislation before the provisions applying to other companies (CA 2006, s. 380(4)).

The law, both within the Act itself and in supporting legislation issued in regulations under it, is clearly presented in its application. There are separate comprehensive codes of accounting and reporting requirements for small and larger companies, defining the generally accepted accounting practice relevant to them.

The small companies regime has been further divided with the changes made to CA 2006 by the *Small Companies (Micro-Entities' Accounts) Regulations* 2013 (SI 2013/3008). The introduction of the concept of the 'micro-entity' provides further options for the preparers of the accounts of the smallest companies.

The small companies' regime (which includes micro-entities as a subset of small companies) applies for a financial year in relation to which the company:

- qualifies as small (CA 2006, s. 382–383); and
- is not excluded from the regime (CA 2006, s. 384).

Implementation

Provisions of CA 2006 were introduced by statutory instrument by means of 'commencement orders' and other supporting regulations in the months leading up to October 2009, the date by which all parts of the Act came into force.

The accounts and report provisions of the Act relate to financial years *commencing on or after 6 April 2008.*

The micro-entities regime contained in the *Small Companies (Micro-Entities' Accounts) Regulations 2013* (SI 2013/3008) may be applied for financial years which ended on or after 30 September 2013.

Small companies' and micro-entities' accounts regimes

The Act presents the 'small companies' regime' within:

- Pt. 15 (s. 380–474) – 'Accounts and reports'; and
- Pt. 16 (s. 475–539) – 'Audit' (where relevant for the smaller company).

Preparing small company accounts is governed by reference to:

- CA 2006, Pt. 15 (relevant sections) (the 'primary legislation'); and
- regulations made under statutory instruments for small companies ('secondary legislation'), covering the form and content of accounts and directors' report – the *Small Companies and Groups (Accounts and Directors' Report) Regulations* 2008 (SI 2008/409).

All of the above are as amended by other legislation, such as the *Small Companies (Micro-Entities' Accounts) Regulations 2013* (SI 2013/3008) and the *Companies, Partnerships and Groups (Accounts and Reports) Regulations* 2015 (SI 2015/980).

SI 2008/409

The *Small Companies and Groups (Accounts and Directors' Report) Regulations* 2008 (SI 2008/409) (hereinafter referred to as 'the Small Companies Regulations') specify the form and content of the accounts and directors' report of companies subject to the small companies regime under CA 2006, Pt. 15.

The full text of SI 2008/409 is contained in **Appendix B**.

Chapter 6 covers the form and content of the accounts of micro-entities.

Chapter 3   General accounting provisions

3.1   Introduction

This chapter summarises the accounting provisions of the CA 2006 which relate to: the prescriptive formats of accounts; the content of accounts; and the principles and rules for determining amounts to be included in the accounts.

Annual accounts may be prepared:

- as 'Companies Act individual accounts' (CA 2006, s. 396) or 'Companies Act group accounts' (CA 2006, s. 404); or
- in accordance with international accounting standards ('IAS individual accounts' or 'IAS group accounts') (CA 2006, s. 395(1)).

This book is concerned only with the accounts of micro-entities prepared in accordance with that regime under the Companies Act and therefore this chapter summarises and comments upon the accounts provisions of the CA 2006 insofar as they relate to Companies Act individual accounts, that is, prepared in accordance with the requirements of the CA 2006.

3.2   Accounts

Accounts must be prepared for members for all companies, irrespective of size (except some dormant companies).

Chapter 6 provides more detailed guidance on the company accounts provisions of the CA 2006 as they affect the accounts of companies under the micro-entities' regime. **Chapters 7** to **9** consider the additional impact on the accounts of micro-entities of FRS 105.

A small company applying the micro-entity exemptions are required to file only the balance sheet, together with the information disclosed at the foot of the balance sheet, with Companies House. More information on filing of accounts is covered in **Chapter 10**.

Depending on certain criteria, small companies may be exempt from the requirement for audit although they may voluntarily choose an audit. Notwithstanding this, as discussed later at **3.3**, it is unlikely that micro-entities would neither choose to have an audit nor would any auditor prepared to undertake one given the lack of disclosures given in a set of micro-entity accounts.

Company accounts are produced from the company's underlying financial records ('adequate accounting records') as explained at **3.5** (CA 2006, s. 386–389 'Accounting Records').

Table 3.1 summarises the requirements which directors must follow in respect of a company's 'individual accounts' which are set out in CA 2006, s. 396.

> **Table 3.1   Individual accounts (CA 2006, s. 396)**
>
> For each financial year, the directors must prepare individual accounts comprising:
>
> * a balance sheet; and
> * a profit and loss account;
>
> showing a true and fair view of:
>
> * the state of affairs at the year end; and
> * the profit or loss for the financial year;
>
> complying with:
>
> * the provisions of the *Small Companies and Groups (Accounts and Directors' Report) Regulations* 2008 (SI 2008/409) (as to form, content and notes);
>
> containing:
>
> * any additional information (or departure from requirement) necessary to show a true and fair view. In the case of the accounts of a micro-entity, the micro-entity minimum accounting items (see **3.3.2**) included in the company's accounts for the year are presumed to give the true and fair view.

3.3   True and fair view

The concept

The concept of a true and fair view lies at the heart of financial reporting in the UK. This requirement was recently reconfirmed by the FRC in its June 2014 document 'True and Fair'; the true and fair requirement remains of fundamental importance in both UK GAAP and IFRS.

The directors of a company must not approve accounts unless they are satisfied that they give a true and fair view of the company's assets, liabilities, financial position and profit or loss.

The requirement for full accounts to show a 'true and fair' view applies irrespective of whether or not the accounts are subject to audit. Any decision concerning the method of accounting or means of disclosing information must take this basic requirement into account.

The basic accounting principle is that annual accounts should show a 'true and fair' view, a term that has never been defined in statute or case law.

In essence, accounts are deemed to present a 'true and fair view' if they:

* comply with any relevant legislation or regulatory requirements;
* comply with accounting standards and generally recognised practice (GAAP);
* provide an unbiased (fair and reasonable) presentation;
* are compiled with sufficient accuracy within the bounds of materiality; and
* faithfully represent the underlying commercial activity (the concept of 'substance over legal form').

The Statement of Principles for Financial Reporting issued by the ASB in 1999 states that 'it is inherent in the nature of the true and fair view concept that financial statements will not give a true and fair view unless the information they contain is sufficient in quantity and quality to satisfy the reasonable expectations of the readers to whom they are addressed'.

Companies that prepare Companies Act accounts in accordance with UK accounting standards are subject to the overriding requirement of CA 2006 (and regulations made under it) that accounts give a 'true and fair view', which, in all but highly exceptional cases, requires compliance with UK accounting standards.

UK tax legislation requires that the profits of a trade, profession or vocation be computed in accordance with generally accepted accounting practice on an accounting basis which gives a true and fair view, subject to any adjustment required by tax law in computing those profits.

In 2008, in the absence of statutory definition, the FRC commissioned legal opinion to confirm the continued relevance of the 'true and fair' concept to the preparation and audit of financial statements following the enactment of the CA 2006 and the introduction of IFRS. This legal opinion endorsed the analysis of previous opinions and confirmed the centrality of the 'true and fair view' concept in UK financial reporting. It also confirmed that 'fair presentation' under IFRS is equivalent to a true and fair view.

Accounts are required to give a 'true and fair view' of the state of affairs of the company (and consolidated undertakings (if applicable)) as at the end of the financial year and of the profit or loss of the company (and consolidated undertakings (if applicable) so far as concerns members of the parent company) for the financial year.

Where compliance with the provisions of CA 2006 as to the matters to be included in 'annual accounts' ('individual accounts' or 'group accounts') or the notes would not be sufficient to give a true and fair view, the necessary additional information must be given in the accounts or in a note to them.

Micro-entities deemed true and fair view

With the changes made to CA 2006 by the *Small Companies (Micro-Entities' Accounts) Regulations 2013 (SI 2013/3008)*, the accounts of a micro-entity prepared in compliance with these regulations are **presumed** or **deemed** to give a true and fair view. This is also stated in section 3 of FRS 105.

With the introduction of a significantly reduced disclosure framework for micro-entities, the usual considerations of whether sufficient information is presented in a set of accounts must be ignored, hence the need for the regulations to state that micro-entity accounts are deemed to show a true and fair view.

Audited accounts

The impact of this means that any micro-entity considering a voluntary audit of its accounts is unlikely to find an auditor prepared to take the assignment. An audit of accounts must be carried out by a statutory auditor in accordance with International Standards on Auditing (UK and Ireland) ('ISAs'). Those ISAs prescribe that an auditor shall not undertake any audit assignment unless the accounts are intended to show a true and fair view in accordance with the accounting framework under which they are prepared. It is considered that the 'presumed' true and fair view under the micro-entities framework, coupled with the fact that micro-entities accounts are not required to present any additional information in order to meet the true and fair concept, means that auditors should not accept the assignment as a fundamental precondition for audit has not been met.

Given that the micro-entities regime is designed to reduce the bureaucratic burden on very small companies, it is unlikely any such company would voluntarily choose to have their accounts audited. If there are other reasons why an audit is required (for example, to show to prospective lenders) the directors should prepare accounts in accordance with the regime applicable to small companies or alternatively the full 'UK GAAP' under FRS 102.

3.4 Accounting principles

Company accounts are required to be prepared in accordance with the principles set out in SI 2008/409, Sch. 1. These principles are the fundamental accounting concepts that underlie accounts and are also incorporated within accounting standards generally and (for micro-entities) FRS 105.

The basic statutory accounting principles in SI 2008/409 are as follows.

- Going concern – the company or reporting entity is presumed to be carrying on business as a going concern.
- Consistency – accounting policies must be applied consistently within the same accounts and from one financial year to the next.
- Prudence – the amount of any item must be determined on a prudent basis and in particular:
  - only profits realised at the balance sheet date must be included in the profit and loss account; and
  - all liabilities having arisen in respect of the financial year (or preceding financial years) must be taken into account (including those liabilities becoming apparent up to the date of approval of the accounts (in accordance with CA 2006, s. 414)).
- Accruals – all income and charges relating to the financial year to which the accounts relate must be taken into account, without regard to the date of receipt or payment.
- Individual determination – in determining the aggregate amount of any item, the amount of each individual asset or liability that is taken into account must be determined separately.
- Netting – amounts in respect of items representing assets or income must not be set off against amounts in respect of items representing liabilities or expenditure (as the case may be), or vice versa.
- Substance of transactions – in determining how amounts are presented within the accounts, regard should be had to the substance of the reported transaction or arrangement in accordance with GAAP.

3.5 Adequate accounting records

Companies are required to keep 'adequate accounting records' in accordance with CA 2006, s. 386. Company accounts are produced from these underlying financial records.

Adequate accounting records are those which are sufficient to show and explain the company's transactions. The accounting records must:

- disclose with reasonable accuracy, at any time, the financial position of the company at that time;
- enable the directors to ensure that any accounts required to be prepared comply with the requirements of CA 2006;
- contain entries from day to day of all receipts and expenditure (with sufficient identifying detail); and
- contain a record of company assets and liabilities.

If the company deals in goods, the accounting records must also contain statements of:

- stock held at the year end;
- stocktaking (records and procedures) underlying the year end stock; and
- all goods sold and purchased (except for retail sales), in sufficient detail to identify the goods and the buyers and sellers.

A parent company must ensure that any subsidiary undertaking keeps such accounting records as ensure compliance with CA 2006.

Directors should be constantly aware of the company's financial position and progress. The exact nature and extent of the accounting systems and management information needed to exercise adequate control will depend on the nature, complexity and extent of the company's business. Adequate control over records and transactions involves monitoring:

- cash;
- debtors and creditors;
- stock and work in progress;

- capital expenditure;
- contractual arrangements; and
- plans and budgets.

Accounting records of private companies are required by CA 2006, s. 388(4) to be preserved for three years from the date on which they are made; although, having regard to other legislation, it is generally considered that documents should be kept for at least six years (and 12 years in the event of contracts under seal).

3.6 Approval and signature of the accounts

The statutory accounts require appropriate approval and signature. A company's annual accounts must be approved by the board of directors and signed on behalf of the board by a director of the company. The signature must be on the company's individual balance sheet and the name of the signatory must be stated.

The balance sheet of a small company (including micro-entities) which have been prepared in accordance with the provisions applicable to companies subject to the small companies regime must contain a statement by the directors to that effect in a prominent position above the signature (see **6.8**).

Chapter 4   Financial Reporting Framework in the UK and Republic of Ireland

4.1   Introduction

From late 2012, the Financial Reporting Council (FRC) issued a suite of standards that replaced existing UK accounting standards. This was the culmination of ten years' work and consultation on how to bring UK GAAP up to date and in line with international standards whilst maintaining consistency with UK law.

4.2   The new financial reporting standards

The FRC has issued the following financial reporting standards:

- FRS 100 – *Application of financial reporting requirements;*
- FRS 101 – *Reduced disclosure framework;*
- FRS 102 – *The financial reporting standard applicable in the UK and Republic of Ireland;*
- FRS 103 – *Insurance contracts;*
- FRS 104 – *Interim financial statements;* and
- FRS 105 – *The financial reporting standard applicable to the micro-entities regime.*

These standards replace all extant Statements of Standard Accounting Practice (SSAPs), Financial Reporting Standards (FRSs) and Urgent Issues Task Force Abstracts (UITFs) with effect from accounting periods commencing 1 January 2015 with the exception of section 1A of FRS 102 and FRS 105 which apply for periods commencing on or after 1 January 2016.

The Financial Reporting Standard for Smaller Entities (FRSSE 2015) remained in existence for small companies for periods commencing in 2015.

4.3   Application of financial reporting requirements (FRS 100)

FRS 100 sets out the financial reporting requirements for UK and Republic of Ireland entities preparing accounts that are intended to give a true and fair view of the assets, liabilities, financial position and profit or loss for a period.

The standard requires entities prepare their accounts, depending on eligibility, in accordance with either EU-adopted IFRS, FRS 101, 102 or 105.

- EU-adopted IFRS is applied when required by law or regulation, e.g. in consolidated accounts of fully listed or AIM companies. It is optional for other entities.
- FRS 101 sets out a reduced disclosure framework for individual accounts of qualifying entities that apply EU-adopted IFRS for recognition and measurement.
- FRS 102 replaces the current suite of standards which comprise UK GAAP. It includes a reduced disclosure requirements for small companies and other disclosure exemptions for qualifying group entities.
- FRS 105 may be applied by eligible micro entities.

4.4   Statement of compliance

Companies are required to include a statement of compliance in the notes to the accounts specifying whether they are applying FRS 101, FRS 102, FRS 102 with reduced disclosures, FRS 102 section 1A or the FRS 105. Companies applying EU-adopted IFRS are required by IAS 1 to make an equivalent statement of compliance.

4.5   Consistency with company law

CA 2006, s. 395 requires that companies prepare either 'Companies Act accounts' or 'IAS accounts'. Accounts prepared in accordance with FRS 101, FRS 102, FRS 102 with reduced disclosures FRS 102 section 1A or the FRS 105 are 'Companies Act accounts'. Only those accounts prepared under EU-adopted IFRS (with full disclosures) are 'IAS accounts'. Charitable companies are prohibited by company law from applying EU-adopted IFRS and must prepare 'Companies Act accounts'.

4.6   Effective date and transitional arrangements

FRS 100 is applicable to accounting periods commencing on or after 1 January 2015. Early adoption is available subject to provisions set out in FRS 101, 102 and the 105. A company applying the standard early is required to state that fact.

On first application of FRS 100 a company shall apply the following transitional arrangements if transitioning to:

- EU-adopted IFRS – the requirements of IFRS 1;
- FRS 101 unless the company previously applied EU-adopted IFRS – IFRS 1, para. 6–33;
- FRS 101 where the company previously applied EU-adopted IFRS – the company does not reapply;
- IFRS 1 but considers whether adjustments are necessary to comply with FRS 101.5(b);
- FRS 102 – the transitional arrangements set out in FRS 102 section 35.
- FRS 105 – the transitional arrangements set out in FRS 105 section 28.

Companies eligible to apply FRS 101 are likely to apply that standard early, particularly if they currently already prepare their accounts under EU-adopted IFRS and would benefit from the exemption from certain disclosures.

FRS 102 and 105 are likely to be early adopted by recently incorporated companies about to prepare accounts for their first period to avoid the needless conversion from 'old' UK GAAP to 'new' UK GAAP after one or two accounting periods.

Chapter 5   Eligibility

In order to qualify as a micro-entity, the following three factors must be considered:

- whether the entity is excluded from the micro-entities' regime;
- whether group considerations exclude the entity; and
- whether the size criteria are satisfied

The micro-entities' regime is not mandatory but is a choice for those that qualify.

5.1   Excluded entities

An entity that does not fall under the *Companies Act* 2006 is not eligible to be treated as a micro-entity. In particular, limited liability partnerships and charitable companies are not eligible. In addition, other entities are excluded, see **Table 5.1**.

Table 5.1   Entities excluded from the micro-entities' regime

An entity is excluded if, at any time during the financial period to which the accounts relate it was:

- a company excluded from the small companies' regime (see **Table 5.2**);
- an investment undertaking;
- a financial holding undertaking;
- a credit institution;
- an insurance undertaking;
- a charity;
- a qualifying partnership;
- a limited liability partnership;
- an overseas company;
- an unregistered company;
- a company authorised to register pursuant to CA 2006, s. 1040;
- a company voluntarily preparing group accounts (or whose accounts are included in consolidated group accounts prepared by another company).

Table 5.2   Companies excluded from the small companies' regime

A company is excluded from the small companies' regime if it was at any time during the financial period to which the accounts relate:

- a public limited company (plc);
- an authorised insurance company;
- a banking company;
- an e-money issuer;
- a Markets in Financial Instruments Directive (MiFID) investment firm;
- a UCITS management company;
- a company that carries on an insurance market activity*;
- a member of an ineligible group**.

A group is ineligible if any of its members is:

- a traded company***;
- a body corporate (other than a company) whose shares are admitted to trading on a regulated market in an EEA state;
- a person (other than a small company) who has permission under the *Financial Services and Markets Act* 2000, Pt. 4 to carry on a regulated activity;
- a small company that is an authorised insurance company, a banking company, an e-money issuer, a MiFID investment firm or a UCITS management company; or
- a person who carries on insurance market activity*.

*As defined by the *Financial Services and Markets Act* 2000, s. 316(3), 'insurance market activity' means a regulated activity relating to contracts of insurance written at Lloyd's.
** A group is defined in CA 2006, s. 474 as 'a parent undertaking and its subsidiary undertakings', as defined in CA 2006, s. 1162. A company is generally a subsidiary if more than 50% of its voting shares are held by another (parent) company.
*** A 'traded company' is defined in CA 2006, s. 474 as a company any of whose transferable securities are admitted trading on a regulated market.

5.2 Group considerations

A parent company which is not ineligible can qualify as a micro-entity for the purpose of its individual accounts if:

- it qualifies as a micro-entity;
- the group headed by it is small; and
- it does not prepare group accounts.

As noted above, a subsidiary company (whether it is itself a parent or not) cannot qualify as a micro-entity if its accounts are included in consolidated accounts. This means that the company is included in group accounts by way of full consolidation (i.e. not proportional).

5.3 Size criteria

Micro-entities are a sub-category of small companies and therefore to be considered as a micro-entity the company must first satisfy the small company criteria (and in the case of a parent the small group criteria). The relevant size criteria are shown in **Table 5.3**.

Table 5.3 Group and company size criteria under CA 2006			
A company must not exceed more than one of the following			
	Small Group	Small Company	Micro-entity
Turnover	£10.2m (net) or £12.2m (gross)	£10.2m	£632,000
Balance sheet total	£5.1m (net) or £6.1m (gross)	£5.1m	£316,000
Monthly average number of employees	50	50	10

Turnover figures should be proportionately adjusted where the financial 'year' is not 12 months.

'Balance sheet total' means the aggregate of the amounts shown as assets in the company's balance sheet (i.e. gross assets before deduction of liabilities, accruals and provisions).

The average number of employees is determined by establishing the number of persons employed under contracts of employment by the company each month and calculating an average. This is not a measurement of 'full-time equivalent' employees.

As a general rule, for a company to qualify as micro or small, the criteria must be met for the current (Y1) and previous year (Y0). If the criteria are not met for the following year (Y2), a company may still continue to be treated as micro or small, as appropriate, for that following year (Y2) if it met the criteria and qualified as micro or small in the previous year (Y1). However, if the criteria are not met in the year after that (Y3), then the company must file accounts according to its size for Y3. Growing companies can therefore continue to be treated as micro or small in the first year that they fail to meet the qualifying criteria.

If the company is in its first year and if the criteria are met for that first year, the company will qualify as micro or small in that first year.

When considering the size of a group, the alternative bases for turnover and balance sheet totals are:

- 'net' – aggregate figures for turnover and balance sheet totals after any set-offs and consolidation adjustments made for the elimination of group transactions; and
- 'gross' – aggregate figures for turnover and balance sheet totals without such set-offs and consolidation adjustments.

The aggregate figures are ascertained by aggregating the relevant figures from individual statutory accounts (determined in accordance with CA 2006, s. 382) for each member of the group.

CA 2006 under SI 2008/409, Sch. 6 consolidation adjustments include:

- elimination of intra-group transactions and assets and liabilities;
- elimination of intra-group unrealised profits or losses; and
- adjustments to effect uniform accounting policies within the group.

It is important to note that the 'net' and 'gross' bases may be mixed in determining whether the criteria have been met. For example, if a group has a turnover of £12.5m (gross) and £9.8m (net), a balance sheet total of £5.8m (gross) and £5.5m (net) and 60 employees, on the size criteria the group would qualify as a small group. Although it exceeds the employee number threshold, it does not exceed the net turnover threshold or gross balance sheet threshold.

Chapter 6   Contents of micro-entity accounts

6.1   Introduction

This chapter summarises the micro-entities accounts provisions of the CA 2006 as they affect companies under the 'micro-entities regime'.

The *Small Companies (Micro-Entities' Accounts) Regulations* 2013 (SI 2013/3008) modified Pt. 15 and 16 of the CA 2006 and the *Small Companies and Groups (Accounts and Directors' Report) Regulations* 2008 (SI 2008/409) for financial years ended on or after 30 September 2013. The *Companies, Partnerships and Groups (Accounts and Reports) Regulations* 2015 (SI 2015/980) made further modifications with effect for financial years commencing on or after 1 January 2016.

6.2   Accounts – provisions for micro-entities

The accounts of a company qualifying as a 'micro-entity' (see **Chapter 5**) have significantly reduced statutory disclosure requirements compared even to 'small' companies.

A micro-entity also has reduced requirements with respect to filing with the Registrar of Companies.

A micro-entity wishing to file these reduced accounts with the Registrar of Companies has to produce two sets of accounts: the annual accounts for members and the reduced accounts for filing.

Company accounts prepared in accordance with the micro-entities regime are referred to as 'micro-entity accounts' in this book. These always refer to the individual accounts of the entity; note that entities preparing group accounts cannot apply the micro-entities regime to their individual financial statements. See **Chapter 5** for more details.

A micro-entity does not have to take advantage of all the exemptions and modifications permitted if it does not wish to do so.

Consideration must be given to other users of the financial statements (such as banks) before an entity opts to prepare accounts under this regime. As the disclosure requirements are minimal, these users may require additional information to be prepared.

6.3   Format of micro-entity accounts

The form and content of individual accounts prepared by micro-entities are determined in accordance with regulations provided by the newly updated the *Small Companies and Groups (Accounts and Directors' Report) Regulations* 2008 (SI 2008/409).

The statutory formats

The accounts formats from which a micro-entity may choose are given in SI 2008/409, Sch. 1 (Pt. 1, Section C). There is a choice of two balance sheet formats and there are no choices with respect to profit and loss account format.

Balance sheet

In its annual accounts, a micro-entity must adopt one of the formats of balance sheet set out in SI 2008/409, Sch. 1 (Pt. 1, Section C). The formats are also illustrated in **Table 6.1**.

Profit and loss account

The profit and loss account format for a micro-entity is set out in SI 2008/409, Sch. 1 (Pt. 1, Section C). The format is also illustrated in **Table 6.2**.

Accounting principles

The general accounting principles of the small company regulations must be applied by micro-entities unless they are specifically amended by the micro-entities regulations. See **7.9** for details of differences.

Accounting principles are explained further in **3.4** (**Chapter 3**).

Micro-entity accounts, properly prepared, are deemed by law to give a true and fair view however it is unlikely they can be audited.

6.4 Micro-entity balance sheet

The formats of balance sheet from which a micro-entity must choose for its annual accounts are reproduced in **Table 6.1**.

Table 6.1 *Micro-entity balance sheets*	
Format 1	**Format 2**
A. Called up share capital not paid	ASSETS
B. Fixed assets	A. Called up share capital not paid
C. Current assets	B. Fixed assets
D. Prepayments and accrued income	C. Current assets
E. Creditors: amounts falling due within one year	D. Prepayments and accrued income
F. Net current assets (liabilities)	LIABILITIES
G. Total assets less current liabilities	A. Capital and reserves
H. Creditors: amounts falling due after more than one year	B. Provisions for liabilities
I. Provisions for liabilities	C. Creditors (aggregate amounts falling due within and after more than one year must be shown separately)
J. Accruals and deferred income	D. Accruals and deferred income
K. Capital and reserves	

Format 2 requires balance sheet totals of ASSETS and LIABILITIES to be given.

6.5 Micro-entity profit and loss account

The format of the profit and loss account which a micro-entity must prepare is reproduced in **Table 6.2**.

Table 6.2   *Micro-entity profit and loss account format*

A.   Turnover

B.   Other income

C.   Cost of raw materials and consumables

D.   Staff costs

E.   Depreciation and other amounts written off assets

F.   Other charges

G.   Tax

H.   Profit or loss

Note that the above headings cannot be changed.

6.6   Footnotes to the balance sheet – micro-entities

No notes to the accounts are required under the micro-entities regime; however there are two additional items that must appear at the foot of the balance sheet. These are disclosures relating to the following:

Directors' benefits – advances, credit and guarantees

CA 2006, s. 413 provides for the disclosure of advances and credits granted by a company to its directors, and guarantees of any kind entered into by a company on behalf of its directors.

Guarantees and other financial commitments

Particulars of charges on assets, contingent liabilities, capital commitments not provided for, pension commitments and other financial commitments.

6.7   Directors' reports of a micro-entity

The changes to the regulations made in 2015 exempt micro-entities from the requirement to prepare a directors' report and strategic report.

This exemption is automatic and there is no requirement to make any statement about the exemption.

6.8   Directors' statements

A company which qualifies as a micro-entity in relation to a financial year (other than a dormant company) and takes advantage of the provisions applicable to companies subject to the micro-entities regime with respect to the preparation of annual accounts must include statements in its accounts, on the balance sheet, confirming preparation in accordance with the micro-entities regime.

For small (unquoted) companies, every copy of any balance sheet and directors' report that is published by or on behalf of the company must state the name of the person who signed it on behalf of the board.

Directors' statement – micro-entity accounts preparation: s. 414

A company's annual accounts must be approved by the board of directors and signed on behalf of the board by a director of the company. The signature must be on the company's balance sheet.

If the accounts are prepared in accordance with the provisions applicable to companies subject to the micro-entities regime, the balance sheet must contain (in a 'prominent position' above the signature of a director required by s. 414(1–2)) a statement that the accounts have been prepared in accordance with the provisions applicable to companies subject to the micro-entities regime within CA 2006, Pt. 15. Reference to FRS 105 should also be made in this statement.

Example 6.1   Section 414 Directors' statement – balance sheet

These accounts have been prepared in accordance with the provisions applicable to companies subject to the micro-entities regime as set out within the *Companies Act* 2006, Pt. 15 and with FRS 105 the *Financial Reporting Standard applicable to the Micro-entities Regime*.

Chapter 7   Essentials of FRS 105

7.1   Contents of FRS 105

This chapter provides the essential elements and requirements of FRS 105 by summarising its main contents and making cross-references to the standard itself. The full text of FRS 105 is at **Appendix A**. Throughout this chapter references are made to the sections of FRS 105 unless otherwise specified.

FRS 105 is effective for periods commencing on or after 1 January 2016 although earlier adoption is permitted.

FRS 105 is based on FRS 102, however its accounting requirements are modified to satisfy the legal requirements applicable to micro-entities and to reflect the simpler nature of such entities. As a result, there are no accounting policy choices available in FRS 105.

The application of the micro-entities regime is optional however a company that chooses to apply the regime is required to apply FRS 105.

The standard is set out in sections as shown in **Table 7.1**.

Table 7.1   Contents of FRS 105
Section
Summary
1   Scope
2   Concepts and Pervasive Principles
3   Financial Statement Presentation
4   Statement of Financial Position
5   Income Statement
6   Notes to the Financial Statements
Appendix: Company law disclosure requirements
7   Subsidiaries, Associates, Jointly Controlled Entities and Intermediate Payment Arrangements
8   Accounting Policies, Estimates and Errors
9   Financial Instruments
10   Inventories
11   Investments in Joint Ventures
12   Property, Plant and Equipment and Investment Property
13   Intangible Assets other than Goodwill
14   Business Combinations and Goodwill
15   Leases
16   Provisions and Contingencies
Appendix: Examples of recognising and measuring provisions
17   Liabilities and Equity
18   Revenue

7.2   Scope, concepts and pervasive principles (sections 1 and 2)

FRS 105 applies to the accounts of micro-entities.

The accounts prepared in accordance with the standard that include the micro-entity minimum accounting items are presumed in law to show a true and fair view. See **3.3.2** for more details of the impact of this.

The FRS permits a micro-entity to include additional information in its financial statements. If additional information is included it should be done with regard to the requirement of section 1A of FRS 102.

Section 2 sets out the fundamental concepts and basic principles that underlie the recognition and measurement of transactions of micro-entities within the scope of FRS 105.

These concepts define the financial position (assets, liabilities and equity) and performance (income, expenses and profit or loss) and are no different to the concepts used across the UK GAAP framework.

7.3   Financial statement presentation (sections 3–6)

Sections 3–6 set out what makes up a set of micro-entity accounts. The standard has been written in the context of the micro-entities regime of CA 2006 as explained in **Chapter 6** and is therefore consistent.

A set of accounts shall contain:

- a statement of financial position (balance sheet) at the reporting date with notes included at the foot of the statement; and
- an income statement (profit and loss account) for the reporting period.

Comparative figures are required for both primary statements.

The formats to be used for the balance sheet and profit and loss account are explained at **6.4** and **6.5**.

The notes to be included are explained at **6.6** and the details of the company law requirements are included in FRS 102 in the appendix to section 6 (see **Appendix A**).

A micro-entity is not required to show any additional information but is permitted to do so.

7.4 Subsidiaries, associates, jointly-controlled entities and intermediate payment arrangements (section 7)

Subsidiaries, associates and jointly controlled entities

A micro-entity that is a parent is excluded from adopting FRS 105 (and the micro-entities regime) if it chooses to present consolidated financial statements. Therefore any investment in subsidiaries, associates and jointly-controlled entities are accounted for as financial instruments in accordance with section 9.

Intermediate payment arrangements

Intermediate payment arrangements may take a variety of forms.

- The intermediary is usually established by the micro-entity and constituted as a trust, although other arrangements are possible.
- The relationship between the micro-entity and the intermediary may take different forms. For example, when the intermediary is constituted as a trust, the micro-entity will not have a legal right to direct the intermediary's activities however, in these and other cases the micro-entity may give advice to the intermediary or may be relied on by the intermediary to provide the information it needs to carry out its activities. Sometimes, the way the intermediary has been set up gives it little discretion in the broad nature of its activities.
- The arrangements are most commonly used to pay employees or used to compensate suppliers of goods and services other than employee services. Sometimes, the micro-entity's employees and other suppliers are not the only beneficiaries of the arrangement. Other beneficiaries may include past employees and their dependants, and the intermediary may be entitled to make charitable donations.
- The precise identity of the persons or entities that will receive payments from the intermediary, and the amounts that they will receive, are not usually agreed at the outset.
- The micro-entity often has the right to appoint or veto the appointment of the intermediary's trustees (or its directors or the equivalent).
- The payments made to the intermediary and the payments made by the intermediary are often cash payments but may involve other transfers of value.

Examples of intermediate payment arrangements are employee share ownership plans (ESOPs) and employee benefit trusts that are used to facilitate employee shareholdings under remuneration schemes.

Although the trustees of an intermediary must act at all times in accordance with the interests of the beneficiaries of the intermediary, most intermediaries (particularly those established as a means of remunerating employees) are specifically designed so as to serve the purposes of the micro-entity, and to ensure that there will be minimal risk of any conflict arising between the duties of the trustees of the intermediary and the interest of the micro-entity, such that there is nothing to encumber implementation of the wishes of the micro-entity in practice. Where this is the case, the micro-entity has *de facto* control.

Accounting for intermediate payment arrangements

When a micro-entity makes payments (or transfers assets) to an intermediary, there is a rebuttable presumption that the entity has exchanged one asset for another and that the payment itself does not represent an immediate expense. To rebut this presumption at the time the payment is made to the intermediary, the micro-entity must demonstrate:

*   it will not obtain future economic benefit from the amounts transferred; or
*   it does not have control of the right or other access to the future economic benefit it is expected to receive.

Where a payment to an intermediary is an exchange by the micro-entity of one asset for another, any assets that the intermediary acquires in a subsequent exchange transaction will also be under the control of the micro-entity. Accordingly, assets and liabilities of the intermediary shall be accounted for by the micro-entity as an extension of its own business and recognised in its financial statements. An asset will cease to be recognised as an asset of the micro-entity when, for example, the asset of the intermediary vests unconditionally with identified beneficiaries.

A micro-entity may distribute its own equity instruments, or other equity instruments, to an intermediary in order to facilitate employee shareholdings under a remuneration scheme. Where this is the case and the micro-entity has control, or de facto control, of the assets and liabilities of the intermediary, the commercial effect is that the micro-entity is, for all practical purposes, in the same position as if it had purchased the shares directly.

Where an intermediary holds the micro-entity's equity instruments, the micro-entity shall account for the equity instruments as if it had purchased them directly. The micro-entity shall account for the assets and liabilities of the intermediary in its financial statements as follows.

*   The consideration paid for the equity instruments of the sponsoring entity shall be deducted from equity until such time that the equity instruments vest unconditionally with employees.
*   Other assets and liabilities of the intermediary shall be recognised as assets and liabilities of the micro-entity.
*   No gain or loss shall be recognised in profit or loss on the purchase, sale, issue or cancellation of the micro-entity's own equity instruments.
*   Finance costs and any administration expenses shall be recognised on an accruals basis rather than as funding payments are made to the intermediary.
*   Any dividend income arising on the micro-entity's own equity instruments shall be excluded from profit or loss and deducted from the aggregate of dividends paid.

7.5   Accounting policies, estimates and errors (section 8)

This section explains the overall procedure for selecting and applying accounting policies and how to deal with estimates and errors.

Accounting policies

FRS 105 is prescriptive in the accounting policies to be applied by a micro-entity. There are no policy choices as is the case in some areas when accounts are prepared in accordance with FRS 102 for instance. This approach makes the accounting simpler for very small companies. Section 8 does, however, state that where FRS 105 is specific the entity shall apply the policy, however it need not follow the policy if the effect is not material.

Where FRS 105 does not address a transaction, condition or other event, management should use its judgment to develop and apply an appropriate policy that is a faithful representation, reflects the economic substance, is neutral and free from bias and is prudent. In making this judgment, management should refer to the definitions, recognition criteria and measurement concepts in section 2. No additional information is required to be given in the accounts explaining the policy in such situations.

Changes in accounting policies and estimates and correction of errors

FRS 105 follows the generally accepted principles adopted in FRS 102 and IFRS namely:

- changes in accounting policy shall only be made if required by the FRS or result in the accounts being more reliable and relevant;
- changes in accounting policy shall be made retrospectively by way of a prior period adjustment as far as is practicable (or in accordance with transitional provisions if applicable);
- changes in accounting estimates shall be made prospectively in the accounts of the year in which the change is determined; and
- correction of prior period errors, if material, shall be adjusted retrospectively by way of a prior period adjustment.

Note that the FRSSE previously required a prior period adjustment in respect of fundamental errors rather than material ones.

Chapter 8   Accounting requirements of FRS 105

This chapter summarises the recognition and measurement requirements of FRS 105 as set out in sections 9–27. The full text of the sections of the standard are in **Appendix A**.

Throughout this chapter references are made to the sections of FRS 105 unless otherwise specified.

No note disclosures are required in micro-entity accounts other than the specific requirements noted at **6.6**.

8.1   Financial instruments (section 9)

Scope

All financial instruments are covered by this section unless specifically excluded on the basis they are subject to a separate section of the standard. The section therefore covers instruments such as:

- cash;
- accounts receivable and payable (trade debtors and creditors);
- commercial paper and commercial bills held;
- demand and fixed-term deposits with banks or similar institutions;
- bonds, loans and similar instruments;
- investments;
- derivatives, such as options, warrants, futures contracts, forward contracts and interest rate swaps.

The section does not apply to:

- financial instruments that meet the definition of a micro-entity's own equity, and the equity component of compound financial instruments issued by the reporting micro-entity that contain both a liability and an equity component (see section 17);
- leases, to which section 15 applies. However, the de-recognition requirements and impairment accounting requirements in section 9 apply to de-recognition and impairment of receivables recognised by a lessor and the de-recognition requirements in section 9 apply to payables recognised by a lessee arising under a finance lease;
- employers' rights and obligations under employee benefit plans, to which section 23 applies;
- financial instruments, contracts and obligations to which section 21 applies;
- reimbursement assets and financial guarantee contracts accounted for in accordance with section 16;
- contracts for contingent consideration in a business combination (see section 14). This exemption applies only to the acquirer.

Initial recognition

A financial asset or financial liability is initially measured at cost.

Cost will usually be the transaction price for loans, invoice value for trade debtors or creditors or the consideration given in the case of an investment or purchase of an option.

Transaction costs shall be added or subtracted from the cost of a financial asset or liability unless not material, in which case they are recognised as an expense.

When a micro-entity purchases inventory, property, plant and equipment or investment property or sells goods or services with settlement deferred beyond normal credit terms, the transaction price will be the cash price available on the date of the transaction.

Subsequent measurement

Trade investments in ordinary or preference shares and investments in subsidiaries, associates and jointly-controlled entities shall be measured at cost less impairment.

The transaction price of a derivative (plus transaction costs if applicable) less any impairment losses recognised to date shall be allocated to profit and loss over the term of the contract on a straight line basis (or other more appropriate systematic method). Any contractual payments or receipts under a derivative contract shall be recognised in profit and loss as they accrue.

All other financial instruments shall be measured at amortised cost as follows:

* transaction price plus or minus transaction costs as appropriate;
* **plus** the cumulative interest income or expense to date;
* **less** repayments of principal or interest;
* **less** in the case of a financial asset, any impairment provision.

Total interest income or expense is the difference between the transaction price and the aggregate receipts or payments (excluding transaction costs) and is allocated to profit and loss as follows:

* for transactions where settlement is deferred beyond normal credit terms, on a straight line basis;
* in all other cases at a constant rate on the asset's or liability's carrying amount (excluding transaction costs). This will usually be the contracted rate.

Transaction costs not immediately recognised in profit and loss shall be allocated on a straight line basis over the life of the contract.

Impairment

At the end of each reporting period, an assessment is made whether there is evidence that any financial asset is impaired. If so, an impairment loss is measured as follows:

* a trade investment in ordinary or preference shares or investment in a subsidiary, associate or jointly-controlled entity is impaired if the carrying amount exceeds the best estimate of the assets selling price at the reporting date;
* a derivative asset is impaired if the carrying amount exceeds the assets fair value less costs to sell;
* all other financial assets are impaired if the carrying amount exceeds the expected net cash flows that can be generated from the asset. If discounting is material the cash flows shall be measured at their present value (the discount rate shall be the contractual interest rate).

Impairment losses may be reversed if the impairment decreases and the change is due to an event that occurred after the original impairment was recognised.

Onerous derivative contracts

At the end of each reporting period, an assessment is made whether a derivative constitutes an onerous contract. This occurs when the unavoidable payments exceed the economic benefits expected to be received. A derivative which does not mitigate a specific risk or risks is onerous when the expected payments exceed the expected cash receipts.

For example, a company has a variable rate loan and mitigates the risk of fluctuating exchange rates by taking out a variable to fixed rate swap. During the life of the loan, interest rates are falling and the fixed payments are higher than the variable receipts however the derivative is not onerous as the company is still receiving the benefits of risk mitigation. If, on the other hand, the company repays the loan but is not able to terminate the swap, if payments exceed the receipts the contract is onerous as there are no other benefits received.

De-recognition

The principles of de-recognition are unchanged from those in the FRSSE.

Offsetting

A financial asset and liability shall be offset only when a micro-entity:

* currently has a legally enforceable right of set off; and
* intends to settle on a net basis or to realise the asset and settle the liability simultaneously.

8.2 Inventories (section 10)

Scope

This section applies to all inventories, except:

* work in progress arising under construction contracts, including directly related service contracts (see section 18 Revenue); and
* biological assets related to agricultural activity and agricultural produce at the point of harvest (see section 27 Specialised Activities).

Measurement

Inventories are measured at the lower of cost and estimated selling price less costs to complete and sell.

8.3 Investments in joint ventures (section 11)

Scope

This section applies to investment in joint ventures that are jointly controlled operations or jointly controlled assets and **not** joint ventures that are jointly controlled entities (refer to section 9).

Joint ventures defined

Joint control is the contractually agreed sharing of control over an economic activity, and exists only when the strategic financial and operating decisions relating to the activity require the unanimous consent of the parties sharing control (the venturers).

A joint venture is a contractual arrangement whereby two or more parties undertake an economic activity that is subject to joint control. Joint ventures can take the form of jointly controlled operations, jointly controlled assets, or jointly controlled entities.

Jointly controlled operations

The operation of some joint ventures involves the use of the assets and other resources of the venturers rather than the establishment of a corporation, partnership or other entity, or a financial structure that is separate from the venturers themselves. Each venturer uses its own property, plant and equipment and carries its own inventories. It also incurs its own expenses and liabilities and raises its own finance, which represent its own obligations. The joint venture activities may be carried out by the venturer's employees alongside the venturer's similar activities. The joint venture agreement usually provides a means by which the revenue from the sale of the joint product and any expenses incurred in common are shared among the venturers.

In respect of its interests in jointly controlled operations, a venturer shall recognise in its financial statements:

- the assets that it controls and the liabilities that it incurs; and
- the expenses that it incurs and its share of the income that it earns from the sale of goods or services by the joint venture.

Jointly controlled assets

Some joint ventures involve the joint control, and often the joint ownership, by the venturers of one or more assets contributed to, or acquired for the purpose of, the joint venture and dedicated to the purposes of the joint venture.

In respect of its interest in a jointly controlled asset, a venturer shall recognise in its financial statements:

- its share of the jointly controlled assets, classified in accordance with the format adopted set out in section 4 Statement of Financial Position;
- any liabilities that it has incurred;
- its share of any liabilities incurred jointly with the other venturers in relation to the joint venture;
- any income from the sale or use of its share of the output of the joint venture, together with its share of any expenses incurred by the joint venture; and
- any expenses that it has incurred in respect of its interest in the joint venture.

8.4   Property, plant and equipment and investment property (section 12)

Scope

This section applies to the accounting for property, plant and equipment and investment property but excludes biological assets related to agricultural activity (see section 27).

Recognition and de-recognition

The cost of an item of property, plant and equipment or investment property shall be recognised as an asset if, and only if:

- it is probable that future economic benefits associated with the item will flow to the micro-entity; and
- the cost of the item can be measured reliably.

An item of property, plant and equipment or investment property is derecognised:

- on disposal; or
- when no future economic benefits are expected from its use or disposal.

Spare parts and servicing equipment are usually carried as inventory. However, major spare parts and stand-by equipment are property, plant and equipment when they are used during more than one period. Similarly, if the spare parts and servicing equipment can be used only in connection with an item of property, plant and equipment, they are considered property, plant and equipment.

Land and buildings are separable assets, and a micro-entity shall account for them separately, even when they are acquired together.

Measurement at initial recognition

An item of property, plant and equipment or investment property is measured at initial recognition at its cost. The FRS contains details of the costs which may or may not be included.

The income and related expenses of incidental operations during construction or development of an item of property, plant and equipment or investment property are recognised in profit or loss if those operations are not necessary to bring the item to its intended location and operating condition.

Measurement after initial recognition

All items of property, plant and equipment and investment property shall be measured after initial recognition at cost less any accumulated depreciation and any accumulated impairment losses. A micro-entity shall recognise the costs of day-to-day servicing of an item of property, plant and equipment or investment property in profit or loss in the period in which the costs are incurred.

No revaluation of property plant and equipment or investment property is permitted

Depreciation

Assets shall be depreciated over their useful lives as a single asset.

Land generally has an unlimited useful life and therefore is not usually depreciated.

The depreciation charge for each period shall be recognised in profit or loss unless another section of the FRS requires the cost to be recognised as part of the cost of an asset. For example, the depreciation of manufacturing property, plant and equipment is included in the costs of inventories (see section 10).

Depreciable amount and depreciation period

The depreciable amount of an asset shall be allocated on a systematic basis over its useful life. Useful life shall be determined considering the following factors:

- the expected usage of the asset;
- expected physical wear and tear;

- technical or commercial obsolescence arising from changes or improvements in production, or from a change in the market demand for the product or service output of the asset;
- legal or similar limits on the use of the asset, such as the expiry dates of related leases.

Factors may indicate that the residual value or useful life of an asset has changed since the most recent annual reporting date. If such indicators are present, the entity shall review its previous estimates and, if current expectations differ, amend the residual value, depreciation method or useful life. The micro-entity shall account for the change in residual value, depreciation method or useful life prospectively as a change in an accounting estimate.

Depreciation of an asset begins when it is available for use, i.e. when it is in the location and condition necessary for it to be capable of operating in the manner intended by management. Depreciation of an asset ceases when the asset is derecognised.

Depreciation does not cease when the asset becomes idle or is retired from active use unless the asset is fully depreciated. However, under usage methods of depreciation the depreciation charge can be zero while there is no production.

Impairment

At each reporting date, a micro-entity shall apply section 22 to determine whether an item or group of items of property, plant and equipment or investment property is impaired. That section explains when and how a micro-entity reviews the carrying amount of its assets, how it determines the recoverable amount of an asset, and when it recognises or reverses an impairment loss.

An entity shall include in profit or loss, compensation from third parties for items of property, plant and equipment or investment property that were impaired, lost or given up only when the compensation is virtually certain.

A plan to dispose of an asset before the previously expected date is an indicator of impairment that triggers the calculation of the asset's recoverable amount for the purpose of determining whether the asset is impaired.

8.5   Intangible assets other than goodwill (section 13)

Scope

This section applies to the accounting for all separately acquired intangible assets and internally generated intangible assets, other than intangible assets held for sale in the ordinary course of business (Inventories). For the accounting of intangible assets acquired as part of a business combination including goodwill, see section 14.

Recognition and derecognition

All separately acquired intangible assets shall be recognised.

An internally generated intangible shall not be recognised as an asset and shall be recognised as an expense immediately in profit or loss. The following is a non-exhaustive list included in the FRS of such internal activities which shall be recognised as an expense:

- expenditure on research and development activities;
- internally generated brands, logos, publishing titles, customer lists and items similar in substance;
- start-up activities (i.e. start-up costs), which include establishment costs such as legal and secretarial costs incurred in establishing a legal entity, expenditure to open a new facility or

business (i.e. pre-opening costs) and expenditure for starting new operations or launching new products or processes (i.e. pre-operating costs);
- training activities;
- advertising and promotional activities;
- relocating or reorganising part or all of a micro-entity;
- internally generated goodwill.

A separately acquired intangible asset shall be derecognised:

- on disposal; or
- when no future economic benefits are expected from its use or disposal.

Initial measurement

Intangible assets shall be measured initially at cost. The FRS contains details of the costs which may or may not be included.

Measurement after initial recognition

A separately acquired intangible asset shall be measured after initial recognition at cost less any accumulated amortisation and any accumulated impairment losses.

Amortisation over useful life

Intangible assets shall be considered to have a finite useful life. The useful life of an intangible asset that arises from contractual or other legal rights shall not exceed the period of the contractual or other legal rights, but may be shorter depending on the period over which the entity expects to use the asset.

If, in exceptional cases, a micro-entity is unable to make a reliable estimate of the useful life of an intangible asset, the life shall not exceed ten years.

Amortisation period and amortisation method

The depreciable amount of an intangible asset shall be allocated on a systematic basis over its useful life. The amortisation charge for each period shall be recognised in profit or loss, unless another section of the FRS requires the cost to be recognised as part of the cost of an asset. For example, the amortisation of an intangible asset may be included in the costs of inventories or property, plant and equipment.

Amortisation begins when the intangible asset is available for use, i.e. when it is in the location and condition necessary for it to be usable in the manner intended by management. Amortisation ceases when the asset is derecognised. The entity shall choose an amortisation method that reflects the pattern in which it expects to consume the asset's future economic benefits. If the entity cannot determine that pattern reliably, it shall use the straight-line method.

Residual value

A micro-entity shall assume that the residual value of an intangible asset is zero unless:

- there is a commitment by a third party to purchase the asset at the end of its useful life; or
- there is an active market for the asset and:
    - residual value can be determined by reference to that market; and
    - it is probable that such a market will exist at the end of the asset's useful life.

Impairment

To determine whether a separately acquired intangible asset is impaired, refer to section 22. That section explains when and how a micro-entity reviews the carrying amount of its assets, how it determines the recoverable amount of an asset, and when it recognises or reverses an impairment loss.

8.6 Business combinations and goodwill (section 14)

Trade and asset acquisitions

Where a business combination occurs by the acquisition of the trade and assets of another business, a micro-entity shall apply the provisions of section 19 of FRS 102, with the following **exceptions**:

- a micro-entity shall not separately identify and recognise intangible assets;
- a micro-entity shall not recognise a deferred tax asset or liability;
- a micro-entity shall not recognise and measure a share-based payment transaction in accordance with section 28 of FRS 102, but instead apply section 23 of FRS 105; and
- a micro-entity is not required to provide any of the disclosures.

Goodwill arising on a trade and asset acquisition

Where a micro-entity has recognised goodwill acquired in a trade and asset acquisition (in accordance with paragraph 19.22 of FRS 102), the micro-entity shall measure that goodwill at cost less accumulated amortisation and accumulated impairment losses.

- A micro-entity shall follow the principles in section 13 of FRS 105 (see **8.5** above) for amortisation of goodwill. Goodwill shall be considered to have a finite useful life, and shall be amortised on a systematic basis over its life. If, in exceptional cases, a micro-entity is unable to make a reliable estimate of the useful life of goodwill, the life shall not exceed ten years.
- A micro-entity shall follow section 22 of FRS 105 for recognising and measuring the impairment of goodwill.

8.7 Leases (section 15)

Scope

This section covers all leases other than licensing agreements for such items as motion picture films, video recordings, plays, manuscripts, patents and copyrights which are accounted for as intangible assets.

This section applies to agreements that transfer the right to use assets even though substantial services by the lessor may be called for in connection with the operation or maintenance of such assets. This section does not apply to agreements that are contracts for services that do not transfer the right to use assets from one contracting party to the other.

Some arrangements do not take the legal form of a lease but convey rights to use assets in return for payments. Examples of such arrangements may include outsourcing arrangements, telecommunication contracts that provide rights to capacity and take-or-pay contracts.

Determining whether an arrangement is, or contains, a lease shall be based on the substance of the arrangement.

Classification of leases

A lease is classified as a finance lease if it transfers substantially all the risks and rewards incidental to ownership. A lease is classified as an operating lease if it does not transfer substantially all the risks and rewards incidental to ownership.

The approach to classification does not differ substantially from that which applies under SSAP21 or the FRSSE.

Recognition and measurement – lessees

At the commencement of the lease term, a lessee shall recognise its rights of use and obligations under **finance leases** as assets and liabilities in its statement of financial position at amounts equal to the fair value of the leased asset or, if lower, the present value of the minimum lease payments, determined at the inception of the lease.

Any initial direct costs of the lessee (incremental costs that are directly attributable to negotiating and arranging a lease) are added to the amount recognised as an asset.

The present value of the minimum lease payments shall be calculated using the interest rate implicit in the lease. If this cannot be determined, the lessee's incremental borrowing rate shall be used.

A lessee shall apportion minimum lease payments between the finance charge and the reduction of the outstanding liability. The lessee shall allocate the finance charge to each period during the lease term so as to produce a constant periodic rate of interest on the remaining balance of the liability. A lessee shall charge contingent rents as expenses in the periods in which they are incurred.

A lessee shall recognise lease payments under **operating leases** (excluding costs for services such as insurance and maintenance) as an expense over the lease term on a straight-line basis unless another systematic basis is representative of the time pattern of the user's benefit, even if the payments are not on that basis.

Lease incentives

A lessee shall recognise the aggregate benefit of lease incentives as a reduction to the expense recognised over the lease term, on a straight-line basis unless another systematic basis is representative of the time pattern of the lessee's benefit from the use of the leased asset.

Recognition and measurement – lessors

A lessor shall recognise assets held under a **finance lease** in its statement of financial position and present them as a receivable at an amount equal to the net investment in the lease. The net investment in a lease is the lessor's gross investment in the lease discounted at the interest rate implicit in the lease. The gross investment in the lease is the aggregate of:

• the minimum lease payments receivable by the lessor under a finance lease; and
• any unguaranteed residual value accruing to the lessor.

The recognition of finance income shall be based on a pattern reflecting a constant periodic rate of return on the lessor's net investment in the finance lease. Lease payments relating to the period, excluding costs for services, are applied against the gross investment in the lease to reduce both the principal and the unearned finance income. If there is an indication that the estimated unguaranteed residual value used in computing the lessor's gross investment in the lease has changed significantly, the income allocation over the lease term is revised, and any reduction in respect of amounts accrued is recognised immediately in profit or loss.

The FRS includes additional requirements in the case of manufacturer or dealer lessors which are not covered in this book.

A lessor shall recognise lease income from **operating leases** (excluding amounts for services such as insurance and maintenance) in profit or loss on a straight-line basis over the lease term unless another systematic basis is representative of the time pattern of the lessee's benefit from the leased asset, even if the receipt of payments is not on that basis.

Lease incentives

A lessor shall recognise the aggregate cost of lease incentives as a reduction to the income recognised over the lease term on a straight-line basis, unless another systematic basis is representative of the time pattern over which the lessor's benefit from the leased asset is diminished.

Sale and leaseback arrangements

If a sale and leaseback transaction results in a finance lease, the seller-lessee shall not recognise immediately, as income, any excess of sales proceeds over the carrying amount. Instead, the seller-lessee shall defer such excess and amortise it over the lease term.

If a sale and leaseback transaction results in an operating lease, and it is clear that the transaction is established at fair value, the seller-lessee shall recognise any profit or loss immediately. If the sale price is below fair value, the seller-lessee shall recognise any profit or loss immediately unless the loss is compensated for by future lease payments at below market price. In that case the seller-lessee shall defer and amortise such loss in proportion to the lease payments over the period for which the asset is expected to be used. If the sale price is above fair value, the seller-lessee shall defer the excess over fair value and amortise it over the period for which the asset is expected to be used.

8.8   Provisions and contingencies (section 16)

Scope

This section applies to all provisions, contingent liabilities and contingent assets except those provisions covered by other sections of the FRS. Where those other sections contain no specific requirements to deal with contracts that have become onerous, this section applies to those contracts

This section does not apply to financial instruments that are within the scope of section 9 unless the contracts are onerous contracts or financial guarantee contracts.

The requirements in this section do not apply to executory contracts unless they are onerous contracts. Executory contracts are contracts under which neither party has performed any of its obligations or both parties have partially performed their obligations to an equal extent.

The FRS makes it clear that the word 'provision' is sometimes used in the context of such items as depreciation, impairment of assets, and uncollectible receivables however those are adjustments of the carrying amounts of assets, rather than recognition of liabilities, and therefore are not covered by this section.

Recognition and measurement

The principles and methods of recognising and accounting for provisions, onerous contracts, contingent liabilities and contingent assets are consistent with the requirements of FRS 12 and the FRSSE and are not covered in detail here.

The FRS includes as an appendix to section 16 examples of recognising and measuring provisions in connection with:

- future operating losses;
- onerous contracts;
- warranties;
- refunds policy;
- closure of a division: no implementation before the end of reporting period;
- closure of a division: communication and implementation before end of reporting period;
- staff retraining as a result of changes in the income tax system;
- a court case.

8.9 Liabilities and equity (section 17)

Scope

This section establishes principles for classifying financial instruments as either liabilities or equity and deals with the accounting for compound financial instruments, such as convertible debt. It also addresses the issue of equity instruments, distributions to individuals or other parties acting in their capacity as investors in equity instruments (i.e. in their capacity as owners) and the accounting for purchases of own equity.

The section shall be applied to all types of financial instruments except:

- investments in subsidiaries and associates and interests in jointly controlled entities that are accounted for in accordance with section 9;
- employers' rights and obligations under employee benefit plans to which section 23 applies;
- financial instruments, contracts and obligations under share-based payment transactions to which section 21 applies (except for treasury shares issued, purchased, sold, transferred or cancelled in connection with employee share option plans, employee share purchase plans, and all other share-based payment arrangements);
- financial guarantee contracts (section 16).

Classification

Equity is the residual interest in the assets of a micro-entity after deducting all its liabilities. Equity includes investments by the owners of the micro-entity, plus additions to those investments earned through profitable operations and retained for use in the micro-entity's operations, minus reductions to owners' investments as a result of unprofitable operations and distributions to owners.

A financial instrument is a **financial liability** of the issuer where the issuer does not have an unconditional right to avoid settling an obligation in cash or by delivery of another financial asset. However a financial instrument is classified as equity where the issuer can be required to settle an obligation in cash or by delivery of another financial asset only in the event of the liquidation of the issuer.

Measurement

A micro-entity shall recognise the issue of shares or other equity instruments as equity when it issues those instruments and another party is obliged to provide cash or other resources to the micro-entity in exchange for the instruments.

A micro-entity shall measure the equity instruments at the fair value of the cash or other resources received or receivable, net of direct costs of issuing the equity instruments.

A micro-entity shall account for the transaction costs of an equity transaction as a deduction from equity, net of any related income tax benefit.

Convertible debt or similar compound instruments

The proceeds of the issue of convertible debt, or a similar compound financial instrument, shall be allocated between the liability component and the equity component of the instrument as follows:

- determine the amount of the liability component as the fair value of a similar liability that does not have a conversion feature or similar associated equity component;
- allocate the residual amount as the equity component;
- transaction costs shall be allocated between the debt component and the equity component on the basis of their relative fair values.

The allocation shall not be revised in subsequent periods.

The liability component shall be accounted for as a financial instrument in accordance with section 9. An example is shown in the appendix to section 22 of FRS 102 illustrating the accounting for convertible debt by an issuer.

Treasury shares

Treasury shares are the equity instruments of a micro-entity that have been issued and subsequently reacquired by the micro-entity. A micro-entity shall deduct from equity the fair value of the consideration given for the treasury shares. The micro-entity shall not recognise a gain or loss in profit or loss on the purchase, sale, transfer or cancellation of treasury shares.

Distributions to owners

A micro-entity shall reduce its equity reserves for the amount of distributions to its owners (holders of its equity instruments).

8.10 Revenue (section 18)

Scope

This section is applied in accounting for revenue arising from:

- the sale of goods (whether produced for the purpose of sale or purchased for resale);
- the rendering of services;
- construction contracts in which the micro-entity is the contractor; and
- the use by others of micro-entity assets yielding interest, royalties or dividends.

Revenue or other income arising from lease agreements is dealt with in section 15.

Measurement

Revenue shall be measured at the amount receivable, taking into account any trade discounts, prompt settlement discounts and volume rebates allowed.

Revenue includes only the gross inflows of economic benefits received and receivable by the micro-entity on its own account.

A micro-entity shall exclude from revenue all amounts collected on behalf of third parties such as sales taxes, goods and services taxes and value added taxes.

In an agency relationship, a micro-entity (the agent) shall include in revenue only the amount of its commission. The amounts collected on behalf of the principal are not revenue of the micro-entity.

Deferred payment

If payment is deferred beyond normal credit terms, the amount of revenue recognised is equal to the cash price available on the transaction date. Any excess of the deferred payment amount over the cash price available on the transaction date is recognised as interest and accounted for on a straight line basis over the period of the credit terms.

Exchanges of goods or services

A micro-entity shall not recognise revenue:

- when goods or services are exchanged for goods or services that are of a similar nature and value; or
- when goods or services are exchanged for dissimilar goods or services but the transaction lacks commercial substance.

A micro-entity shall recognise revenue when goods are sold or services are exchanged for dissimilar goods or services in a transaction that has commercial substance. In that case, the micro-entity shall measure the transaction:

- at the fair value of the goods or services received, adjusted by the amount of any cash transferred;
- if the amount cannot be measured reliably, then at the fair value of the goods or services given up adjusted by the amount of any cash transferred; or
- if the fair value of neither the goods or services received nor the goods or services given up can be measured reliably, then at the carrying amount of the goods or services given up adjusted by the amount of any cash transferred.

Identification of the revenue transaction

A micro-entity shall apply the recognition criteria to the separately identifiable components of a transaction when necessary to reflect the substance of the transaction.

The recognition criteria shall be applied to two or more transactions together when they are linked in such a way that the commercial effect cannot be understood without reference to the series of transactions as a whole.

Recognition

Sales of goods: revenue from the sale of goods is recognised when all the following conditions are satisfied:

- the micro-entity has transferred to the buyer the significant risks and rewards of ownership of the goods;
- the micro-entity retains neither continuing managerial involvement to the degree usually associated with ownership nor effective control over the goods sold;
- the amount of revenue can be measured reliably;
- it is probable that the economic benefits associated with the transaction will flow to the micro-entity; and
- the costs incurred or to be incurred in respect of the transaction can be measured reliably.

Rendering of services: When the outcome of a transaction involving the rendering of services can be estimated reliably, a micro-entity shall recognise revenue associated with the transaction by reference to the stage of completion of the transaction at the end of the reporting period (sometimes referred to as the percentage of completion method). The outcome of a transaction can be estimated reliably when all the following conditions are satisfied:

- the amount of revenue can be measured reliably;
- it is probable that the economic benefits associated with the transaction will flow to the micro-entity;
- the stage of completion of the transaction at the end of the reporting period can be measured reliably; and
- the costs incurred for the transaction and the costs to complete the transaction can be measured reliably.

When services are performed by an indeterminate number of acts over a specified period of time, a micro-entity recognises revenue on a straight-line basis over the specified period unless there is evidence that some other method better represents the stage of completion. When a specific act is much more significant than any other act, the micro-entity postpones recognition of revenue until the significant act is executed.

When the outcome of the transaction involving the rendering of services cannot be estimated reliably, a micro-entity shall recognise revenue only to the extent of the expenses recognised that are recoverable.

Construction contracts: When the outcome of a construction contract can be estimated reliably, a micro-entity shall recognise contract revenue and contract costs associated with the construction contract as revenue and expenses respectively by reference to the stage of completion of the contract activity at the end of the reporting period (often referred to as the percentage of completion method). Reliable estimation of the outcome requires reliable estimates of the stage of completion, future costs and collectability of billings.

The requirements of this section are usually applied separately to each construction contract. However, in some circumstances, it is necessary to apply this section to the separately identifiable components of a single contract or to a group of contracts together in order to reflect the substance of a contract or a group of contracts.

The FRS provides further guidance on the application of the percentage of completion method referred to above.

Interest, royalties and dividends: A micro-entity shall recognise revenue arising from the use by others of micro-entity assets yielding interest, royalties and dividends as follows:

- interest income shall be recognised in accordance with section 9;
- royalties shall be recognised on an accrual basis in accordance with the substance of the relevant agreement; and
- dividends shall be recognised when the shareholder's right to receive payment is established;

when it is probable that the economic benefits associated with the transaction will flow to the micro-entity; and the amount of the revenue can be measured reliably.

An appendix to section 18 provides a number of examples as guidance in applying the requirements of the FRS in recognising income.

8.11 Borrowing costs (section 20)

Borrowing costs shall be recognised as an expense in profit and loss in the period in which they are incurred.

Borrowing costs include:

- interest expense recognised in accordance with section 9;
- finance charges in respect of finance leases recognised in accordance with section 15; and
- exchange differences arising from foreign currency borrowings to the extent that they are regarded as an adjustment to interest costs.

8.12 Share-based payment (section 21)

Scope

This section specifies the accounting for all share-based payment transactions including:

- equity-settled share-based payment transactions;
- cash-settled share-based payment transactions; and
- transactions in which the micro-entity receives or acquires goods or services and the terms of the arrangement provide either the micro-entity or the supplier of those goods or services with a choice of whether the micro-entity settles the transaction in cash (or other assets) or by issuing equity instruments.

Recognition

Equity settled share-based payments shall not be accounted for until shares are issued at which point the requirements of section 17 are applied.

The goods or services received in a cash settled share-based payment transaction shall be recognised (in accordance with the measurement requirements for a provision in section 16) when the entity obtains the goods or as the services are received and at the same time recognise a corresponding liability.

If the cash-settled share-based payments granted to employees vest immediately, on grant date the micro-entity shall recognise the services received in full, with a corresponding liability.

If the cash-settled share-based payments do not vest until the employee completes a specified period of service, the micro-entity shall presume that the services to be rendered by the employee as consideration for those cash-settled share-based payments will be received in the future, during the vesting period. The micro-entity shall account for those services as they are rendered by the employee during the vesting period, with a corresponding increase in the liability.

When the goods or services received or acquired in a cash-settled share-based payment transaction do not qualify for recognition as assets, the micro-entity shall recognise them as expenses.

Share-based payment transactions with cash alternatives

Some share-based payment transactions give either the entity or the counterparty a choice of settling the transaction in cash (or other assets) or by the transfer of equity instruments.

When the entity has a choice of settlement of the transaction, the entity shall account for the whole transaction as equity settled unless:

- the choice of settlement in equity instruments has no commercial substance (e.g. because the micro-entity is legally prohibited from issuing shares); or
- the micro-entity has a past practice or a stated policy of settling in cash, or generally settles in cash whenever the counterparty asks for cash settlement,

in such cases the entity shall account for the transaction as a wholly cash-settled transaction.

When the counterparty has a choice of settlement of the transaction, the entity shall account for the transaction as a wholly cash-settled share-based payment transaction unless the choice of settlement in cash (or other assets) has no commercial substance because the cash settlement amount (or value of the other assets) bears no relationship to, and is likely to be lower in value than, the fair value of the equity instruments. In such circumstances the entity shall account for the whole transaction as equity settled.

8.13   Impairment of assets (section 22)

Scope and objective

An impairment loss occurs when the carrying amount of an asset exceeds its recoverable amount. This section shall be applied in accounting for the impairment of all assets (including goodwill), other than the following, for which other sections of the FRS provide guidance:

- assets arising from construction contracts (see section 18);
- financial assets within the scope of section 9; and
- inventories (see section 10).

General principles

If, and only if, the recoverable amount of an asset is less than its carrying amount, the micro-entity shall reduce the carrying amount of the asset to its recoverable amount.

If it is not possible to estimate the recoverable amount of the individual asset, a micro-entity shall estimate the recoverable amount of the cash-generating unit to which the asset belongs. This may be the case because measuring the recoverable amount requires forecasting cash flows, and sometimes individual assets do not generate cash flows by themselves. An impairment loss for a cash-generating unit shall be recognised and measured in accordance with the relevant requirements of section 27 of FRS 102.

A micro-entity that has goodwill acquired in a business combination shall apply the additional impairment requirements applicable to goodwill in section 27 of FRS 102.

An impairment loss shall be recognised immediately in profit or loss.

Indicators of impairment

A micro-entity shall assess at each reporting date whether there is any indication that an asset may be impaired. If any such indication exists, the micro-entity shall then estimate the recoverable amount of the asset. If there is no indication of impairment, it is not necessary to estimate the recoverable amount.

In assessing whether there is any indication that an asset may be impaired, the following indications shall be considered as a minimum.

- Declining asset market value significantly more than would be expected as a result of the passage of time or normal use.
- Significant changes with an adverse effect on the micro-entity have taken place during the period, or in the near future, in the technological, market, economic or legal environment in which the micro-entity operates or in the market to which an asset is dedicated.
- Market interest rates or other market rates of return on investments have increased during the period, and those increases are likely to affect materially the discount rate used in calculating an asset's value in use and decrease the asset's fair value less costs to sell.
- The carrying amount of the net assets of the micro-entity is more than the estimated fair value of the micro-entity as a whole
- Evidence of obsolescence or physical damage of an asset.
- Significant changes with an adverse effect in the extent to which, or manner in which, an asset is used or is expected to be used. For example the asset becoming idle, plans to discontinue or restructure the operations, and plans to dispose of an asset before the previously expected date.
- Evidence is available from internal reporting that indicates that the economic performance of an asset is, or will be, worse than expected.

If there is an indication that an asset may be impaired, this may indicate that the micro-entity should review the remaining useful life, the depreciation or amortisation method or the residual value for the asset and adjust it in accordance with the relevant section of the FRS, even if no impairment loss is recognised for the asset.

Measuring recoverable amount

The recoverable amount of an asset is the higher of its fair value less costs to sell and its value in use. It is not always necessary to determine both an asset's fair value less costs to sell and its value in use. If either of these amounts exceeds the asset's carrying amount, the asset is not impaired and it is not necessary to estimate the other amount.

Section 22 provides detailed guidance on the methods of determining both fair value less costs to sell and the value in use.

Reversal of an impairment loss

An impairment loss recognised for goodwill shall not be reversed in a subsequent period

For all other assets, if and only if the reasons for the impairment loss have ceased to apply, an impairment loss shall be reversed in a subsequent period.

The micro-entity shall recognise the reversal immediately in profit or loss.

The reversal of an impairment loss shall not increase the carrying amount of the asset above the carrying amount that would have been determined (net of amortisation or depreciation) had no impairment loss been recognised for the asset in prior years.

After a reversal of an impairment loss is recognised, the micro-entity shall adjust the depreciation (amortisation) charge for the asset in future periods to allocate the asset's revised carrying amount, less its residual value (if any), on a systematic basis over its remaining useful life.

8.14   Employee benefits (section 23)

Scope

Employee benefits are all forms of consideration given by a micro-entity in exchange for service rendered by employees, including directors and management and applies to all employee benefits, except for share-based payment transactions, which are covered by section 21.

Employee benefits will be one of the following four types:

- short-term employee benefits expected to be settled wholly before 12 months after the end of the reporting period in which the employees render the related service including:
  - wages, salaries and social security contributions;
  - paid annual leave and paid sick leave;
  - profit-sharing and bonuses; and
  - non-monetary benefits (such as medical care, housing, cars and free or subsidised goods or services) for current employees;
- post-employment benefits that are payable after the completion of employment including:
  - retirement benefits, such as pensions; and
  - other post-employment benefits, such as post-employment life insurance and post-employment medical care;
- other long-term employee benefits including
  - long-term paid absences such as long-service or sabbatical leave;
  - other long-service benefits;
  - long-term disability benefits;
  - profit-sharing and bonuses; and
  - deferred remuneration; or
- termination benefits provided in exchange for the termination of an employee's employment as a result of either:
  - a micro-entity's decision to terminate an employee's employment before the normal retirement date; or
  - an employee's decision to accept voluntary redundancy in exchange for those benefits.

General recognition principle

A micro-entity shall recognise the cost of all employee benefits to which its employees have become entitled as a result of service rendered to the micro-entity during the reporting period:

Recognition and measurement

Short-term benefits

When an employee has rendered service to a micro-entity during the reporting period, the micro-entity shall measure the amounts recognised at the undiscounted amount of short-term employee benefits expected to be paid in exchange for that service.

Accumulating short-term absences (for example paid annual leave or sick leave) occur where they can be carried forward and used in future periods. A micro-entity shall recognise the expected cost of accumulating compensated absences when the employees render service that increases their entitlement to future compensated absences. The micro-entity shall measure the expected cost of accumulating compensated absences at the undiscounted additional amount might expect to pay as a result of the unused entitlement that has accumulated at the end of the reporting period.

The expected cost of profit-sharing and bonus plans shall be recognised only when there is, at the reporting date, a present legal or constructive obligation to make such payments as a result of past events and a reliable estimate of the obligation can be made.

Post-employment benefits

Post-employment benefit plans are classified as either defined contribution plans or defined benefit plans, depending on their principal terms and conditions.

- Defined contribution plans are post-employment benefit plans under which a micro-entity pays fixed contributions into a separate entity (a fund) and has no legal or constructive obligation to pay further contributions or to make direct benefit payments to employees if the fund does not hold sufficient assets to pay all employee benefits relating to employee service in the current and prior periods. The amount of the post-employment benefits received by the employee is determined by the amount of contributions paid by a micro-entity (and perhaps also the employee) to a post-employment benefit plan or to an insurer, together with investment returns arising from the contributions.
- Defined benefit plans are post-employment benefit plans other than defined contribution plans. Under defined benefit plans, the micro-entity's obligation is to provide the agreed benefits to current and former employees, and actuarial risk (that benefits will cost more or less than expected) and investment risk (that returns on assets set aside to fund the benefits will differ from expectations) are borne, in substance, by the micro-entity. If actuarial or investment experience is worse than expected, the micro-entity's obligation may be increased, and vice versa if actuarial or investment experience is better than expected.

When contributions to a defined contribution or defined benefit plan are not expected to be settled wholly within 12 months after the end of the reporting period in which the employees render the related service, the liability recognised shall be measured at the present value of the contributions payable. The rate used to discount the future payments shall be determined by reference to market yields at the reporting date on high quality corporate bonds.

When a micro-entity participates in a defined benefit plan (which may include a multiemployer plan or state plan) and has entered into an agreement that determines how the micro-entity will fund a deficit (such as a schedule of contributions), the micro-entity shall recognise a liability for the contributions payable that arise from the agreement (to the extent that they relate to the deficit) and the resulting expense in profit or loss.

Where a micro-entity participates in a defined benefit plan that shares risks between entities under common control it shall recognise a cost equal to its contribution payable for the period. If a micro-entity is legally responsible for the plan and has entered into an agreement that determines how a deficit will be funded, the micro-entity shall recognise a liability for the contributions payable that arise from the agreement (to the extent that they relate to the deficit) and the resulting expense in profit or loss.

Long-term employee benefits

A micro-entity shall recognise a liability for other long-term employee benefits measured at the present value of the benefit obligation at the reporting date calculated. The rate used to discount the future payments shall be determined by reference to market yields at the reporting date on high quality corporate bonds.

Termination benefits

Termination benefits do not provide a micro-entity with future economic benefits and shall be recognised as an expense in profit or loss immediately.

A micro-entity shall recognise termination benefits as a liability and an expense only when the micro-entity is demonstrably committed either:

- to terminate the employment of an employee or group of employees before the normal retirement date; or
- to provide termination benefits as a result of an offer made in order to encourage voluntary redundancy.

A micro-entity is demonstrably committed to a termination only when the micro-entity has a detailed formal plan for the termination and is without realistic possibility of withdrawal from the plan.

A micro-entity shall measure termination benefits at the best estimate of the expenditure that would be required to settle the obligation at the reporting date. In the case of an offer made to encourage voluntary redundancy, the measurement of termination benefits shall be based on the number of employees expected to accept the offer.

When termination benefits are due more than 12 months after the end of the reporting period, they shall be measured at their discounted present value. The rate used to discount the future payments shall be determined by reference to market yields at the reporting date on high quality corporate bonds.

8.15   Income tax (section 24)

Scope

Income tax includes all domestic and foreign taxes that are based on taxable profit.

This section requires a micro-entity to recognise the current tax consequences of transactions and other events that have been recognised in the financial statements. Current tax is tax payable (refundable) in respect of the taxable profit (tax loss) for the current period or past reporting periods.

This section prohibits the recognition of deferred tax which represents the future tax consequences of transactions and events recognised in the financial statements of the current and previous periods.

This section also covers accounting for Value Added Tax (VAT) and other similar sales taxes, which are not income taxes.

Current tax

A micro-entity shall recognise a current tax liability for tax payable on taxable profit for the current and past periods. If the amount of tax paid for the current and past periods exceeds the amount of tax payable for those periods, the micro-entity shall recognise the excess as a current tax asset.

A current tax asset shall be recognised for the benefit of a tax loss that can be carried back to recover tax paid in a previous period.

The current tax liability (asset) shall be measured at the undiscounted amount of tax it expects to pay (recover) using the tax rates and laws that have been enacted or substantively enacted by the reporting date.

Deferred tax

A micro-entity shall not recognise deferred tax.

Withholding tax on dividends

When a micro-entity pays dividends to its shareholders, it may be required to pay a portion of the dividends to taxation authorities on behalf of shareholders. Outgoing dividends and similar amounts payable shall be recognised at an amount that includes any withholding tax but excludes other taxes, such as attributable tax credits. Incoming dividends and similar income receivable shall be recognised at an amount that includes any withholding tax but excludes other taxes, such as attributable tax credits. Any withholding tax suffered shall be shown as part of the tax charge.

In the UK, company dividends are not subject to withholding taxes but rather attributable tax credits are available for some non-corporate shareholders.

Value Added Tax and other similar sales taxes

Turnover included in profit or loss shall exclude VAT and other similar sales taxes on taxable outputs and VAT imputed under the flat rate VAT scheme. Expenses shall exclude recoverable VAT and other similar recoverable sales taxes. Irrecoverable VAT allocable to fixed assets and to other items separately recognised shall be included in their cost where practicable and material.

Presentation

A micro-entity shall present changes in a current tax liability (asset) as tax expense (income).

A micro-entity shall offset current tax assets and current tax liabilities, if and only if, it has a legally enforceable right to set off the amounts (usually where these relate to the same tax authority and it intends either to settle on a net basis or to realise the asset and settle the liability simultaneously.

8.16   Foreign currency translation (section 25)

Scope

A micro-entity may have transactions in foreign currencies. This section prescribes how to include foreign currency transactions in the financial statements.

Where a micro-entity has a foreign branch, the micro-entity should refer to the requirements of section 30 of FRS 102 to determine if the foreign branch has a different functional currency, and if so, should apply the requirements of that section to those transactions undertaken by the foreign branch.

Reporting foreign currency transactions

A micro-entity shall record a foreign currency transaction by applying to the foreign currency amount the spot exchange rate at the date of the transaction unless:

- the transaction is to be settled at a contracted rate, in which case that rate shall be used; or
- where a trading transaction is covered by a related or matching forward contract, in which case the rate of exchange specified in that contract shall be used.

For practical reasons, a rate that approximates the actual rate at the date of the transaction is often used, for example, an average rate for a week or a month might be used for all transactions in each foreign currency occurring during that period. However, if exchange rates fluctuate significantly, the use of the average rate for a period is inappropriate.

At the end of each reporting period, unless a contracted rate is being applied a micro-entity shall:

- translate foreign currency monetary items using the closing rate; and
- translate non-monetary items that are measured in terms of historical cost in a foreign currency using the exchange rate at the date of the transaction.

A micro-entity shall recognise, in profit or loss in the period in which they arise, exchange differences arising on the settlement of monetary items or on translating monetary items at rates different from those at which they were translated on initial recognition during the period or in previous periods.

8.17 Events after the end of the reporting period (section 26)

Scope and principles

This section of FRS 105 defined events after the end of the reporting period and set out the principles for recognising and measuring those events.

The requirements of the section do not differ from the principles and requirements of FRS 22 or the FRSSE under old UK GAAP.

Going concern

A micro-entity shall not prepare its financial statements on a going concern basis if management determines after the end of the reporting period that it either intends to liquidate the micro-entity or to cease trading, or that it has no realistic alternative but to do so.

Deterioration in operating results and financial position after the reporting period may lead management to determine that they intend to liquidate the micro-entity or to cease trading or that they have no realistic alternative but to do so. If the going concern basis of accounting is no longer appropriate, the effect is so pervasive that this section requires a fundamental change in the basis of accounting.

8.18 Specialised activities (section 27)

Scope

This section sets out the financial reporting requirements for micro-entities involved in agriculture.

Recognition and measurement

A micro-entity that is engaged in agricultural activity shall recognise a biological asset or an item of agricultural produce when, and only when:

- the micro-entity controls the asset as a result of past events;
- it is probable that future economic benefits associated with the asset will flow to the micro-entity; and
- the cost of the asset can be measured reliably.

A micro-entity shall measure biological assets at cost less any accumulated depreciation and any accumulated impairment losses.

Agricultural produce harvested from a micro-entity's biological assets shall be measured at the point of harvest at the lower of cost and estimated selling price less costs to complete and sell. Such measurement is the cost at that date when applying section 10 or another applicable section of the FRS.

Chapter 9   Transition to FRS 105

9.1   FRS 105 section 28

This chapter summarises the requirements of section 28 which apply to a first-time adopter of FRS 105.

A micro-entity that has applied this FRS in a previous reporting period, but whose most recent previous annual financial statements were prepared in accordance with a different accounting framework, must either apply this section or else apply this FRS retrospectively in accordance with section 8 of the FRS as if the micro-entity had never stopped applying this FRS.

The full text of the sections of the FRS are in **Appendix A**.

No disclosures about the transition to FRS 105 or adjustments that have been necessary are required.

9.2   First-time adoption

A first-time adopter of this FRS shall apply this section in its first financial statements that conform to this FRS.

A micro-entity's first financial statements that conform to this FRS are the first financial statements prepared in accordance with this FRS if, for example, the micro-entity:

- did not present financial statements for previous periods; or
- presented its most recent previous financial statements under previous UK and Republic of Ireland requirements or FRS 102 and that are therefore not consistent with this FRS in all respects.

A micro-entity shall disclose, in a complete set of financial statements, comparative information in respect of the preceding period for all amounts presented in the financial statements. Therefore, a micro-entity's date of transition to this FRS is the beginning of the earliest period for which the micro-entity presents full comparative information in accordance with this FRS in its first financial statements that comply with this FRS.

9.3   Procedures for preparing financial statements at the date of transition

Subject to specific exceptions and exemptions (see **9.4**), a micro-entity shall, in its opening statement of financial position as of its date of transition to this FRS:

- recognise all assets and liabilities whose recognition is required by the FRS;
- not recognise items as assets or liabilities if this FRS does not permit such recognition;
- reclassify items that it recognised under its previous financial reporting framework as one type of asset, liability or component of equity, but are a different type of asset, liability or component of equity under the FRS; and
- apply this FRS in measuring all recognised assets and liabilities.

The opening statement of financial position is not required to be presented.

The accounting policies that a micro-entity uses in its opening statement of financial position under the FRS may differ from those that it used for the same date using its previous financial reporting framework. The resulting adjustments arise from transactions, other events or conditions before the date of transition to the FRS. Therefore, a micro-entity shall recognise those adjustments directly in equity reserves at the date of transition to the FRS.

9.4   Exceptions and exemptions

Exceptions

On first-time adoption of the FRS, a micro-entity shall not retrospectively change the accounting that it followed under its previous financial reporting framework for:

- Financial assets and financial liabilities derecognised under a previous accounting framework before the date of transition shall not be recognised upon adoption of FRS 105. Conversely, for financial assets and liabilities that would have been derecognised under this FRS in a transaction that took place before the date of transition, but that were not derecognised under a micro-entity's previous accounting framework, a micro-entity may choose:
  - to derecognise them on adoption of the FRS; or
  - to continue to recognise them until disposed of or settled.
- Accounting estimates. If it is determined that an accounting estimate made in a financial period before the date of transition was incorrect, the effect of correction shall be made prospectively in the first period after transition.

Exemptions

A micro-entity may use one or more of the following exemptions in preparing its first financial statements that conform to FRS 105:

Business combinations and goodwill

A first-time adopter is not required to apply section 14 to business combinations that were effected before the date of transition to this FRS. However, if a first-time adopter restates any business combination to comply with section 14, it shall restate all later business combinations.

Share-based payment transactions

A first-time adopter is not required to apply section 21 to obligations arising from share-based payment transactions that were settled before the date of transition to the FRS.

Investment properties

A first-time adopter is not required to retrospectively determine the depreciated cost of each of the major components of an investment property at the date of transition to the FRS. If this exemption is applied, a first-time adopter shall:

- Determine the total cost of the investment property including all of its components. Where no depreciation had been charged under the previous financial reporting framework, this can be calculated by reversing any revaluation gains or losses previously recorded in equity reserves.
- The cost of land, if any, shall be separated from buildings.
- Estimate the total depreciated cost of the investment property (excluding land) at the date of transition to this FRS, by recognising accumulated depreciation since the date of initial

acquisition calculated on the basis of the useful life of the most significant component of the item of investment property (e.g. the main structural elements of the building).

- A portion of the estimated total depreciated cost shall then be allocated to each of the other major components (i.e. excluding the most significant component identified above) to determine their depreciated cost. The allocation should be made on a reasonable and consistent basis.
- Any amount of the total depreciated cost not allocated shall be allocated to the most significant component of the investment property.

Compound financial instruments

A first-time adopter need not separate those two components if the liability component is not outstanding at the date of transition to the FRS.

Arrangements containing a lease

A first-time adopter may elect to determine whether an arrangement existing at the date of transition to the FRS contains a lease (see section 15) on the basis of facts and circumstances existing at that date, rather than when the arrangement was entered into.

Decommissioning liabilities included in the cost of property, plant and equipment or investment property

A first-time adopter may elect to measure this component of the cost of an item of property, plant and equipment or investment property at the date of transition to this FRS, rather than on the date(s) when the obligation initially arose.

Dormant companies

A company within the Act's definition of a dormant company may elect to retain its accounting policies for reported assets, liabilities and equity at the date of transition to the FRS until there is any change to those balances or the company undertakes any new transactions.

Lease incentives

A first-time adopter is not required to apply section 15 to lease incentives provided the term of the lease commenced before the date of transition to the FRS. The first-time adopter shall continue to recognise any residual benefit or cost associated with these lease incentives on the same basis as that applied at the date of transition to the FRS.

Chapter 10   Filing of accounts

10.1   Introduction

This book does not aim to cover the finer details of the filing requirements for the accounts of companies but this chapter gives guidance on filing with both the Registrar of Companies and HMRC and explains some of the current filing methods which are introducing changes to the process which has existed for many years of paper filing of accounts with the Registrar and tax authorities.

In general, company accounts need to be filed:

- with the Registrar of Companies within nine months after the end of the reporting period; and
- with HMRC with the company's tax return (if the company is required to file a tax return) not more than 12 months following the end of the year to which they relate.

One recent development in filing accounts with the Registrar of Companies is that electronic filing of accounts is permitted and the number of accounts being submitted electronically is growing. This chapter sets out the various options for a company in relation to filing accounts electronically.

10.2   Filing exemptions for micro-entities

For periods commencing before 1 January 2016, a company eligible under the small companies' regime (and therefore also micro-entities) preparing companies act accounts, i.e. under UK GAAP not IAS, was permitted to deliver 'abbreviated accounts' in place of full statutory accounts ('individual accounts') to the Registrar of Companies.

Under the new regulations, this option is no longer available and companies must deliver a copy of the accounts which were prepared for the members however small companies will still be able to take advantage of certain filing exemptions.

A small or micro-entity also the option not to file with the Registrar of Companies a copy of the profit and loss account. If the company takes advantage of this exemption there should be disclosure of that fact on the balance sheet that is filed.

10.3   Filing deadlines

In general, private companies (i.e. those that are not public companies) are required to file accounts with the Registrar of Companies within nine months from the end of the accounting period (accounting reference date or ARD).

When filing the company's first accounts, the deadline for delivery is nine months after the anniversary of incorporation (i.e. 21 months). The deadline remains the same even if this company extends its first accounting period to the maximum of 18 months. It is calculated to the exact corresponding date in the 21st month following the incorporation. For example, a company incorporated on 29 January 2013 has until midnight on 29 October 2014 to submit its first accounts.

When the accounting period is extended, other than for the first accounts, the filing deadline remains as nine months after the end of the period. However, when a private company shortens the accounting period, the filing deadline for that period is the longer of the following:

- nine months after the new ARD; or
- three months after the date of the notice of the ARD change being delivered to the Registrar.

Companies submitting their accounts after the filing deadline has passed will incur a late filing penalty of at least £150. The penalty increases in line with the period of late submission. The maximum penalty for a private company which submits accounts six months after the normal filing deadline is £1,500. However, if the company files its accounts late two years in a row, the penalty in the second year is doubled.

10.4   Registrar of Companies

The Registrar of Companies is given authority under CA 2006 to make rules governing the filing of documents at Companies House. These 'Registrar's Rules' are secondary legislation, made under s. 1117 of the Act, and include the form, delivery and method of authentication for documents (including accounts) to be delivered to the Registrar.

The rules specify differing filing requirements for hard copy and electronic filings. For example, although the Companies Act requirement for an original signature to be included on the accounts that are filed was repealed as from 1 October 2009, signatures are still required by the Registrar's Rules to be included on balance sheets filed in paper form.

Furthermore, Companies House has recently reviewed its policy on filing documents with original signatures and has concluded that the Registrar of Companies will 'accept in good faith that documents presented for filing which have automatically generated signatures have been properly approved by the signatory'. And that 'documents will no longer be rejected simply because the signature does not appear to be original'.

www.companieshouse.gov.uk/about/policyDocuments/documentSignatures.shtml

A detailed list of the Registrar's Rules, including when amendments came into force, is available at www.companieshouse.gov.uk/about/policyDocuments/registrarsRules/infoRegistrarsRules.shtml.

The most significant recent change came into force on 30 November 2012 when Volume 1 of the Registrar's Rules 2009 (Documents delivered in electronic form) was revoked and the new Registrar's (Electronic Form) Rules 2012—Volume 1 came into force.

The rules contained in Volumes 2, 3, 4 and 5 of the Registrar's Rules 2009 (as amended) remain in force.

10.5   Filing accounts in paper form

Of particular relevance to the filing of accounts on paper at Companies House are the following rules relating to registered number, signatures and the form and content of documents.

The Registrar's (requirements for paper documents) Rules 2009

Registered number

Paragraph 22(3) of Volume 2 of the amended Registrar's Rules 2009 lists the documents (delivered on paper) which must contain the name and registered number of the company to which the document relates (but only one of the documents filed must show this information).

Only one of the following documents filed must contain the name and registered number of the company:

- copy of balance sheet or abbreviated accounts;
- (where applicable): copy of profit and loss account; copy of directors' report; or directors' remuneration report;
- (where applicable) copy of auditor's report.

The company name or registered number required as above must be in black typescript or handwritten in black ink in a 'prominent position' in the document filed; this does not, however, include, for example, the cover of an annual accounts package.

Signature – the following documents (filed in paper form) must be signed by a director:

- copy of balance sheet; or
- annual accounts.

The signature must be applied to the document in a prominent position, at the end of the balance sheet.

Form and content of documents:

Generally, paper documents sent to Companies House must state in a prominent position the registered name and number of the company. Paper documents must be:

- on A4 size, plain white paper with a matt finish (note – Companies House does usually accept accounts on US letter sized paper and off-white paper as long as the document can be scanned legibly to A4);
- black, clear and legible text, of uniform density; and
- clear and legible bold letters and numbers.

Documents should not be poor lettering or photocopies, carbon copies, or produced from a dot matrix printer (note – as this may cause problems scanning the documents).

10.6   Common reasons for accounts rejections at Companies House

In 2010, Companies House published a document listing the most common reasons why paper accounts had been rejected, which were:

- incorrect statements to the accounts, e.g. referring to the wrong Act (this was more common in 2010 due to the recent change from CA 1985 to CA 2006);
- filing accounts with the same date as previously filed accounts (see amended accounts below); signatory name missing on the balance sheet;
- balance sheet signature missing;
- audit exemption statements missing or incorrect; and
- accounting reference date (ARD)/made up date absent or incorrect.

www.companieshouse.gov.uk/about/pdf/commonAccountsRejections.pdf

In response to this, the ICAEW issued a document entitled 'Rejected Accounts' which gives guidance on preventing accounts being rejected by the Registrar.

If such accounts are submitted close to the filing deadline and the corrected accounts cannot be returned before the filing deadline expires, an automatic late filing penalty will be issued. There used to be a grace period of 14 days for accounts that were rejected near the deadline, however this ceased to exist on 1 October 2009.

10.7   Filing accounts in electronic form

There are four ways to file accounts electronically at Companies House.

- WebFiling;
- Filing of iXBRL accounts:
  - joint filing with HMRC;
  - electronic filing using enabled accounts production software;
  - electronic filing of iXBRL accounts using enabled company secretarial software or a third party web-based service.

WebFiling accounts

Companies House's WebFiling service allows the filing of a number of documents electronically, including (with some restrictions):

- dormant company accounts (DCA) AA02;
- audit exempt micro-entity accounts; and
- audit exempt full accounts.

Audited companies, Community Interest Companies (CIC) and Limited Liability Partnerships (LLP) cannot file annual accounts using the WebFiling service.

The Dormant Company Accounts (DCA) AA02 and the Audit Exempt Abbreviated Accounts are online WebFilings where the information is completed on screen.

Electronic filing is particularly useful if accounts are filed near to the filing deadline when there is invariably a risk of incurring penalties for late filing in the event that Companies House does not receive the document in time.

For more information on WebFiling and filing of iXBRL accounts, refer to guidance provided by Companies House or HMRC.

10.8   Amended accounts

If it is found that a set of accounts submitted to Companies House is defective (i.e. containing errors or not compliant with a requirement of the Companies Act), then the directors may submit amending financial statements to the Registrar of Companies. This may be because the company has realised that the accounts are defective or because the Registrar has written to the directors to request that they either give a satisfactory explanation for the accounts or prepare revised accounts.

The rules relating to revised accounts are set out in CA 2006 (s. 454–459), Pt. 15 and the *Companies (Revision of Defective Accounts and Reports) Regulations* 2008 (SI 2008/373):

www.legislation.gov.uk/uksi/2008/373/contents/made#.

10.9   HMRC

A UK Corporation Tax Return for a limited company (preparing Companies Act or IAS individual accounts) includes form CT600, the accounts and the tax computation together with any accompanying information as required. This must be submitted to HMRC electronically. The accounts forming part of the return must be in iXBRL format (see **10.10** below).

iXBRL tagging of UK statutory financial statements has been required for tax purposes since 2011. It has been mandatory for organisations since accounting periods ending after 31 March 2010 and filing their tax return after 31 March 2011.

A dormant company will not have to deliver a return unless it is sent a statutory notice to do so. In most cases, if HMRC has been notified that a company is dormant, no notice to deliver a return will be issued.

10.10   Electronic tagging of accounts (iXBRL)

In March 2006, a review was carried out of HMRC's online services. One of the recommendations of the review, which was supported by government, was that HMRC and Companies House should work together to provide a joint filing facility. In support of these recommendations, Companies House has encouraged online filing wherever possible.

Inline Extensible Business Reporting Language (iXBRL) is an electronic format for embedding XBRL 'tags' into financial statements. XBRL itself is an open and global standard for exchanging business information.

The accounts tagged under iXBRL are still in a format which can be read 'manually' (as opposed to by a computer only): this is what the 'inline' refers to – the tags applied are hidden behind the scenes, in line with the normal text.

Embedding tags into an annual report and accounts document can by performed in a variety of ways:

- using an accounts preparation package which has the tagging facility built in;
- using tagging software to apply the tags to accounts created in a word-processed document; or
- engaging a third party tagging firm or accountant to create the iXBRL file from the word processed document file ('managed tagging').

HMRC maintain a list of approved providers of software and managed tagging providers at www.hmrc.gov.uk/efiling/ctsoft_dev.htm.

HMRC have produced taxonomies (a dictionary of tags) for UK GAAP and IFRS which set out the available tags to be used in a set of financial statements. The items listed in the taxonomies must be tagged if they are present in any given set of accounts and computations. The tags will be applied to both financial and narrative information.

New taxonomies for accounts prepared under FRS 101 (IFRS with reduced disclosure) and FRS 102 (new UK GAAP) are currently being developed by HMRC. It is hoped they will be published by the middle of 2015.

HMRC have made provision for transitional arrangements which allows companies to use a Minimum Tagging List (for UK GAAP of around 1,200 tags) rather than the Full Taxonomy during the transition period, although companies may adopt full tagging immediately. Full tagging was expected to be mandatory from April 2013. However, in May 2012 HMRC indicated that, following consultation, they now have no plans to move to full tagging.

10.11   Planned changes in accounts filing

As part of the journey towards Companies House's aim of becoming a fully electronic registry, in 2010 Companies House announced that it expected all incorporations and filings of annual returns, accounts and the main company changes would be digital-only (electronic) by March 2013 for the standard company types.

Although mandatory electronic filing at Companies House has been put on hold until the Government's moratorium on new regulation for small businesses has ended in 2014, the number of accounts being filed electronically has grown rapidly over the recent past. The Companies House register is not yet fully electronic, but a significant proportion (almost 66% in 2014–15) of the accounts submitted are being filed electronically. It can only be anticipated that this proportion will increase 'voluntarily' and will, indeed, become a requirement over the coming years.

Appendices

Appendix A   FRS 105 The Financial Reporting Standard applicable to the Micro-entities Regime

FRS 105 *The Financial Reporting Standard applicable to the Micro-entities Regime* is an accounting standard. It is issued by the Financial Reporting Council in respect of its application in the United Kingdom and promulgated by the Institute of Chartered Accountants in Ireland in respect of its application in the Republic of Ireland.

Contents

SUMMARY

With effect from 1 January 2015 the Financial Reporting Council (FRC) revised financial reporting standards in the   **(i)**
United Kingdom and Republic of Ireland. The revisions fundamentally reformed financial reporting, replacing the extant
standards with five Financial Reporting Standards:

(a)   FRS 100 *Application of Financial Reporting Requirements*;
(b)   FRS 101 *Reduced Disclosure Framework*;
(c)   FRS 102 *The Financial Reporting Standard applicable in the UK and Republic of Ireland*;
(d)   FRS 103 *Insurance Contracts*; and
(e)   FRS 104 *Interim Financial Reporting*.

The revisions made by the FRC followed a sustained and detailed period of consultation. The FRC made these fundamental   **(ii)**
changes recognising that the introduction of International Financial Reporting Standards for listed groups in 2002 (with
application from 2005) called into question the need for two sets of financial reporting standards. Evidence from
consultation supported a move towards an international-based framework for financial reporting, but one that was
proportionate to the needs of preparers and users.

The FRC's overriding objective in setting accounting standards is to enable users of accounts to receive high-quality   **(iii)**
understandable financial reporting proportionate to the size and complexity of the entity and users' information needs.

In meeting this objective, the FRC aims to provide succinct financial reporting standards that: **(iv)**

(a)   have consistency with international accounting standards through the application of an IFRS-based solution unless
      an alternative clearly better meets the overriding objective;
(b)   reflect up-to-date thinking and developments in the way entities operate and the transactions they undertake;
(c)   balance consistent principles for accounting by all UK and Republic of Ireland entities with practical solutions,
      based on size, complexity, public interest and users' information needs;
(d)   promote efficiency within groups; and
(e)   are cost-effective to apply.

FRS 105 *The Financial Reporting Standard applicable to the Micro-entities Regime* is an accounting standard intended   **(v)**
for financial statements of companies which qualify for the micro-entities regime. FRS 105 is effective for accounting
periods beginning on or after 1 January 2016. Early application is permitted. The FRC withdraws the Financial Reporting
Standard for Smaller Entities from the effective date of this FRS.

Development of FRS 105

In November 2013, *The Small Companies (Micro-entities'Accounts) Regulations 2013* (SI 2013/3008) were made which   **(vi)**
amended *The Small Companies and Groups (Accounts and Directors' Report) Regulations 2008* (SI 2008/409). The
amendment introduced a new optional reporting framework for companies that meet the qualifying criteria of a micro-
entity. In response to this change of UK company law and the revision of financial reporting standards in the United
Kingdom and Republic of Ireland set out in paragraph (i), the FRC developed FRS 105.

In February 2015 the FRC issued Financial Reporting Exposure Draft (FRED) 58 *Draft FRS 105 The Financial Reporting*   **(vii)**
Standard applicable to the Micro-entities Regime to consult on the new accounting standard for micro-entities. Respondents
were generally supportive of the proposed requirements and comments made during the consultation were taken into
account when FRS 105 was finalised.

FRS 105 is based on FRS 102, but its accounting requirements are adapted to satisfy the legal requirements applicable to   **(viii)**
micro-entities and to reflect the simpler nature and smaller size of micro-entities.

The application of the micro-entities regime is optional, however, a micro-entity that chooses to prepare its financial   **(ix)**
statements in accordance with the micro-entities regime is required to apply FRS 105. A company that qualifies for this
regime, but chooses not to apply it, is required to apply another accounting standard. The possible options are set out in
FRS 100 *Application of Financial Reporting Requirements*.

(x) At the same time as the FRC issues FRS 105, the FRC also makes amendments to FRS 102 to incorporate consequential changes resulting from the *The Companies, Partnerships and Groups (Accounts and Reports) Regulations 2015* (SI 2015/980). FRS 105 takes into account any relevant changes made to FRS 102 in this regard.

Organisation of FRS 105

(xi) FRS 105 is organised by topic with each topic presented in a separate numbered section. Cross-references to paragraphs are identified by section followed by paragraph number. Paragraph numbers are in the form of xx.yy, where xx is the section number and yy is the sequential paragraph number within that section.

(xii) In examples that include monetary amounts, the measuring unit is Currency Unit (abbreviated as CU).

(xiii) All the paragraphs of FRS 105 have equal authority. Some sections include appendices of implementation guidance or examples. Some of these are an integral part of this FRS while others provide guidance concerning its application; each specifies its status.

(xiv) FRS 105 is set out in Sections 1 to 28 and the Glossary (Appendix I). Terms defined in the glossary are in **bold type** the first time they appear in each section.

(xv) Where references to other sections or paragraphs are made, these are in reference to FRS 105 unless otherwise stated.

FRS 105 THE FINANCIAL REPORTING STANDARD APPLICABLE TO THE MICRO-ENTITIES REGIME

Section 1 Scope

Scope of this Financial Reporting Standard

1.1 This FRS applies to the **financial statements** of a **micro-entity**. The financial statements of a micro-entity prepared in accordance with this FRS that include the **micro-entity minimum accounting items** are presumed in law to show a true and fair view of the micro-entity's **financial position** and **profit or loss** in accordance with the **micro-entities regime**.

1.2 References to a micro-entity in this FRS are to a micro-entity that chooses to apply the micro-entities regime.

1.3 This FRS permits, but does not require, a micro-entity to include information additional to the micro-entity minimum accounting items in its financial statements. If a micro-entity includes additional information it shall have regard to any requirement of Section 1A *Small Entities* of **FRS 102** that relates to that information.

Date from which effective

1.4 A micro-entity applying the micro-entities regime shall apply this FRS for accounting periods beginning on or after 1 January 2016. Early application is permitted.

Section 2 Concepts and Pervasive Principles

Scope of this section

2.1 This section sets out the concepts and basic principles that generally underlie the **recognition** and **measurement** of transactions of **micro-entities** within the scope of this FRS.

Financial position

2.2 The **financial position** of a micro-entity is the relationship of its **assets**, **liabilities** and **equity** as of a specific date as presented in the **statement of financial position**. These are defined as follows:

    (a) An asset is a resource controlled by the micro-entity as a result of past events and from which future economic benefits are expected to flow to the micro-entity.

    (b) A liability is a present obligation of the micro-entity arising from past events, the settlement of which is expected to result in an outflow from the micro-entity of resources embodying economic benefits.

    (c) Equity is the residual interest in the assets of the micro-entity after deducting all its liabilities.

Some items that meet the definition of an asset or a liability may not be recognised as assets or liabilities in the statement of financial position because they do not satisfy the criteria for recognition in paragraphs 2.22 and 2.24. In particular, the expectation that future economic benefits will flow to or from a micro-entity must be sufficiently certain to meet the probability criterion before an asset or liability is recognised.   **2.3**

Assets

The future economic benefit of an asset is its potential to contribute, directly or indirectly, to the flow of cash to the micro-entity. Those cash flows may come from using the asset or from disposing of it.   **2.4**

Many assets, for example **property, plant and equipment**, have a physical form. However, physical form is not essential to the existence of an asset. Some assets are intangible.   **2.5**

In determining the existence of an asset, the right of ownership is not essential. Thus, for example, property held on a **lease** is an asset if the micro-entity controls the benefits that are expected to flow from the property.   **2.6**

Liabilities

An essential characteristic of a liability is that the micro-entity has a present obligation to act or perform in a particular way. The obligation may be either a legal obligation or a **constructive obligation**. A legal obligation is legally enforceable as a consequence of a binding contract or statutory requirement. A constructive obligation is an obligation that derives from a micro-entity's actions when: **2.7**

(a)   by an established pattern of past practice, published policies or a sufficiently specific current statement, the micro-entity has indicated to other parties that it will accept certain responsibilities; and

(b)   as a result, the micro-entity has created a valid expectation on the part of those other parties that it will discharge those responsibilities.

The settlement of a present obligation usually involves the payment of cash, transfer of other assets, provision of services, the replacement of that obligation with another obligation, or conversion of the obligation to equity. An obligation may also be extinguished by other means, such as a creditor waiving or forfeiting its rights.   **2.8**

Equity

Equity is the residual interest in the assets of the micro-entity after deducting all its liabilities.   **2.9**

Performance

Performance is the relationship of the **income** and **expenses** of a micro-entity during a **reporting period**. Income and expenses are defined as follows: **2.10**

(a)   Income is increases in economic benefits during the reporting period in the form of inflows or enhancements of assets or decreases of liabilities that result in increases in equity, other than those relating to contributions from equity investors.

(b)   Expenses are decreases in economic benefits during the reporting period in the form of outflows or depletions of assets or incurrences of liabilities that result in decreases in equity, other than those relating to distributions to equity investors.

The recognition of income and expenses results directly from the recognition and measurement of assets and liabilities. Criteria for the recognition of income and expenses are discussed in paragraphs 2.26 and 2.27.   **2.11**

Income

The definition of income encompasses both **revenue** and **gains**.   **2.12**

(a)   Revenue is income that arises in the course of the ordinary activities of a micro-entity and is referred to by a variety of names including sales, fees, interest, dividends, royalties and rent.

(b)   Gains are other items that meet the definition of income but are not revenue.

Expenses

The definition of expenses encompasses losses as well as those expenses that arise in the course of the ordinary activities of the micro-entity.   **2.13**

(a) Expenses that arise in the course of the ordinary activities of the micro-entity include, for example, cost of sales, wages and **depreciation**. They usually take the form of an outflow or depletion of assets such as cash, **inventory**, or property, plant and equipment.

(b) Losses are other items that meet the definition of expenses and may arise in the course of the ordinary activities of the micro-entity.

Recognition of assets, liabilities, income and expenses

2.14 Recognition is the process of incorporating in the statement of financial position or **income statement** an item that meets the definition of an asset, liability, equity, income or expense and satisfies the following criteria:

(a) it is **probable** that any future economic benefit associated with the item will flow to or from the micro-entity; and

(b) the item has a cost or value that can be measured reliably.

2.15 The uncertainties that inevitably surround many events and circumstances are acknowledged by the exercise of **prudence** in the preparation of the financial statements. Prudence is the inclusion of a degree of caution in the exercise of the judgements needed in making the estimates required under conditions of uncertainty, such that assets or income are not overstated and liabilities or expenses are not understated. However, the exercise of prudence does not allow the deliberate understatement of assets or income, or the deliberate overstatement of liabilities or expenses. In short, prudence does not permit bias.

The probability of future economic benefit

2.16 The concept of probability is used in the first recognition criterion to refer to the degree of uncertainty that the future economic benefits associated with the item will flow to or from the micro-entity. Assessments of the degree of uncertainty attaching to the flow of future economic benefits are made on the basis of the evidence relating to conditions at the end of the reporting period available when the financial statements are prepared. Those assessments are made individually for individually significant items, and for a group for a large population of individually insignificant items.

Reliability of measurement

2.17 The second criterion for the recognition of an item is that it possesses a cost or value that can be measured with reliability. In many cases, the cost or value of an item is known. In other cases it must be estimated. The use of reasonable estimates is an essential part of the preparation of financial statements and does not undermine their reliability. When a reasonable estimate cannot be made, the item is not recognised in the financial statements.

2.18 An item that fails to meet the recognition criteria may qualify for recognition at a later date as a result of subsequent circumstances or events.

Measurement of assets, liabilities, income and expenses

2.19 Measurement is the process of determining the monetary amounts at which a micro-entity measures assets, liabilities, income and expenses in its financial statements. Measurement involves the selection of a basis of measurement. This FRS specifies which measurement basis a micro-entity shall use for many types of assets, liabilities, income and expenses.

Pervasive recognition and measurement principles

2.20 In the absence of a requirement in this FRS that applies specifically to a transaction or other event or condition, paragraph 8.4 provides guidance for making a judgement and paragraph 8.5 requires a micro-entity to look to the definitions, recognition criteria and measurement concepts for assets, liabilities, income and expenses and the pervasive principles set out in this section.

Accrual basis

2.21 A micro-entity shall prepare its financial statements using the **accrual basis** of accounting. On the accrual basis, items are recognised as assets, liabilities, equity, income or expenses when they satisfy the definitions and recognition criteria for those items.

Recognition in financial statements

Assets

2.22 A micro-entity shall recognise an asset in the statement of financial position when it is probable that the future economic benefits will flow to the micro-entity and the asset has a cost or value that can be measured reliably. An asset is not recognised in the statement of financial position when expenditure has been incurred for which it is considered not probable that economic benefits will flow to the micro-entity beyond the current reporting period. Instead such a transaction results in the recognition of an expense in the income statement.

A micro-entity shall not recognise a **contingent asset** as an asset. When the flow of future economic benefits to the micro-entity is virtually certain, then the related asset is not a contingent asset, and its recognition is appropriate. **2.23**

Liabilities

A micro-entity shall recognise a liability in the statement of financial position when: **2.24**

(a)   the micro-entity has an obligation at the end of the reporting period as a result of a past event;
(b)   it is probable that the micro-entity will be required to transfer resources embodying economic benefits in settlement; and
(c)   the settlement amount can be measured reliably.

A **contingent liability** is either a possible but uncertain obligation or a present obligation that is not recognised because it fails to meet one or both of the conditions (b) and (c) in paragraph 2.24. **2.25**

Income

The recognition of income results directly from the recognition and measurement of assets and liabilities. A micro-entity shall recognise income in the income statement when an increase in future economic benefits related to an increase in an asset or a decrease of a liability has arisen that can be measured reliably. **2.26**

Expenses

The recognition of expenses results directly from the recognition and measurement of assets and liabilities. A micro-entity shall recognise expenses in the income statement when a decrease in future economic benefits related to a decrease in an asset or an increase of a liability has arisen that can be measured reliably. **2.27**

Profit or loss

Profit or loss is the arithmetical difference between income and expenses. It is not a separate element of financial statements, and a separate recognition principle is not needed for it. **2.28**

Generally this FRS does not allow the recognition of items in the statement of financial position that do not meet the definition of assets or of liabilities regardless of whether they result from applying the notion commonly referred to as the 'matching concept' for measuring profit or loss. **2.29**

Measurement at initial recognition

At initial recognition, a micro-entity shall measure assets and liabilities at cost. **2.30**

Under limited circumstances this FRS requires a micro-entity to estimate the cost of an asset or liability based on its **fair value**. Where this FRS requires a micro-entity to determine the fair value of an asset or liability, it shall use the following hierarchy to estimate the fair value: **2.31**

(a)   The best evidence of fair value is the open market price for an identical asset or liability in an **active market**.
(b)   When an open market price is not available, the price of a recent transaction for an identical asset or liability provides evidence of fair value as long as there has not been significant change in economic circumstances or a significant lapse of time since the transaction took place.
(c)   If neither (a) nor (b) above are available, the fair value shall be estimated using a valuation technique. The objective of using a valuation technique is to estimate what the price of a recent transaction for an identical asset or liability would have been on the measurement date in an arm's length exchange motivated by normal business considerations.

Subsequent measurement

Financial assets and financial liabilities

A micro-entity measures **financial assets** and **financial liabilities** as follows: **2.32**

(a)   Investments in preference shares or **ordinary shares** and investments in **subsidiaries** and **associates** and interests in **jointly controlled entities** shall be measured at cost less impairment.

(b) **Derivatives** are measured at cost adjusted for amounts recognised in profit or loss over the term of the instruments and any impairment loss.

(c) **Financial instruments** other than financial instruments covered by paragraphs (a) and (b) are measured at cost adjusted for the allocation of interest, the amortisation of any **transaction costs** included in the cost of the instruments and any impairment loss.

Non-financial assets

2.33 **Property, plant and equipment**, **investment property** and **biological assets** are measured at cost less accumulated depreciation and accumulated **impairment losses**.

2.34 **Inventories** are measured at the lower of cost and selling price less costs to complete and sell.

2.35 Measurement of assets at amounts lower than their initial historical cost is intended to ensure that an asset is not measured at an amount greater than the micro-entity expects to recover from the sale or use of that asset.

Liabilities other than financial liabilities

2.36 Most liabilities other than financial liabilities are measured at the best estimate of the amount that would be required to settle the obligation at the **reporting date**.

Offsetting

2.37 A micro-entity shall not offset assets and liabilities, or income and expenses, unless required or permitted by this FRS.

(a) Measuring assets net of valuation allowances (for example, allowances for inventory obsolescence and allowances for uncollectible receivables) is not offsetting.

(b) If a micro-entity's normal **operating activities** do not include buying and selling **fixed assets**, including investments and operating assets, then the micro-entity reports gains and losses on disposal of such assets by deducting from the proceeds on disposal the **carrying amount** of the asset and related selling expenses.

Section 3 Financial Statement Presentation

Scope of this section

3.1 This section explains what compliance with this FRS requires and what makes up a complete set of **financial statements** for a **micro-entity**.

Presumed true and fair view

3.2 The financial statements of a micro-entity that comply with this FRS are presumed in law to give a true and fair view of the **financial position** and **profit or loss** of the micro-entity in accordance with the **micro-entities regime**.

Going concern

3.3 When preparing financial statements using this FRS, the management of a micro-entity shall make an assessment of whether the going concern basis of accounting is appropriate. The going concern basis of accounting is appropriate unless management either intends to liquidate the micro-entity or to cease trading, or has no realistic alternative but to do so. In assessing whether the going concern basis of accounting is appropriate, management takes into account all available information about the future, which is at least, but is not limited to, 12 months from the date when the financial statements are authorised for issue.

Frequency of reporting

3.4 A micro-entity shall present a complete set of financial statements (including comparative information as set out in paragraph 3.7) at the end of each **reporting period**.

Consistency of presentation

3.5 A micro-entity shall retain the presentation and classification of items in the financial statements from one period to the next unless:

The Financial Reporting Standard applicable to the Micro-entities Regime FRS 105

(a)   it is apparent, following a significant change in the nature of the micro-entity's operations or a review of its financial statements, that another presentation or classification would be more appropriate having regard to the criteria for the selection and application of **accounting policies** in Section 8 *Accounting Policies, Estimates and Errors*; or

(b)   this FRS requires a change in presentation.

When the presentation or classification of items in the financial statements is changed, a micro-entity shall reclassify comparative amounts unless the reclassification is **impracticable**.   **3.6**

Comparative information

Except when this FRS permits or requires otherwise, a micro-entity shall present comparative information in respect of the preceding period for all amounts presented in the current period's financial statements.   **3.7**

Materiality

A micro-entity need not provide a specific disclosure required by this FRS if the information is not **material**. This exemption does not apply to the disclosures required by paragraph 6.2(a).   **3.8**

Complete set of financial statements

A complete set of financial statements of a micro-entity shall include the following: **3.9**

(a)   a **statement of financial position** as at the **reporting date** with **notes** included at the foot of the statement; and

(b)   an **income statement** for the reporting period.

Because paragraph 3.7 requires comparative amounts in respect of the previous period for all amounts presented in the financial statements, a complete set of financial statements means that a micro-entity shall present, as a minimum, two of each of the required financial statements and related notes.   **3.10**

In a complete set of financial statements, a micro-entity shall present each financial statement with equal prominence.   **3.11**

A micro-entity may use titles for the financial statements other than those used in this FRS as long as they are not misleading.   **3.12**

Identification of the financial statements

A micro-entity shall clearly identify each of the financial statements and the notes. In addition, a micro-entity shall display the following information prominently, and repeat it when necessary for an understanding of the information presented: **3.13**

(a)   the name of the reporting entity and any change in its name since the end of the preceding reporting period;

(b)   the date of the end of the reporting period and the period covered by the financial statements;

(c)   the presentation currency; and

(d)   the level of rounding, if any, used in presenting amounts in the financial statements.

Statement of compliance with the micro-entity provisions

In accordance with section 414(3) of the **Act**, financial statements prepared in accordance with the **micro-entity provisions** shall on the **statement of financial position**, in a prominent position above the signature, contain a statement that the financial statements are prepared in accordance with the micro-entity provisions.   **3.14**

Section 4 Statement of Financial Position

Scope of this section

This section sets out the information that is to be presented in a **statement of financial position** and how to present it. The statement of financial position (which is referred to as the balance sheet in the **Act**) presents a **micro-entity's assets, liabilities** and **equity** as of a specific date – the end of the **reporting period**.   **4.1**

A micro-entity is permitted, but not required, to present information additional to that required by this section. Paragraph 1.3 applies to any additional information presented.   **4.2**

Information to be presented in the statement of financial position

4.3 A micro-entity shall present a statement of financial position in accordance with one of the formats set out in Section C of Part 1 of Schedule 1 to the **Small Companies Regulations**, as follows:

Format 1	CU	CU
Called up share capital not paid		X
Fixed assets		X
Current assets	X	
Prepayments and accrued income	X	
Creditors: amounts falling due within one year	(X)	
Net current assets / (liabilities)		X/(X)
Total assets less current liabilities		X
Creditors: amounts falling due after more than one year		(X)
Provisions for liabilities		(X)
Accruals and deferred income		(X)
		X
Capital and reserves		X

Format 2	CU	CU
Assets		
Called up share capital not paid		X
Fixed assets		X
Current assets		X
Prepayments and accrued income		X
		X
Capital, Reserves and Liabilities		
Capital and reserves		X
Provisions for liabilities		X
Creditors		
Amounts falling due within one year	X	
Amounts falling due after one year	X	
		X
Accruals and deferred income		X
		X

Creditors: amounts falling due within one year

4.4 A micro-entity shall classify a creditor as due within one year when the micro-entity does not have an unconditional right, at the end of the reporting period, to defer settlement of the creditor for at least 12 months after the **reporting date**.

Section 5 Income Statement

Scope of this section

This section requires a **micro-entity** to present its **profit or loss** for a period, ie its financial **performance** for the period. It sets out the information that is to be presented in the **income statement** (which is referred to as the profit and loss account in the **Act**) and how to present it. **5.1**

A micro-entity is permitted, but not required, to present information additional to that required by this section. Paragraph 1.3 applies to any additional information presented. **5.2**

Presentation of profit or loss

A micro-entity shall present its profit or loss for a period in an income statement in accordance with Section C of Part 1 of Schedule 1 to the **Small Companies Regulations**, as follows: **5.3**

	CU
Turnover	X
Other income	X
Cost of raw materials and consumables	(X)
Staff costs	(X)
Depreciation and other amounts written off assets	(X)
Other charges	(X)
Tax	(X)
Profit or loss	X / (X)

Under this FRS, the effects of corrections of **material errors** and changes in **accounting policies** are presented as retrospective adjustments of prior periods rather than as part of profit or loss in the period in which they arise (see Section 8 *Accounting Policies, Estimates and Errors*). **5.4**

Section 6 Notes to the Financial Statements

Scope of this section

This section sets out the information that shall be disclosed in the **notes** to the **financial statements** and where. A **micro-entity** is permitted, but not required, to disclose information additional to that required by this section. Paragraph 1.3 applies to any additional information disclosed. **6.1**

Structure and content of the notes

In accordance with section 472(1A) of the **Act**, the notes to the financial statements of a micro-entity shall be presented at the foot of the **statement of financial position** and shall include the following information: **6.2**

(a) advances, credit and guarantees granted to directors as required by section 413 of the Act (see paragraph 6A.1 in the Appendix to this Section); and

(b) financial commitments, guarantees and contingencies as required by regulation 5A of, and paragraph 57 of Part 3 of Schedule 1 to, the **Small Companies Regulations** (see paragraphs 6A.2 and 6A.3 in the Appendix to this Section).

Appendix to Section 6

Company law disclosure requirements

This appendix is an integral part of this FRS.

This appendix sets out the company law disclosure requirements referred to in paragraph 6.2. Other than substituting company law terminology with the equivalent terminology used in this FRS (see Appendix II Table of equivalence for UK Companies Act terminology), the text is as close as possible to that set out in company law.

Where this FRS contains a disclosure requirement related to a company law requirement this has been indicated.

6A.1   *Details of advances and credits granted by a micro-entity to its directors and guarantees of any kind entered into by a micro-entity on behalf of its directors must be shown in the notes to the financial statements.*

The details required of an advance or credit are:

(a)   *its amount;*
(b)   *an indication of the interest rate;*
(c)   *its main conditions;*
(d)   *any amounts repaid;*
(e)   *any amounts written off; and*
(f)   *any amounts waived.*

There must also be stated in the notes to the financial statements the totals of amounts stated under (a), (d), (e) and (f).

The details required of a guarantee are:

(a)   *its main terms;*
(b)   *the amount of the maximum liability that may be incurred by a micro-entity;*
(c)   *any amount paid and any liability incurred by a micro-entity for the purpose of fulfilling the guarantee (including any loss incurred by reason of enforcement of the guarantee).*

There must also be stated in the notes to the financial statements the totals of amounts stated under (b) and (c). (Section 413 of the Act)

6A.2   *The total amount of any financial commitments, guarantees and contingencies that are not included in the statement of financial position must be stated. (Schedule 1, paragraph 57(1))*

The total amount of any commitments concerning pensions must be separately disclosed. (Schedule 1, paragraph 57(3))

The total amount of any commitments which are undertaken on behalf of or for the benefit of:

(a)   *any parent, fellow subsidiary or any subsidiary of a micro-entity; or*
(b)   *any undertaking in which a micro-entity has a participating interest,*

must be separately stated and those within (a) must also be stated separately from those within (b). (Schedule 1, paragraph 57(4))

The following paragraphs in this FRS address these disclosure requirements within the context of specific transactions:

(a)   Section 9 *Financial Instruments*: paragraph 9.28
(b)   Section 11 *Investments in Joint Ventures*: paragraph 11.9
(c)   Section 12 *Property, Plant and Equipment and Investment Property*: paragraph 12.28
(d)   Section 13 *Intangible Assets other than Goodwill*: paragraph 13.17
(e)   Section 14 *Business Combinations and Goodwill*: paragraph 14.3
(f)   Section 15 *Leases*: paragraphs 15.17 and 15.33.
(g)   Section 16 *Provisions and Contingencies*: paragraph 16.19
(h)   Section 23 *Employee Benefits*: paragraph 23.22.
(i)   Section 27 *Specialised Activities*: paragraph 27.5.

6A.3   *An indication of the nature and form of any valuable security given by the micro-entity in respect of commitments, guarantees and contingencies within paragraph 6A.2. must be given. (Schedule 1, paragraph 57(2))*

The following paragraphs in this FRS address these disclosure requirements within the context of specific transactions:

(a)   Section 9 *Financial Instruments*: paragraph 9.29.
(b)   Section 10 *Inventories*: paragraph 10.22.
(c)   Section 12 *Property, Plant and Equipment and Investment Property*: paragraph 12.29.
(d)   Section 13 *Intangible Assets other than Goodwill*: paragraph 13.18.
(e)   Section 27 *Specialised Activities*: paragraph 27.6.

Section 7 Subsidiaries, Associates, Jointly Controlled Entities and Intermediate Payment Arrangements

Scope of this section

This section sets out how a **micro-entity** shall account for investments in **subsidiaries** and **associates,** interests in **jointly** **7.1** **controlled entities** and intermediate payment arrangements.

Investments in subsidiaries, associates and interests in jointly controlled entities

A micro-entity shall account for any investments in subsidiaries and associates and any interests in jointly controlled **7.2** entities in accordance with Section 9 *Financial Instruments.*

Consolidated financial statements

An entity that is required or chooses to present **consolidated financial statements** is excluded from the **micro-entities** **7.3** **regime** (sections 384A(8) and 384B(2) of the **Act**) and shall not apply this FRS.

Intermediate payment arrangements (eg ESOPs)

Intermediate payment arrangements may take a variety of forms: **7.4**

(a)   The intermediary is usually established by the micro-entity and constituted as a trust, although other arrangements are possible.

(b)   The relationship between the micro-entity and the intermediary may take different forms. For example, when the intermediary is constituted as a trust, the micro-entity will not have a right to direct the intermediary's activities. However, in these and other cases the micro-entity may give advice to the intermediary or may be relied on by the intermediary to provide the information it needs to carry out its activities. Sometimes, the way the intermediary has been set up gives it little discretion in the broad nature of its activities.

(c)   The arrangements are most commonly used to pay employees, although they are sometimes used to compensate suppliers of goods and services other than employee services. Sometimes the micro-entity's employees and other suppliers are not the only beneficiaries of the arrangement. Other beneficiaries may include past employees and their dependants, and the intermediary may be entitled to make charitable donations.

(d)   The precise identity of the persons or entities that will receive payments from the intermediary, and the amounts that they will receive, are not usually agreed at the outset.

(e)   The micro-entity often has the right to appoint or veto the appointment of the intermediary's trustees (or its directors or the equivalent).

(f)   The payments made to the intermediary and the payments made by the intermediary are often cash payments but may involve other transfers of value.

Examples of intermediate payment arrangements are employee share ownership plans (ESOPs) and employee benefit trusts that are used to facilitate employee shareholdings under remuneration schemes. In a typical employee benefit trust arrangement for **share-based payment transactions**, a micro-entity makes payments to a trust or guarantees borrowing by the trust, and the trust uses its funds to accumulate assets to pay the micro-entity's employees for services the employees have rendered to the micro-entity.

Although the trustees of an intermediary must act at all times in accordance with the interests of the beneficiaries of the intermediary, most intermediaries (particularly those established as a means of remunerating employees) are specifically designed so as to serve the purposes of the micro-entity, and to ensure that there will be minimal risk of any conflict arising between the duties of the trustees of the intermediary and the interest of the micro-entity, such that there is nothing to encumber implementation of the wishes of the micro-entity in practice. Where this is the case, the micro-entity has de facto **control**.

Accounting for intermediate payment arrangements

When a micro-entity makes payments (or transfers **assets**) to an intermediary, there is a rebuttable presumption that the **7.5** entity has exchanged one asset for another and that the payment itself does not represent an immediate **expense**. To rebut this presumption at the time the payment is made to the intermediary, the micro-entity must demonstrate:

(a)   it will not obtain future economic benefit from the amounts transferred; or

(b)   it does not have control of the right or other access to the future economic benefit it is expected to receive.

Where a payment to an intermediary is an exchange by the micro-entity of one asset for another, any assets that the **7.6** intermediary acquires in a subsequent exchange transaction will also be under the control of the micro-entity. Accordingly, assets and **liabilities** of the intermediary shall be accounted for by the micro-entity as an extension of its own business and recognised in its **financial statements**. An asset will cease to be recognised as an asset of the micro-entity when, for example, the asset of the intermediary **vests** unconditionally with identified beneficiaries.

7.7   A micro-entity may distribute its own equity instruments, or other equity instruments, to an intermediary in order to facilitate employee shareholdings under a remuneration scheme. Where this is the case and the micro-entity has control, or de facto control, of the assets and liabilities of the intermediary, the commercial effect is that the micro-entity is, for all practical purposes, in the same position as if it had purchased the shares directly.

7.8   Where an intermediary holds the micro-entity's equity instruments, the micro-entity shall account for the equity instruments as if it had purchased them directly. The micro-entity shall account for the assets and liabilities of the intermediary in its financial statements as follows:

(a)   The consideration paid for the equity instruments of the sponsoring entity shall be deducted from equity until such time that the equity instruments vest unconditionally with employees.

(b)   Other assets and liabilities of the intermediary shall be recognised as assets and liabilities of the micro-entity.

(c)   No **gain** or loss shall be recognised in **profit or loss** on the purchase, sale, issue or cancellation of the micro-entity's own equity instruments.

(d)   Finance costs and any administration expenses shall be recognised on an **accruals basis** rather than as funding payments are made to the intermediary.

(e)   Any dividend income arising on the micro-entity's own equity instruments shall be excluded from profit or loss and deducted from the aggregate of dividends paid.

Section 8 Accounting Policies, Estimates and Errors

Scope of this section

8.1   This section provides guidance for selecting and applying the **accounting policies** used in preparing **financial statements**. It also covers **changes in accounting estimates** and corrections of **errors** in prior period financial statements.

Selection and application of accounting policies

8.2   Accounting policies are the specific principles, bases, conventions, rules and practices applied by a **micro-entity** in preparing and presenting financial statements.

8.3   If this FRS specifically addresses a transaction, other event or condition, a micro-entity shall apply this FRS. However, the micro-entity need not follow a requirement in this FRS if the effect of doing so would not be **material**. This exemption does not apply to the disclosures required by paragraph 6.2(a).

8.4   If this FRS does not specifically address a transaction, other event or condition, a micro-entity's management shall use its judgement in developing and applying an accounting policy that results in information that:

(a)   represents faithfully the transactions, other events or conditions;

(b)   reflects the economic substance of the transactions, other events and conditions, and not merely the legal form;

(c)   is neutral, ie free from bias; and

(d)   is **prudent**.

8.5   In making the judgement described in paragraph 8.4, management shall refer to and consider the definitions, **recognition** criteria and **measurement** concepts for **assets**, **liabilities**, **income** and **expenses** and the pervasive principles in Section 2 *Concepts and Pervasive Principles*. A micro-entity is not required to provide any disclosures other than those required by Section 6 *Notes to the Financial Statements* in respect of these transactions or events.

Consistency of accounting policies

8.6   A micro-entity shall select and apply its accounting policies consistently for similar transactions, other events and conditions.

Changes in accounting policies

8.7   A micro-entity shall change an accounting policy only if the change:

(a)   is required by this FRS; or

(b)   results in the financial statements providing reliable and more relevant information about the effects of transactions, other events or conditions on the micro-entity's **financial position** and financial **performance**.

The following are not changes in accounting policies: **8.8**

(a) the application of an accounting policy for transactions, other events or conditions that differ in substance from those previously occurring; and

(b) the application of a new accounting policy for transactions, other events or conditions that did not occur previously or were not material.

Applying changes in accounting policies

A micro-entity shall account for changes in accounting policy as follows: **8.9**

(a) a micro-entity shall account for a change in accounting policy resulting from a change in the requirements of this FRS in accordance with the transitional provisions, if any, specified in that amendment; and

(b) a micro-entity shall account for all other changes in accounting policy retrospectively (see paragraph 8.10).

Retrospective application

When a change in accounting policy is applied retrospectively in accordance with paragraph 8.9, the micro-entity shall **8.10** apply the new accounting policy to comparative information for prior periods to the earliest date for which it is practicable, as if the new accounting policy had always been applied. When it is **impracticable** to determine the individual-period effects of a change in accounting policy on comparative information for one or more prior periods presented, the micro-entity shall apply the new accounting policy to the **carrying amounts** of assets and liabilities as at the beginning of the earliest period for which **retrospective application** is practicable, which may be the current period, and shall make a corresponding adjustment to the opening balance of each affected component of **equity** for that period.

Changes in accounting estimates

A **change in accounting estimate** is an adjustment of the carrying amount of an asset or a liability, or the amount of the **8.11** periodic consumption of an asset, that results from the assessment of the present status of, and expected future benefits and obligations associated with, assets and liabilities. Changes in accounting estimates result from new information or new developments and, accordingly, are not corrections of errors. When it is difficult to distinguish a change in an accounting policy from a change in an accounting estimate, the change is treated as a change in an accounting estimate.

A micro-entity shall recognise the effect of a change in an accounting estimate, other than a change to which **8.12** paragraph 8.13 applies, **prospectively** by including it in **profit or loss** in:

(a) the period of the change, if the change affects that period only; or

(b) the period of the change and future periods, if the change affects both.

To the extent that a change in an accounting estimate gives rise to changes in assets and liabilities, or relates to an item of **8.13** equity, the micro-entity shall recognise it by adjusting the carrying amount of the related asset, liability or equity item in the period of the change.

Corrections of prior period errors

Prior period errors are omissions from, and misstatements in, a micro-entity's financial statements for one or more prior **8.14** periods arising from a failure to use, or misuse of, reliable information that:

(a) was available when financial statements for those periods were authorised for issue; and

(b) could reasonably be expected to have been obtained and taken into account in the preparation and presentation of those financial statements.

Such errors include the effects of mathematical mistakes, mistakes in applying accounting policies, oversights or **8.15** misinterpretations of facts, and fraud.

To the extent practicable, a micro-entity shall correct a material prior period error retrospectively in the first financial **8.16** statements authorised for issue after its discovery by:

(a) restating the comparative amounts for the prior period(s) presented in which the error occurred; or

(b) if the error occurred before the earliest prior period presented, restating the opening balances of assets, liabilities and equity for the earliest prior period presented.

When it is impracticable to determine the period-specific effects of a material error on comparative information for one **8.17** or more prior periods presented, the micro-entity shall restate the opening balances of assets, liabilities and equity for the earliest period for which retrospective restatement is practicable (which may be the current period).

Section 9 Financial Instruments

Scope of this section

9.1 This section deals with the **recognition**, **derecognition**, **measurement** and disclosure of **financial instruments** (**financial assets** and **financial liabilities**).

9.2 All financial instruments are accounted for in accordance with this section, unless they are excluded by paragraph 9.3. Examples of financial instruments in the scope of this section include:

(a) cash;

(b) accounts receivable and payable (trade debtors and creditors);

(c) commercial paper and commercial bills held;

(d) demand and fixed-term deposits with banks or similar institutions;

(e) bonds, loans and similar instruments;

(f) investments;

(g) options, warrants, futures contracts, forward contracts and interest rate swaps.

9.3 This section does not apply to the following financial instruments:

(a) Financial instruments that meet the definition of a **micro-entity's** own **equity**, and the equity component of **compound financial instruments** issued by the reporting micro-entity that contain both a **liability** and an equity component (see Section 17 *Liabilities and Equity*).

(b) **Leases**, to which Section 15 *Leases* applies. However, the derecognition requirements in paragraphs 9.21 to 9.23 and impairment accounting requirements in paragraphs 9.16 to 9.19 apply to derecognition and impairment of receivables recognised by a lessor and the derecognition requirements in paragraphs 9.25 and 9.26 apply to payables recognised by a lessee arising under a **finance lease**.

(c) Employers' rights and obligations under employee benefit plans, to which Section 23 *Employee Benefits* applies.

(d) Financial instruments, contracts and obligations to which Section 21 *Share-based Payment* applies.

(e) Reimbursement assets and **financial guarantee contracts** accounted for in accordance with Section 16 *Provisions and Contingencies*.

(f) Contracts for contingent consideration in a **business combination** (see Section 14 *Business Combinations and Goodwill*). This exemption applies only to the acquirer.

Initial recognition of financial assets and liabilities

9.4 A micro-entity shall recognise a financial asset or a financial liability only when the micro-entity becomes a party to the contractual provisions of the instrument.

Initial measurement

9.5 A financial asset or financial liability is recognised initially at its cost. The cost is measured at the transaction price.

Examples – Transaction price of a financial asset or liability

1   For a loan the transaction price is the amount borrowed or loaned.
2   For trade receivables or payables (trade debtors or trade creditors) the transaction price equals the invoice price unless payment is deferred beyond normal credit terms (see paragraph 9.6).
3   For an investment the transaction price is the consideration given (eg cash paid to acquire the investment).
4   For an option the transaction price is the premium paid to purchase the option.

9.6 When a micro-entity purchases **inventory, property, plant and equipment, investment property** or sells goods or services with settlement deferred beyond normal credit terms, the transaction price is the cash price available on the date of the transaction (see Sections 10 *Inventories*, 12 *Property, Plant and Equipment and Investment Property* and 18 *Revenue* respectively).

Example – Transaction price when payment is deferred

A micro-entity sells goods to a customer for CU100. Customers are usually required to pay within 14 days of the invoice date, but the micro-entity agrees with the customer that payment will be deferred for one year. The micro-entity sells the same item for CU90, if payment is received within the usual credit terms.

The cash price for the goods and thereby the transaction price is CU90.

Transaction costs shall be added to the cost of a financial asset or shall be deducted from the cost of a financial liability, unless they are not **material** in which case they are recognised immediately as an **expense** in **profit or loss**.   **9.7**

Examples – Transaction costs

1   A micro-entity receives a bank loan of CU500. The bank charges CU5 in arrangement fees. The micro-entity determines that the transaction costs are immaterial and recognises them immediately in profit or loss as an expense. The cost of the loan is CU500.

2   A micro-entity is making an investment and buys shares in another entity for CU1,000. The micro-entity incurs legal fees and other transaction costs totalling CU100. The micro-entity determines that the transaction costs are material and includes them in the cost of the investment. The total cost of the investment is CU1,100.

3   A micro-entity takes out a forward foreign currency exchange contract and is charged a fee of CU30. The micro-entity determines that the transaction costs are material. The total cost of the forward foreign currency exchange contract is CU30.

Subsequent measurement

At the end of each **reporting period**, a micro-entity shall measure financial instruments as follows, without any deduction for transaction costs the micro-entity may incur on sale or other disposal: **9.8**

(a)   Investments in preference shares or **ordinary shares** and investments in **subsidiaries** and **associates** and interests in **jointly controlled entities** shall be measured at cost less impairment.

(b)   **Derivatives** shall be measured as set out in paragraph 9.10.

(c)   Financial instruments other than those covered by paragraphs (a) and (b) shall be measured as set out in paragraphs 9.12 to 9.15.

All financial assets must be assessed for impairment or uncollectability. See paragraphs 9.16 to 9.19.

Derivatives

Derivatives include forward foreign currency exchange contracts and interest rate swaps. More examples are given in paragraph 9.2(g).   **9.9**

The transaction price of a financial instrument that is a derivative plus any transaction costs not immediately recognised in profit or loss (see paragraph 9.7) less any **impairment losses** recognised to date, is allocated to profit or loss over the term of the contract on a straight-line basis, unless another systematic basis of allocation is more appropriate.   **9.10**

Contractual payments

Under a derivative contract a micro-entity may be required to make or may be entitled to receive payments. A micro-entity shall recognise amounts payable or receivable as they accrue.   **9.11**

Financial instruments measured in accordance with paragraph 9.8(c)

Financial instruments other than those covered in paragraphs 9.8(a) and 9.8(b) are measured as follows: **9.12**

(a)   the transaction price (see paragraph 9.5);

(b)   plus, in the case of a financial asset, or minus in the case of a financial liability, transaction costs not yet recognised in profit or loss (see paragraph 9.15);

(c)   plus the cumulative interest income or expense recognised in profit or loss to date (see paragraphs 9.13 and 9.14);

(d)   minus all repayments of principal and all interest payments or receipts to date;

(e)   minus, in the case of a financial asset, any reduction (directly or through the use of an allowance account) for impairment or uncollectability (see paragraphs 9.16 to 9.19).

Allocation of interest income or expense

Total interest income or expense is the difference between the initial transaction price and the total amount of the subsequent contractual receipts or payments, excluding transaction costs.   **9.13**

A micro-entity shall allocate total interest income or expense over the term of the contract as follows: **9.14**

(a)   For transactions where settlement is deferred beyond normal credit terms (see paragraph 9.6), total interest income or expense shall be allocated on a straight-line basis over the term of the contract.

(b)   In all other cases, interest income or expense is allocated at a constant rate on the financial asset's or financial liability's **carrying amount** excluding transaction costs not yet recognised in profit or loss (see paragraph 9.12(b)). The applicable rate will normally be the contractual rate of interest and may be a variable or a fixed rate.

Transaction costs

9.15   Transaction costs not immediately recognised in profit or loss in accordance with paragraph 9.7, are recognised in profit or loss on a straight-line basis over the term of the contract.

Example 1: Measurement of a loan liability

A micro-entity receives a loan of CU1,000 on 1 January 20X0. The micro-entity pays loan arrangement fees of CU50. The contractual interest rate is five per cent payable annually in arrears on 31 December. The loan is repayable after two years. The micro-entity's annual reporting period ends on 31 December.

The micro-entity determines that the loan arrangement fees (transaction costs) are material and on 1 January 20X0 recognises the loan at its transaction price of CU1,000 less the transaction costs of CU50. The transactions costs of CU50 are recognised in the profit and loss account on a straight-line basis over two years, ie CU25 each year.

The carrying value of the loan is as follows:

Year	Carrying amount at 1 Jan	Interest at 5%	Transaction costs in profit or loss	Cash payments	Carrying amount at 31 Dec
	CU	CU	CU	CU	CU
20X0	(950)	(50)	(25)	50	(975)
20X1	(975)	(50)	(25)	1,050	0

Example 2: Measurement of a loan asset

A micro-entity makes an interest-free loan of CU900 on 1 January 20X0. The loan is repayable after two years. In 20X1 the micro-entity agrees that the borrower only needs to repay CU450 which is paid on 31 December 20X1. The micro-entity's annual reporting period ends on 31 December.

The loan is recognised at its transaction price of CU900 on 1 January 20X0. In 20X1 an impairment loss for the uncollectability of CU450 is recognised. The carrying amount of the loan is as follows:

Year	Carrying amount at 1 Jan	Impairment	Cash receipts	Carrying amount at 31 Dec
	CU	CU	CU	CU
20X0	900	–	–	900
20X1	900	(450)	(450)	0

Impairment of financial assets

Recognition and measurement

9.16   At the end of each reporting period, a micro-entity shall assess whether there is evidence of impairment of any financial asset.

9.17   Evidence that a financial asset could be impaired includes the following events:

(a)   significant financial difficulty of the debtor;

(b)   a breach of contract, such as a default or delinquency in interest or principal payments;

(c)   the creditor, for economic or legal reasons relating to the debtor's financial difficulty, granting to the debtor a concession that the creditor would not otherwise consider;

(d)   it has become **probable** that the debtor will enter bankruptcy or other financial reorganisation;

(e)   declining market values of the asset or similar assets;

(f)   significant changes with an adverse effect on the asset that have taken place in the technological, market, economic or legal environment; and

(g)   the contract has become an **onerous contract**.

A micro-entity shall measure an impairment loss for financial assets as set out below. An impairment loss is immediately **9.18** recognised in profit or loss.

(a) An investment in preference shares or ordinary shares and an investment in subsidiaries and associates and an interest in jointly controlled entities is impaired and an impairment loss shall be recognised if the asset's carrying amount exceeds the best estimate of the asset's selling price as at the **reporting date**.

(b) An asset that is a derivative is impaired and an impairment loss shall be recognised if the asset's carrying value exceeds the asset's **fair value less costs to sell**.

(c) An asset measured in accordance with paragraph 9.8(c), is impaired and an impairment loss shall be recognised, if the asset's carrying amount exceeds the total of estimated net cash flows that can be generated from the asset. When the effect of the time value of money is material, the amount of the net cash flows shall be the present value of the estimated net cash flows. The discount rate shall be the asset's current contractual interest rate.

Reversal

A micro-entity shall reverse a previously recognised impairment loss if in a subsequent period the amount of an **9.19** impairment loss decreases and the decrease can be related to an event occurring after the impairment was recognised (eg an improvement in the debtor's credit rating). The micro-entity shall recognise the amount of the reversal in profit or loss immediately.

Onerous contracts

At each reporting date a micro-entity shall assess whether a derivative constitutes an onerous contract. A derivative is an **9.20** onerous contract when the expected unavoidable payments exceed the economic benefits expected to be received from the derivative. A derivative which does not mitigate a specific risk or risks of a micro-entity is an onerous contract when the expected payments exceed the expected cash receipts under the contract. The present obligation arising from an onerous contract shall be measured in accordance with Section 16.

Example: Assessment of whether a derivative is onerous

A micro-entity takes out a loan with a variable rate of interest. In order to mitigate the risk of fluctuating interest payments, the micro-entity enters into an interest rate swap. Through the interest rate swap the micro-entity pays a fixed rate of interest and receives a variable rate of interest equal to the interest on the loan.

Scenario 1:

Interest rates are going down and as a result the payments made by the micro-entity under the interest rate swap are higher than the receipts. The interest rate swap is not an onerous contract because the micro-entity continues to benefit from the interest rate swap by effectively paying a fixed rate of interest on the loan.

Scenario 2:

The micro-entity repays the loan early, but the interest rate swap cannot be terminated. The micro-entity expects that the payments due under the interest rate swap exceed the receipts. The interest rate swap is an onerous contract because the micro-entity no longer derives a benefit from it.

Derecognition of a financial asset

A micro-entity shall derecognise a financial asset only when: **9.21**

(a) the contractual rights to the cash flows from the financial asset expire or are settled;

(b) the micro-entity transfers to another party substantially all of the risks (eg slow or non-payment risk) and rewards of ownership (eg future cash flows from a debtor); or

(c) when no future economic benefits are expected from holding it or its disposal.

A micro-entity shall recognise any **gain** or loss on the derecognition of a financial asset in profit or loss when the item is **9.22** derecognised.

If a micro-entity received any proceeds from the transfer of a financial asset, but the conditions in paragraph 9.21 are not **9.23** met, a micro-entity shall continue to recognise the asset in its entirety and shall recognise a financial liability for the consideration received. The asset and liability shall not be offset. In subsequent periods, the micro-entity shall recognise any **income** on the transferred asset and any expense incurred on the financial liability.

Example 1: Debt factoring arrangement that qualifies for derecognition

A micro-entity sells a group of its accounts receivable to a bank at less than their carrying amount. The micro-entity is obliged to remit promptly to the bank all amounts collected, but it has no obligation to the bank for slow payment or nonpayment by the debtors.

In this case, the micro-entity has transferred to the bank substantially all of the risks and rewards of ownership of the receivables. Accordingly, it removes the receivables from its statement of financial position (ie derecognises them), and it shows no liability in respect of the proceeds received from the bank. The micro-entity recognises a loss calculated as the difference between the carrying amount of the receivables at the time of sale and the proceeds received from the bank. The micro-entity recognises a liability to the extent that it has collected funds from the debtors but has not yet remitted them to the bank.

Example 2: Debt factoring arrangement that does not qualify for derecognition

The facts are the same as in the preceding example except that the micro-entity has agreed to buy back from the bank any receivables for which the debtor is in arrears as to principal or interest for more than 120 days.

In this case, the micro-entity has retained the risk of slow payment or non-payment by the debtors – a significant risk with respect to receivables. Accordingly, the micro-entity does not treat the receivables as having been sold to the bank, and it does not derecognise them. Instead, it treats the proceeds from the bank as a loan. The micro-entity continues to recognise the receivables as an asset until they are collected or written off as uncollectible.

Transfers of non-cash collateral

9.24   When a micro-entity participates in arrangements where it provides or receives financial assets other than cash as collateral (eg a micro-entity pledges commercial papers as security against a loan), the micro-entity shall apply the requirements of paragraphs 11.35(b) to 11.35(d) of **FRS 102**.

Derecognition of a financial liability

9.25   A micro-entity shall derecognise a financial liability (or a part of a financial liability) only when it is extinguished – ie when the obligation specified in the contract is discharged, is cancelled or expires.

9.26   A micro-entity shall recognise any gain or loss on the derecognition of a financial liability (or a part of a financial liability) in profit or loss when the item is derecognised.

Presentation

9.27   A financial asset and a financial liability shall be offset and the net amount presented in the **statement of financial position** when, and only when, a micro-entity:

(a)   currently has a legally enforceable right to set off the recognised amounts; and
(b)   intends either to settle on a net basis, or to realise the asset and settle the liability simultaneously.

Disclosures in the notes

9.28   A micro-entity shall determine the amount of any financial commitments, guarantees and contingencies not recognised in the statement of financial position arising from its financial instruments and disclose that amount within the total amount of financial commitments, guarantees and contingencies (see paragraph 6A.2).

9.29   A micro-entity shall disclose an indication of the nature and form of any financial asset given as security in respect of its commitments, guarantees and contingencies (see paragraph 6A.3).

Section 10 Inventories

Scope of this section

This section sets out the principles for recognising and measuring **inventories**. **10.1**

This section applies to all inventories, except: **10.2**

(a) work in progress arising under **construction contracts**, including directly related service contracts (see Section 18 *Revenue*); and

(b) **biological assets** related to **agricultural activity** and **agricultural produce** at the point of harvest (see Section 27 *Specialised Activities*).

Measurement of inventories

A **micro-entity** shall measure inventories at the lower of cost and estimated selling price less costs to complete and sell. **10.3**

Cost of inventories

A micro-entity shall include in the cost of inventories all costs of purchase, costs of conversion and other costs incurred **10.4** in bringing the inventories to their present location and condition.

Where inventories are acquired through a **non-exchange transaction**, their cost shall be measured at their **fair value** at **10.5** the date of acquisition.

Costs of purchase

The costs of purchase of inventories comprise the purchase price, import duties and other taxes (other than those **10.6** subsequently recoverable by the micro-entity from the taxing authorities), and transport, handling and other costs directly attributable to the acquisition of finished goods, materials and services. Trade discounts, rebates and other similar items are deducted in determining the costs of purchase.

If payment is deferred beyond normal credit terms, the purchase price is the cash price available at the date of purchase. **10.7** Any excess of the deferred payment amount over the cash price available at the date of purchase is recognised as interest and accounted for in accordance with paragraph 9.14(a).

Costs of conversion

The costs of conversion of inventories include costs directly related to the units of production, such as direct labour. They **10.8** also include a systematic allocation of fixed and variable production overheads that are incurred in converting materials into finished goods. Fixed production overheads are those indirect costs of production that remain relatively constant regardless of the volume of production, such as **depreciation** and maintenance of factory buildings and equipment, and the cost of factory management and administration. Variable production overheads are those indirect costs of production that vary directly, or nearly directly, with the volume of production, such as indirect materials and indirect labour.

Production overheads include the costs for obligations (recognised and measured in accordance with Section 16 *Provisions* **10.9** *and Contingencies*) for dismantling, removing and restoring a site on which an item of **property, plant and equipment** is located that are incurred during the **reporting period** as a consequence of having used that item of property, plant and equipment to produce inventory during that period.

Allocation of production overheads

A micro-entity shall allocate fixed production overheads to the costs of conversion on the basis of the normal capacity of **10.10** the production facilities. Normal capacity is the production expected to be achieved on average over a number of periods or seasons under normal circumstances, taking into account the loss of capacity resulting from planned maintenance. The actual level of production may be used if it approximates normal capacity. The amount of fixed overhead allocated to each unit of production is not increased as a consequence of low production or idle plant. Unallocated overheads are recognised as an **expense** in the period in which they are incurred. In periods of abnormally high production, the amount of fixed overhead allocated to each unit of production is decreased so that inventories are not measured above cost. Variable production overheads are allocated to each unit of production on the basis of the actual use of the production facilities.

Other costs included in inventories

10.11   A micro-entity shall include other costs in the cost of inventories only to the extent that they are incurred in bringing the inventories to their present location and condition.

Costs excluded from inventories

10.12   Examples of costs excluded from the cost of inventories and recognised as expenses in the period in which they are incurred are:

(a)   abnormal amounts of wasted materials, labour or other production costs;
(b)   storage costs, unless those costs are necessary during the production process before a further production stage;
(c)   administrative overheads that do not contribute to bringing inventories to their present location and condition; and
(d)   selling costs.

Cost of inventories of a service provider

10.13   To the extent that service providers have inventories, they measure them at the costs of their production. These costs consist primarily of the labour and other costs of personnel directly engaged in providing the service, including supervisory personnel, and attributable overheads. Labour and other costs relating to sales and general administrative personnel are not included but are recognised as expenses in the period in which they are incurred. The cost of inventories of a service provider does not include profit margins or non-attributable overheads that are often factored into prices charged by service providers.

Cost of agricultural produce harvested from biological assets

10.14   Section 27 requires that inventories comprising agricultural produce that a micro-entity has harvested from its biological assets should be measured on initial **recognition,** at the point of harvest, at the lower of cost and estimated selling price less costs to complete and sell. This becomes the cost of the inventories at that date for application of this section.

Techniques for measuring cost, such as standard costing, retail method and most recent purchase price

10.15   A micro-entity may use techniques such as the standard cost method, the retail method or most recent purchase price for measuring the cost of inventories if the result approximates cost. Standard costs take into account normal levels of materials and supplies, labour, efficiency and capacity utilisation. They are regularly reviewed and, if necessary, revised in the light of current conditions. The retail method measures cost by reducing the sales value of the inventory by the appropriate percentage gross margin.

Cost formulas

10.16   A micro-entity shall measure the cost of inventories of items that are not ordinarily interchangeable and goods or services produced and segregated for specific projects by using specific identification of their individual costs.

10.17   A micro-entity shall measure the cost of inventories, other than those dealt with in paragraph 10.16, by using the first-in, first-out (FIFO) or weighted average cost formula. A micro-entity shall use the same cost formula for all inventories having a similar nature and use to the micro-entity. For inventories with a different nature or use, different cost formulas may be justified. The last-in, first-out method (LIFO) is not permitted by this FRS.

Impairment of inventories

10.18   Implicit in the requirement for a micro-entity to measure inventories at the lower of cost and estimated selling price less costs to complete, is a requirement that a micro-entity shall assess at the end of each reporting period whether any inventories are impaired, ie the **carrying amount** is not fully recoverable (eg because of damage, obsolescence or declining selling prices). If an item (or group of items) of inventory is impaired, the micro-entity shall recognise an **impairment loss**.

10.19   When the circumstances that previously caused inventories to be impaired no longer exist or when there is clear evidence of an increase in selling price less costs to complete and sell because of changed economic circumstances, the micro-entity shall reverse the amount of the impairment (ie the reversal is limited to the amount of the original impairment loss).

Recognition as an expense

10.20   When inventories are sold, the micro-entity shall recognise the carrying amount of those inventories as an expense in the period in which the related **revenue** is recognised.

Some inventories may be allocated to other asset accounts, for example, inventory used as a component of self-constructed property, plant or equipment. Inventories allocated to another **asset** in this way are accounted for subsequently in accordance with the section of this FRS relevant to that type of asset. **10.21**

Disclosure in the notes

A micro-entity shall disclose an indication of the nature and form of any items of inventory given as security in respect of its commitments, guarantees and contingencies (see paragraph 6A.3). **10.22**

Section 11 Investments in Joint Ventures

Scope of this section

This section applies to the accounting for investments in **joint ventures** that are **jointly controlled** operations and jointly controlled **assets**. **11.1**

A **micro-entity** shall refer to Section 7 *Subsidiaries, Associates, Jointly Controlled Entities and Intermediate Payment Arrangements* which sets out the requirements for investments in joint ventures that are **jointly controlled entities**. **11.2**

Joint ventures defined

Joint control is the contractually agreed sharing of **control** over an economic activity, and exists only when the strategic financial and operating decisions relating to the activity require the unanimous consent of the parties sharing control (the **venturers**). **11.3**

A joint venture is a contractual arrangement whereby two or more parties undertake an economic activity that is subject to joint control. Joint ventures can take the form of jointly controlled operations, jointly controlled assets, or jointly controlled entities. **11.4**

Jointly controlled operations

The operation of some joint ventures involves the use of the assets and other resources of the venturers rather than the establishment of a corporation, partnership or other entity, or a financial structure that is separate from the venturers themselves. Each venturer uses its own **property, plant and equipment** and carries its own **inventories**. It also incurs its own **expenses** and **liabilities** and raises its own finance, which represent its own obligations. The joint venture activities may be carried out by the venturer's employees alongside the venturer's similar activities. The joint venture agreement usually provides a means by which the **revenue** from the sale of the joint product and any expenses incurred in common are shared among the venturers. **11.5**

In respect of its interests in jointly controlled operations, a venturer shall recognise in its **financial statements**: **11.6**

(a) the assets that it controls and the liabilities that it incurs; and
(b) the expenses that it incurs and its share of the **income** that it earns from the sale of goods or services by the joint venture.

Jointly controlled assets

Some joint ventures involve the joint control, and often the joint ownership, by the venturers of one or more assets contributed to, or acquired for the purpose of, the joint venture and dedicated to the purposes of the joint venture. **11.7**

In respect of its interest in a jointly controlled asset, a venturer shall recognise in its financial statements: **11.8**

(a) its share of the jointly controlled assets, classified in accordance with the format adopted set out in Section 4 *Statement of Financial Position*;
(b) any liabilities that it has incurred;
(c) its share of any liabilities incurred jointly with the other venturers in relation to the joint venture;
(d) any income from the sale or use of its share of the output of the joint venture, together with its share of any expenses incurred by the joint venture; and
(e) any expenses that it has incurred in respect of its interest in the joint venture.

Disclosure in the notes

A micro-entity shall determine the amount of any financial commitments, guarantees and contingencies not recognised in the **statement of financial position** arising from its jointly controlled operations and jointly controlled assets and **11.9** disclose that amount within the total amount of financial commitments, guarantees and contingencies (see paragraph 6A.2).

Section 12 Property, Plant and Equipment and Investment Property

Scope of this section

12.1   This section applies to the accounting for **property**, **plant and equipment** and **investment property**.

12.2   Property, plant and equipment does not include **biological assets** related to **agricultural activity** (see Section 27 *Specialised Activities*).

Recognition

12.3   A **micro-entity** shall recognise the cost of an item of property, plant and equipment or investment property as an **asset** if, and only if:

(a)   it is **probable** that future economic benefits associated with the item will flow to the micro-entity; and
(b)   the cost of the item can be measured reliably.

12.4   Spare parts and servicing equipment are usually carried as **inventory** and recognised in **profit or loss** as consumed. However, major spare parts and stand-by equipment are property, plant and equipment when a micro-entity expects to use them during more than one period. Similarly, if the spare parts and servicing equipment can be used only in connection with an item of property, plant and equipment, they are considered property, plant and equipment.

12.5   Parts of some items of property, plant and equipment or investment property may require replacement at regular intervals (eg the roof of a building). A micro-entity shall add to the **carrying amount** of an item of property, plant and equipment or investment property the cost of replacing part of such an item when that cost is incurred if the replacement part is expected to provide incremental future benefits to the micro-entity. The carrying amount of those parts that are replaced is derecognised in accordance with paragraphs 12.26 and 12.27.

12.6   A condition of continuing to operate an item of property, plant and equipment (eg a bus) or investment property may be performing regular major inspections for faults regardless of whether parts of the item are replaced. When each major inspection is performed, its cost is recognised in the carrying amount of the item of property, plant and equipment or investment property as a replacement if the **recognition** criteria are satisfied. Any remaining carrying amount of the cost of the previous major inspection (as distinct from physical parts) is derecognised. This is done regardless of whether the cost of the previous major inspection was identified in the transaction in which the item was acquired or constructed. If necessary, the estimated cost of a future similar inspection may be used as an indication of what the cost of the existing inspection component was when the item was acquired or constructed.

12.7   Land and buildings are separable assets, and a micro-entity shall account for them separately, even when they are acquired together.

Measurement at initial recognition

12.8   A micro-entity shall measure an item of property, plant and equipment or investment property at initial recognition at its cost.

Elements of cost

12.9   The cost of an item of property, plant and equipment or investment property comprises all of the following:

(a)   Its purchase price, including legal and brokerage fees, import duties and non-refundable purchase taxes, after deducting trade discounts and rebates.
(b)   Any costs directly attributable to bringing the asset to the location and condition necessary for it to be capable of operating in the manner intended by management. These can include the costs of site preparation, initial delivery and handling, installation and assembly, and testing of functionality.
(c)   The initial estimate of the costs, recognised and measured in accordance with Section 16 *Provisions and Contingencies,* of dismantling and removing the item and restoring the site on which it is located, the obligation for which a micro-entity incurs either when the item is acquired or as a consequence of having used the item during a particular period for purposes other than to produce inventories during that period.

12.10   The following costs are not costs of an item of property, plant and equipment or investment property, and a micro-entity shall recognise them as an **expense** when they are incurred:

(a)   costs of opening a new facility;

(b)   costs of introducing a new product or service (including costs of advertising and promotional activities);

(c)   costs of conducting business in a new location or with a new class of customer (including costs of staff training); and

(d)   administration and other general overhead costs.

The **income** and related **expenses** of incidental operations during construction or development of an item of property, plant and equipment or investment property are recognised in **profit or loss** if those operations are not necessary to bring the item to its intended location and operating condition.

12.11

Measurement of cost

The cost of an item of property, plant and equipment or investment property is the cash price equivalent at the recognition date. If payment is deferred beyond normal credit terms, the cost is the cash price available at the recognition date. Any excess of the deferred payment amount over the cash price available at the recognition date is recognised as interest and accounted for in accordance with paragraph 9.14(a).

12.12

Exchanges of assets

An item of property, plant or equipment or investment property may be acquired in exchange for a non-monetary asset or assets, or a combination of monetary and non-monetary assets. A micro-entity shall measure the cost of the acquired asset at **fair value** unless:

12.13

(a)   the exchange transaction lacks commercial substance; or

(b)   the fair value of neither the asset received nor the asset given up is reliably measurable. In that case, the asset's cost is measured at the carrying amount of the asset given up.

Measurement after initial recognition

A micro-entity shall measure all items of property, plant and equipment and investment property after initial recognition at cost less any accumulated **depreciation** and any accumulated **impairment losses**. A micro-entity shall recognise the costs of day-today servicing of an item of property, plant and equipment or investment property in profit or loss in the period in which the costs are incurred.

12.14

Depreciation

If the major components of an item of property, plant and equipment or investment property have significantly different patterns of consumption of economic benefits, a micro-entity shall allocate the initial cost of the asset to its major components and depreciate each such component separately over its **useful life**. Other assets shall be depreciated over their useful lives as a single asset. There are some exceptions, such as land which generally has an unlimited useful life and therefore is not usually depreciated.

12.15

The depreciation charge for each period shall be recognised in profit or loss unless another section of this FRS requires the cost to be recognised as part of the cost of an asset. For example, the depreciation of manufacturing property, plant and equipment is included in the costs of inventories (see Section 10 *Inventories*).

12.16

Depreciable amount and depreciation period

A micro-entity shall allocate the **depreciable amount** of an asset on a systematic basis over its useful life.

12.17

Factors may indicate that the **residual value** or useful life of an asset has changed since the most recent annual **reporting date**. If such indicators are present, a micro-entity shall review its previous estimates and, if current expectations differ, amend the residual value, depreciation method or useful life. The micro-entity shall account for the change in residual value, depreciation method or useful life as a change in an accounting estimate in accordance with paragraphs 8.11 to 8.13.

12.18

Depreciation of an asset begins when it is available for use, ie when it is in the location and condition necessary for it to be capable of operating in the manner intended by management. Depreciation of an asset ceases when the asset is derecognised. Depreciation does not cease when the asset becomes idle or is retired from active use unless the asset is fully depreciated. However, under usage methods of depreciation the depreciation charge can be zero while there is no production.

12.19

12.20   A micro-entity shall consider all the following factors in determining the useful life of an asset:

    (a)   The expected usage of the asset. Usage is assessed by reference to the asset's expected capacity or physical output.

    (b)   Expected physical wear and tear, which depends on operational factors such as the number of shifts for which the asset is to be used and the repair and maintenance programme, and the care and maintenance of the asset while idle.

    (c)   Technical or commercial obsolescence arising from changes or improvements in production, or from a change in the market demand for the product or service output of the asset.

    (d)   Legal or similar limits on the use of the asset, such as the expiry dates of related **leases**.

Depreciation method

12.21   A micro-entity shall select a depreciation method that reflects the pattern in which it expects to consume the asset's future economic benefits. The possible depreciation methods include the straight-line method, the diminishing balance method and a method based on usage such as the units of production method.

12.22   If there is an indication that there has been a significant change since the last annual reporting date in the pattern by which a micro-entity expects to consume an asset's future economic benefits, the micro-entity shall review its present depreciation method and, if current expectations differ, change the depreciation method to reflect the new pattern. The micro-entity shall account for the change as a change in an accounting estimate in accordance with paragraphs 8.11 to 8.13.

Impairment

Recognition and measurement of impairment

12.23   At each reporting date, a micro-entity shall apply Section 22 *Impairment of Assets* to determine whether an item or group of items of property, plant and equipment or investment property is impaired and, if so, how to recognise and measure the impairment loss. That section explains when and how a micro-entity reviews the carrying amount of its assets, how it determines the **recoverable amount** of an asset, and when it recognises or reverses an impairment loss.

Compensation for impairment

12.24   An entity shall include in profit or loss, compensation from third parties for items of property, plant and equipment or investment property that were impaired, lost or given up only when the compensation is virtually certain.

Property, plant and equipment or investment property held for sale

12.25   Paragraph 22.7(f) states that a plan to dispose of an asset before the previously expected date is an indicator of impairment that triggers the calculation of the asset's recoverable amount for the purpose of determining whether the asset is impaired.

Derecognition

12.26   A micro-entity shall **derecognise** an item of property, plant and equipment or investment property:

    (a)   on disposal; or

    (b)   when no future economic benefits are expected from its use or disposal.

12.27   A micro-entity shall recognise the **gain** or loss on the derecognition of an item of property, plant and equipment or investment property in profit or loss when the item is derecognised (unless Section 15 *Leases* requires otherwise on a sale and leaseback). The micro-entity shall not classify such gains as **turnover** in the **income statement**.

Disclosure in the notes

12.28   A micro-entity shall determine the amount of any financial commitments not recognised in the **statement of financial position** for the acquisition of property, plant and equipment or investment property and disclose that amount within the total amount of financial commitments, guarantees and contingencies (see paragraph 6A.2).

12.29   A micro-entity shall disclose an indication of the nature and form of any items of property, plant and equipment or investment property given as security in respect of its commitments, guarantees and contingencies (see paragraph 6A.3).

Section 13 Intangible Assets other than Goodwill

Scope of this section

This section applies to the accounting for all separately acquired **intangible assets** and internally generated intangible assets, other than intangible assets held by a **micro-entity** for sale in the ordinary course of business (see Section 10 *Inventories* and Section 18 *Revenue*).   **13.1**

For the accounting of intangible assets acquired as part of a **business combination** including **goodwill** see Section 14 *Business Combinations and Goodwill*.   **13.2**

Recognition

A micro-entity shall recognise all separately acquired intangible assets.   **13.3**

An internally generated intangible shall not be recognised as an **asset**. All expenditure incurred shall be recognised as an **expense** immediately in **profit or loss**.   **13.4**

A micro-entity shall recognise the expenditure on the following items as an expense and shall not recognise such expenditure as intangible assets (the list is not exhaustive):   **13.5**

(a)   Expenditure on **research** and **development** activities.
(b)   Internally generated brands, logos, publishing titles, customer lists and items similar in substance.
(c)   Start-up activities (ie start-up costs), which include establishment costs such as legal and secretarial costs incurred in establishing a legal entity, expenditure to open a new facility or business (ie pre-opening costs) and expenditure for starting new operations or launching new products or processes (ie pre-operating costs).
(d)   Training activities.
(e)   Advertising and promotional activities.
(f)   Relocating or reorganising part or all of a micro-entity.
(g)   Internally generated goodwill.

Initial measurement

A micro-entity shall measure a separately acquired intangible asset initially at cost which comprises: **13.6**

(a)   its purchase price, including import duties and non-refundable purchase taxes, after deducting trade discounts and rebates; and
(b)   any directly attributable cost of preparing the asset for its intended use.

Exchanges of assets

An intangible asset may be acquired in exchange for a non-monetary asset or assets, or a combination of monetary and non-monetary assets. A micro-entity shall measure the cost of such an intangible asset at **fair value** unless: **13.7**

(a)   the exchange transaction lacks commercial substance; or
(b)   the fair value of neither the asset received nor the asset given up is reliably measurable. In that case, the asset's cost is measured at the **carrying amount** of the asset given up.

Measurement after initial recognition

A micro-entity shall measure a separately acquired intangible asset after initial recognition at cost less any accumulated **amortisation** and any accumulated **impairment losses**. The requirements for amortisation are set out in paragraphs 13.9 to 13.14.   **13.8**

Amortisation over useful life

Intangible assets shall be considered to have a finite **useful life**. The useful life of an intangible asset that arises from contractual or other legal rights shall not exceed the period of the contractual or other legal rights, but may be shorter depending on the period over which the micro-entity expects to use the asset. If the contractual or other legal rights are conveyed for a limited term that can be renewed, the useful life of the intangible asset shall include the renewal period(s) only if there is evidence to support renewal by the micro-entity without significant cost.   **13.9**

If, in exceptional cases, a micro-entity is unable to make a reliable estimate of the useful life of an intangible asset, the life shall not exceed ten years.   **13.10**

Amortisation period and amortisation method

13.11 A micro-entity shall allocate the **depreciable amount** of an intangible asset on a systematic basis over its useful life. The amortisation charge for each period shall be recognised in profit or loss, unless another section of this FRS requires the cost to be recognised as part of the cost of an asset. For example, the amortisation of an intangible asset may be included in the costs of **inventories** or **property, plant and equipment**.

13.12 Amortisation begins when the intangible asset is available for use, ie when it is in the location and condition necessary for it to be usable in the manner intended by management. Amortisation ceases when the asset is derecognised. The micro-entity shall choose an amortisation method that reflects the pattern in which it expects to consume the asset's future economic benefits. If the micro-entity cannot determine that pattern reliably, it shall use the straight-line method.

Residual value

13.13 A micro-entity shall assume that the **residual value** of an intangible asset is zero unless:

(a) there is a commitment by a third party to purchase the asset at the end of its useful life; or
(b) there is an **active market** for the asset and:
  (i) residual value can be determined by reference to that market; and
  (ii) it is **probable** that such a market will exist at the end of the asset's useful life.

Review of amortisation period and amortisation method

13.14 Factors may indicate that the residual value or useful life of an intangible asset has changed since the most recent annual **reporting date**. If such indicators are present, a micro-entity shall review its previous estimates and, if current expectations differ, amend the residual value, amortisation method or useful life. The micro-entity shall account for the change in residual value, amortisation method or useful life as a change in an accounting estimate in accordance with paragraphs 8.11 to 8.13.

Recoverability of the carrying amount—impairment losses

13.15 To determine whether a separately acquired intangible asset is impaired, a micro-entity shall apply Section 22 *Impairment of Assets*. That section explains when and how a micro-entity reviews the carrying amount of its assets, how it determines the **recoverable amount** of an asset, and when it recognises or reverses an **impairment loss**.

Retirements and disposals

13.16 A micro-entity shall derecognise a separately acquired intangible asset, and shall recognise a **gain** or loss in profit or loss:

(a) on disposal; or
(b) when no future economic benefits are expected from its use or disposal.

Disclosure in the notes

13.17 A micro-entity shall determine the amount of any financial commitments, guarantees and contingencies not recognised in the **statement of financial position** for the acquisition of separately acquired intangible assets and disclose that amount within the total amount of financial commitments, guarantees and contingencies (see paragraph 6A.2).

13.18 A micro-entity shall disclose an indication of the nature and form of any intangible assets given as security in respect of its commitments, guarantees and contingencies (see paragraph 6A.3).

Section 14 Business Combinations and Goodwill

Accounting for a trade and asset acquisition

14.1 Where a **micro-entity** effects a **business combination** by acquiring the trade and **assets** of another **business,** it shall apply Section 19 *Business Combinations and Goodwill* of **FRS 102**, except for the following:

(a) a micro-entity shall not separately identify and recognise **intangible assets**;
(b) a micro-entity shall not recognise a **deferred tax asset** or **liability**;
(c) a micro-entity shall not apply paragraph 19.23 of FRS 102, but instead apply paragraph 14.2 of this FRS;
(d) a micro-entity shall not recognise and measure a **share-based payment transaction** in accordance with Section 28 *Employee Benefit* of FRS 102, but instead apply Section 23 *Employee Benefits* of this FRS; and
(e) a micro-entity is not required to provide any of the disclosures.

Goodwill arising on a trade and asset acquisition

Where a micro-entity has recognised **goodwill** acquired in a trade and asset acquisition (in accordance with paragraph 19.22 of FRS 102), the micro-entity shall measure that goodwill at cost less accumulated **amortisation** and accumulated **impairment losses**: **14.2**

(a) A micro-entity shall follow the principles in paragraphs 13.9 to 13.14 of this FRS for amortisation of goodwill. Goodwill shall be considered to have a finite **useful life**, and shall be amortised on a systematic basis over its life. If, in exceptional cases, a micro-entity is unable to make a reliable estimate of the useful life of goodwill, the life shall not exceed ten years.

(b) A micro-entity shall follow Section 22 *Impairment of Assets* of this FRS for recognising and measuring the impairment of goodwill.

Disclosure in the notes

A micro-entity shall determine the amount of any financial commitments, guarantees and contingencies not recognised in the **statement of financial position** for trade and asset acquisitions and disclose that amount within the total amount of financial commitments, guarantees and contingencies (see paragraph 6A.2). **14.3**

Section 15 Leases

Scope of this section

This section covers accounting for all **leases** other than licensing agreements for such items as motion picture films, video recordings, plays, manuscripts, patents and copyrights (see Section 13 *Intangible Assets other than Goodwill*). **15.1**

This section applies to agreements that transfer the right to use **assets** even though substantial services by the lessor may be called for in connection with the operation or maintenance of such assets. This section does not apply to agreements that are contracts for services that do not transfer the right to use assets from one contracting party to the other. **15.2**

Some arrangements do not take the legal form of a lease but convey rights to use assets in return for payments. Examples of such arrangements may include outsourcing arrangements, telecommunication contracts that provide rights to capacity and take-or-pay contracts. **15.3**

Determining whether an arrangement is, or contains, a lease shall be based on the substance of the arrangement. **15.4**

Classification of leases

A lease is classified as a **finance lease** if it transfers substantially all the risks and rewards incidental to ownership. A lease is classified as an **operating lease** if it does not transfer substantially all the risks and rewards incidental to ownership. **15.5**

Whether a lease is a finance lease or an operating lease depends on the substance of the transaction rather than the form of the contract. Examples of situations that individually or in combination would normally lead to a lease being classified as a finance lease are: **15.6**

(a) the lease transfers ownership of the asset to the lessee by the end of the **lease term**;

(b) the lessee has the option to purchase the asset at a price that is expected to be sufficiently lower than the **fair value** at the date the option becomes exercisable for it to be reasonably certain, at the **inception of the lease**, that the option will be exercised;

(c) the lease term is for the major part of the economic life of the asset even if title is not transferred;

(d) at the inception of the lease the **present value** of the **minimum lease payments** amounts to at least substantially all of the fair value of the leased asset; and

(e) the leased assets are of such a specialised nature that only the lessee can use them without major modifications.

Indicators of situations that individually or in combination could also lead to a lease being classified as a finance lease are: **15.7**

(a) if the lessee can cancel the lease, the lessor's losses associated with the cancellation are borne by the lessee;

(b) **gains** or losses from the fluctuation in the **residual value** of the leased asset accrue to the lessee (eg in the form of a rent rebate equalling most of the sales proceeds at the end of the lease); and

(c) the lessee has the ability to continue the lease for a secondary period at a rent that is substantially lower than market rent.

15.8 The examples and indicators in paragraphs 15.6 and 15.7 are not always conclusive. If it is clear from other features that the lease does not transfer substantially all risks and rewards incidental to ownership, the lease is classified as an operating lease. For example, this may be the case if ownership of the asset is transferred to the lessee at the end of the lease for a variable payment equal to the asset's then fair value, or if there are **contingent rents**, as a result of which the lessee does not have substantially all risks and rewards incidental to ownership.

15.9 Lease classification is made at the inception of the lease and is not changed during the term of the lease unless the lessee and the lessor agree to change the provisions of the lease (other than simply by renewing the lease), in which case the lease classification shall be re-evaluated.

Financial statements of lessees: finance leases

Initial recognition

15.10 At the **commencement of the lease term**, a lessee shall recognise its rights of use and obligations under finance leases as assets and **liabilities** in its **statement of financial position** at amounts equal to the fair value of the leased asset or, if lower, the present value of the minimum lease payments, determined at the inception of the lease. Any initial direct costs of the lessee (incremental costs that are directly attributable to negotiating and arranging a lease) are added to the amount recognised as an asset.

15.11 The present value of the minimum lease payments shall be calculated using the **interest rate implicit in the lease**. If this cannot be determined, the **lessee's incremental borrowing rate** shall be used.

Subsequent measurement

15.12 A lessee shall apportion minimum lease payments between the finance charge and the reduction of the outstanding liability. The lessee shall allocate the finance charge to each period during the lease term so as to produce a constant periodic rate of interest on the remaining balance of the liability. A lessee shall charge **contingent rents** as **expenses** in the periods in which they are incurred.

15.13 A lessee shall depreciate an asset leased under a finance lease in accordance with Section 12 *Property, Plant and Equipment and Investment Property*. If there is no reasonable certainty that the lessee will obtain ownership by the end of the lease term, the asset shall be fully depreciated over the shorter of the lease term and its **useful life**. A lessee shall also assess at each **reporting date** whether an asset leased under a finance lease is impaired (see Section 22 *Impairment of Assets*).

Financial statements of lessees: operating leases

Recognition and measurement

15.14 A lessee shall recognise lease payments under operating leases (excluding costs for services such as insurance and maintenance) as an expense over the lease term on a straight-line basis unless another systematic basis is representative of the time pattern of the user's benefit, even if the payments are not on that basis.

15.15 A lessee shall recognise the aggregate benefit of **lease incentives** as a reduction to the expense recognised in accordance with paragraph 15.14 over the lease term, on a straight-line basis unless another systematic basis is representative of the time pattern of the lessee's benefit from the use of the leased asset. Any costs incurred by the lessee (for example costs for termination of a pre-existing lease, relocation or leasehold improvements) shall be accounted for in accordance with the applicable section.

15.16 Where an operating lease becomes an **onerous contract** a **micro-entity** shall also apply Section 16 *Provisions and Contingencies*.

Disclosure in the notes

15.17 A micro-entity shall determine the amount of any financial commitments, guarantees and contingencies not recognised in the statement of financial position arising from operating leases and disclose that amount within the total amount of financial commitments, guarantees and contingencies (see paragraph 6A.2).

Financial statements of lessors: finance leases

Initial recognition and measurement

A lessor shall recognise assets held under a finance lease in its statement of financial position and present them as a receivable at an amount equal to the **net investment in the lease**. The net investment in a lease is the lessor's **gross investment in the lease** discounted at the interest rate implicit in the lease. The gross investment in the lease is the aggregate of: **15.18**

(a) the minimum lease payments receivable by the lessor under a finance lease; and

(b) any unguaranteed residual value accruing to the lessor.

For finance leases other than those involving manufacturer or dealer lessors, initial direct costs (costs that are incremental and directly attributable to negotiating and arranging a lease) are included in the initial measurement of the finance lease receivable and reduce the amount of **income** recognised over the lease term. **15.19**

Subsequent measurement

The **recognition** of finance income shall be based on a pattern reflecting a constant periodic rate of return on the lessor's net investment in the finance lease. Lease payments relating to the period, excluding costs for services, are applied against the gross investment in the lease to reduce both the principal and the unearned finance income. If there is an indication that the estimated unguaranteed residual value used in computing the lessor's gross investment in the lease has changed significantly, the income allocation over the lease term is revised, and any reduction in respect of amounts accrued is recognised immediately in **profit or loss**. **15.20**

Manufacturer or dealer lessors

Manufacturers or dealers often offer to customers the choice of either buying or leasing an asset. A finance lease of an asset by a manufacturer or dealer lessor gives rise to two types of income: **15.21**

(a) profit or loss equivalent to the profit or loss resulting from an outright sale of the asset being leased, at normal selling prices, reflecting any applicable volume or trade discounts; and

(b) finance income over the lease term.

The sales **revenue** recognised at the commencement of the lease term by a manufacturer or dealer lessor is the fair value of the asset or, if lower, the present value of the minimum lease payments accruing to the lessor, computed at a market rate of interest. The cost of sale recognised at the commencement of the lease term is the cost, or **carrying amount** if different, of the leased asset less the present value of the unguaranteed residual value. The difference between the sales revenue and the cost of sale is the selling profit, which is recognised in accordance with the micro-entity's policy for outright sales. **15.22**

If artificially low rates of interest are quoted, selling profit shall be restricted to that which would apply if a market rate of interest were charged. Costs incurred by manufacturer or dealer lessors in connection with negotiating and arranging a lease shall be recognised as an expense when the selling profit is recognised. **15.23**

Financial statements of lessors: operating leases

Recognition and measurement

A lessor shall recognise lease income from operating leases (excluding amounts for services such as insurance and maintenance) in profit or loss on a straight-line basis over the lease term unless another systematic basis is representative of the time pattern of the lessee's benefit from the leased asset, even if the receipt of payments is not on that basis. **15.24**

A lessor shall recognise the aggregate cost of lease incentives as a reduction to the income recognised in accordance with paragraph 15.24 over the lease term on a straight-line basis, unless another systematic basis is representative of the time pattern over which the lessor's benefit from the leased asset is diminished. **15.25**

A lessor shall recognise as an expense, costs, including **depreciation**, incurred in earning the lease income. The depreciation policy for depreciable leased assets shall be consistent with the lessor's normal depreciation policy for similar assets. **15.26**

A lessor shall add to the carrying amount of the leased asset any initial direct costs it incurs in negotiating and arranging an operating lease and shall recognise such costs as an expense over the lease term on the same basis as the lease income. **15.27**

15.28   To determine whether a leased asset has become impaired, a lessor shall apply Section 22.

15.29   A manufacturer or dealer lessor does not recognise any selling profit on entering into an operating lease because it is not the equivalent of a sale.

Sale and leaseback transactions

15.30   A sale and leaseback transaction involves the sale of an asset and the leasing back of the same asset. The lease payment and the sale price are usually interdependent because they are negotiated as a package. The accounting treatment of a sale and leaseback transaction depends on the type of lease.

Sale and leaseback transaction results in a finance lease

15.31   If a sale and leaseback transaction results in a finance lease, the seller-lessee shall not recognise immediately, as income, any excess of sales proceeds over the carrying amount. Instead, the seller-lessee shall defer such excess and amortise it over the lease term.

Sale and leaseback transaction results in an operating lease

15.32   If a sale and leaseback transaction results in an operating lease, and it is clear that the transaction is established at fair value, the seller-lessee shall recognise any profit or loss immediately. If the sale price is below fair value, the seller-lessee shall recognise any profit or loss immediately unless the loss is compensated for by future lease payments at below market price. In that case the seller-lessee shall defer and amortise such loss in proportion to the lease payments over the period for which the asset is expected to be used. If the sale price is above fair value, the seller-lessee shall defer the excess over fair value and amortise it over the period for which the asset is expected to be used.

Disclosure in the notes

15.33   A micro-entity shall determine the amount of any financial commitments, guarantees and contingencies not recognised in the statement of financial position arising from a sale and lease back transaction and disclose that amount within the total amount of financial commitments, guarantees and contingencies (see paragraph 6A.2).

Section 16 Provisions and Contingencies

Scope of this section

16.1   This section applies to all **provisions**, **contingent liabilities** and **contingent assets** except those provisions covered by other sections of this FRS. Where those other sections contain no specific requirements to deal with contracts that have become onerous, this section applies to those contracts.

16.2   This section does not apply to **financial instruments** that are within the scope of Section 9 *Financial Instruments* unless the contracts are **onerous contracts** or **financial guarantee contracts**.

16.3   The requirements in this section do not apply to executory contracts unless they are onerous contracts. Executory contracts are contracts under which neither party has performed any of its obligations or both parties have partially performed their obligations to an equal extent.

16.4   The word 'provision' is sometimes used in the context of such items as **depreciation**, impairment of **assets**, and uncollectible receivables. Those are adjustments of the **carrying amounts** of assets, rather than **recognition** of **liabilities**, and therefore are not covered by this section.

Initial recognition

16.5   A **micro-entity** shall recognise a provision only when:

     (a)   the micro-entity has an obligation at the **reporting date** as a result of a past event;

     (b)   it is **probable** (ie more likely than not) that the micro-entity will be required to transfer economic benefits in settlement; and

     (c)   the amount of the obligation can be estimated reliably.

16.6   The micro-entity shall recognise the provision as a liability in the **statement of financial position** and shall recognise the amount of the provision as an **expense**, unless another section of this FRS requires the cost to be recognised as part of the cost of an asset such as **inventories** or **property, plant and equipment**.

The condition in paragraph 16.5(a) means that the micro-entity has no realistic alternative to settling the obligation. This can happen when the micro-entity has a legal obligation that can be enforced by law or when the micro-entity has a **constructive obligation** because the past event (which may be an action of the micro-entity) has created valid expectations in other parties that the micro-entity will discharge the obligation. Obligations that will arise from the micro-entity's future actions (ie the future conduct of its business) do not satisfy the condition in paragraph 16.5(a), no matter how likely they are to occur and even if they are contractual. To illustrate, because of commercial pressures or legal requirements, a micro-entity may intend or need to carry out expenditure to operate in a particular way in the future (for example, by fitting smoke filters in a particular type of factory). Because the micro-entity can avoid the future expenditure by its future actions, for example by changing its method of operation or selling the factory, it has no present obligation for that future expenditure and no provision is recognised.   **16.7**

Initial measurement

A micro-entity shall measure a provision at the best estimate of the amount required to settle the obligation at the reporting date. The best estimate is the amount a micro-entity would rationally pay to settle the obligation at the end of the **reporting period** or to transfer it to a third party at that time.   **16.8**

(a) When the provision involves a large population of items, the estimate of the amount reflects the weighting of all possible outcomes by their associated probabilities. The provision will therefore be different depending on whether the probability of a loss of a given amount is, for example, 60 per cent or 90 per cent. Where there is a continuous range of possible outcomes, and each point in that range is as likely as any other, the mid-point of the range is used.

(b) When the provision arises from a single obligation, the individual most likely outcome may be the best estimate of the amount required to settle the obligation. However, even in such a case, the micro-entity considers other possible outcomes. When other possible outcomes are either mostly higher or mostly lower than the most likely outcome, the best estimate will be a higher or lower amount.

When the effect of the time value of money is **material**, the amount of a provision shall be the **present value** of the amount expected to be required to settle the obligation. The discount rate (or rates) shall be a pre-tax rate (or rates) that reflect(s) current market assessments of the time value of money and risks specific to the liability. The risks specific to the liability shall be reflected either in the discount rate or in the estimation of the amounts required to settle the obligation, but not both.

A micro-entity shall exclude **gains** from the expected disposal of assets from the **measurement** of a provision.   **16.9**

When some or all of the amount required to settle a provision may be reimbursed by another party (eg through an insurance claim), the micro-entity shall recognise the reimbursement as a separate asset only when it is virtually certain that the micro-entity will receive the reimbursement on settlement of the obligation. The amount recognised for the reimbursement shall not exceed the amount of the provision. The reimbursement receivable shall be presented in the statement of financial position as an asset and shall not be offset against the provision. In the **income statement** the expense relating to a provision may be presented net of the amount recognised for a reimbursement.   **16.10**

Subsequent measurement

A micro-entity shall charge against a provision only those expenditures for which the provision was originally recognised.   **16.11**

A micro-entity shall review provisions at each reporting date and adjust them to reflect the current best estimate of the amount that would be required to settle the obligation at that reporting date. Any adjustments to the amounts previously recognised shall be recognised in **profit or loss** unless the provision was originally recognised as part of the cost of an asset (see paragraph 16.6). When a provision is measured at the present value of the amount expected to be required to settle the obligation, the unwinding of the discount shall be recognised as interest expense in profit or loss in the period it arises.   **16.12**

Onerous contracts

If a micro-entity has an onerous contract, the present obligation under the contract shall be recognised and measured as a provision (see Example 2 of the Appendix to this section).   **16.13**

Future operating losses

Provisions shall not be recognised for future operating losses (see Example 1 of the Appendix to this section).   **16.14**

Appendix A

Restructuring

16.15 A **restructuring** gives rise to a constructive obligation only when a micro-entity:

   (a)   has a detailed formal plan for the restructuring identifying at least:
- (i) the business or part of a business concerned;
- (ii) the principal locations affected;
- (iii) the location, function, and approximate number of employees who will be compensated for terminating their services;
- (iv) the expenditures that will be undertaken; and
- (v) when the plan will be implemented; and

   (b)   has raised a valid expectation in those affected that it will carry out the restructuring by starting to implement that plan or announcing its main features to those affected by it.

16.16 A micro-entity recognises a provision for restructuring costs only when it has a legal or constructive obligation at the reporting date to carry out the restructuring.

Contingent liabilities

16.17 A contingent liability is either a possible but uncertain obligation or a present obligation that is not recognised because it fails to meet one or both of the conditions (b) and (c) in paragraph 16.5. A micro-entity shall not recognise a contingent liability as a liability, except for provisions for contingent liabilities of an acquiree in a trade and asset acquisition (see Section 14 *Business Combinations and Goodwill*). Paragraph 16.19 sets out the disclosure requirements for a contingent liability. When a micro-entity is jointly and severally liable for an obligation, the part of the obligation that is expected to be met by other parties is treated as a contingent liability.

Contingent assets

16.18 A micro-entity shall not recognise a contingent asset as an asset. However, when the flow of future economic benefits to the micro-entity is virtually certain, then the related asset is not a contingent asset, and its recognition is appropriate.

Disclosures in the notes

16.19 A micro-entity shall determine the amount of any financial commitments, guarantees and contingencies not recognised in the statement of financial position and disclose that amount within the total amount of financial commitments, guarantees and contingencies (see paragraph 6A.2). A micro-entity is not required to disclose the amount of a contingent liability where the possibility of an outflow of resources is remote.

Appendix to Section 16

Examples of recognising and measuring provisions

This appendix accompanies, but is not part of, Section 16. It provides guidance for applying the requirements of Section 16 in recognising and measuring provisions.

All of the micro-entities in the examples in this appendix have 31 December as their reporting date. In all cases, it is assumed that a reliable estimate can be made of any outflows expected. In some examples the circumstances described may have resulted in impairment of the assets; this aspect is not dealt with in the examples. References to 'best estimate' are to the present value amount, when the effect of the time value of money is material.

Example 1 Future operating losses

16A.1 A micro-entity determines that it is probable that it will incur future operating losses for several years.

Present obligation as a result of a past obligating event: There is no past event that obliges the micro-entity to pay out resources.

Conclusion: The micro-entity does not recognise a provision for future operating losses. Expected future losses do not meet the definition of a liability. The expectation of future operating losses may be an indicator that one or more assets are impaired (see Section 22 *Impairment of Assets* of this FRS).

Example 2 Onerous contracts

An onerous contract is one in which the unavoidable costs of meeting the obligations under the contract exceed the economic benefits expected to be received under it. The unavoidable costs under a contract reflect the least net cost of exiting from the contract, which is the lower of the cost of fulfilling it and any compensation or penalties arising from failure to fulfil it. For example, a micro-entity may be contractually required under an operating lease to make payments to lease an asset for which it no longer has any use.

16A.2

Present obligation as a result of a past obligating event: The micro-entity is contractually required to pay out resources for which it will not receive commensurate benefits.

Conclusion: If a micro-entity has a contract that is onerous, the micro-entity recognises and measures the present obligation under the contract as a provision.

Example 3 Warranties

A manufacturer gives warranties at the time of sale to purchasers of its product. Under the terms of the contract for sale, the manufacturer undertakes to make good, by repair or replacement, manufacturing defects that become apparent within three years from the date of sale. On the basis of experience, it is probable (ie more likely than not) that there will be some claims under the warranties.

16A.3

Present obligation as a result of a past obligating event: The obligating event is the sale of the product with a warranty, which gives rise to a legal obligation.

An outflow of resources embodying economic benefits in settlement: Probable for the warranties as a whole.

Conclusion: The micro-entity recognises a provision for the best estimate of the costs of making good under the warranty products sold before the reporting date.

Illustration of calculations:

In 20X0, goods are sold for CU100,000. Experience indicates that 90 per cent of products sold require no warranty repairs; six per cent of products sold require minor repairs costing 30 per cent of the sale price; and four per cent of products sold require major repairs or replacement costing 70 per cent of sale price. Therefore estimated warranty costs are:

CU100,000 × 90% × 0 =	CU0
CU100,000 × 6% × 30% =	CU1,800
CU100,000 × 4% × 70% =	CU2,800
Total	CU4,600

The expenditures for warranty repairs and replacements for products sold in 20X0 are expected to be made 60 per cent in 20X1, 30 per cent in 20X2, and ten per cent in 20X3, in each case at the end of the period. Because the estimated cash flows already reflect the probabilities of the cash outflows, and assuming there are no other risks or uncertainties that must be reflected, to determine the present value of those cash flows the micro-entity uses a 'risk-free' discount rate based on government bonds with the same term as the expected cash outflows (six per cent for one-year bonds and seven per cent for two-year and three-year bonds). Calculation of the present value, at the end of 20X0, of the estimated cash flows related to the warranties for products sold in 20X0 is as follows:

Year		Expected cash payments (CU)	Discount rate	Discount factor	Present value (CU)
1	60% × CU4,600	2,760	6%	0.9434 (at 6% for 1 year)	2,604
2	30% × CU4,600	1,380	7%	0.8734 (at 7% for 2 years)	1,205
3	10% × CU4,600	460	7%	0.8163 (at 7% for 3 years)	375
Total					4,184

The micro-entity will recognise a warranty obligation of CU4,184 at the end of 20X0 for products sold in 20X0.

Appendix A

Example 4 Refunds policy

16A.4   A retail store has a policy of refunding purchases by dissatisfied customers, even though it is under no legal obligation to do so. Its policy of making refunds is generally known.

Present obligation as a result of a past obligating event: The obligating event is the sale of the product, which gives rise to a constructive obligation because the conduct of the store has created a valid expectation on the part of its customers that the store will refund purchases.

An outflow of resources embodying economic benefits in settlement: Probable that a proportion of goods will be returned for refund.

Conclusion: The micro-entity recognises a provision for the best estimate of the amount required to settle the refunds.

Example 5 Closure of a division: no implementation before end of reporting period

16A.5   On 12 December 20X0 the board of a micro-entity decided to close down a division. Before the end of the reporting period (31 December 20X0) the decision was not communicated to any of those affected and no other steps were taken to implement the decision.

Present obligation as a result of a past obligating event: There has been no obligating event, and so there is no obligation.

Conclusion: The micro-entity does not recognise a provision.

Example 6 Closure of a division: communication and implementation before end of reporting period

16A.6   On 12 December 20X0 the board of a micro-entity decided to close a division making a particular product. On 20 December 20X0 a detailed plan for closing the division was agreed by the board, letters were sent to customers warning them to seek an alternative source of supply, and redundancy notices were sent to the staff of the division.

Present obligation as a result of a past obligating event: The obligating event is the communication of the decision to the customers and employees, which gives rise to a constructive obligation from that date, because it creates a valid expectation that the division will be closed.

An outflow of resources embodying economic benefits in settlement: Probable.

Conclusion: The micro-entity recognises a provision at 31 December 20X0 for the best estimate of the costs that would be incurred to close the division at the reporting date.

Example 7 Staff retraining as a result of changes in the income tax system

16A.7   The government introduces changes to the income tax system. As a result of those changes, a micro-entity will need to retrain a large proportion of its administrative and sales workforce in order to ensure continued compliance with tax regulations. At the end of the reporting period, no retraining of staff has taken place.

Present obligation as a result of a past obligating event: The tax law change does not impose an obligation on a micro-entity to do any retraining. An obligating event for recognising a provision (the retraining itself) has not taken place.

Conclusion: The micro-entity does not recognise a provision.

Example 8 A court case

16A.8   A customer has sued Micro-entity X, seeking damages for injury the customer allegedly sustained from using a product sold by Micro-entity X. Micro-entity X disputes liability on grounds that the customer did not follow directions in using the product. Up to the date the financial statements for the year to 31 December 20X1 were authorised for issue, the micro-entity's lawyers advise that it is probable that the micro-entity will not be found liable. However, when the micro-entity prepares the financial statements for the year to 31 December 20X2, its lawyers advise that, owing to developments in the case, it is now probable that the micro-entity will be found liable.

(a) At 31 December 20X1

Present obligation as a result of a past obligating event: On the basis of the evidence available when the financial statements were approved, there is no obligation as a result of past events.

Conclusion: No provision is recognised, but the micro-entity shall make the disclosures required by paragraph 16.19.

(b) At 31 December 20X2

Present obligation as a result of a past obligating event: On the basis of the evidence available, there is a present obligation. The obligating event is the sale of the product to the customer.

An outflow of resources embodying economic benefits in settlement: Probable.

Conclusion: A provision is recognised at the best estimate of the amount to settle the obligation at 31 December 20X2, and the expense is recognised in profit or loss. It is not a correction of an error in 20X1 because, on the basis of the evidence available when the 20X1 financial statements were approved, a provision should not have been recognised at that time.

Section 17 Liabilities and Equity

Scope of this section

This section establishes principles for classifying **financial instruments** as either **liabilities** or **equity** and deals with the accounting for **compound financial instruments**, such as convertible debt. It also addresses the issue of equity instruments, distributions to individuals or other parties acting in their capacity as investors in equity instruments (ie in their capacity as **owners**) and the accounting for purchases of own equity. | 17.1

This section shall be applied to all types of financial instruments except: | 17.2

(a) Investments in **subsidiaries** and **associates** and interests in **jointly controlled entities** that are accounted for in accordance with Section 9 *Financial Instruments.*
(b) Employers' rights and obligations under employee benefit plans to which Section 23 *Employee Benefits* applies.
(c) Financial instruments, contracts and obligations under **share-based payment transactions** to which Section 21 *Share-based Payment* applies, except that paragraph 17.14 shall be applied to **treasury shares** issued, purchased, sold, transferred or cancelled in connection with employee share option plans, employee share purchase plans, and all other share-based payment arrangements.
(d) **Financial guarantee contracts** (see Section 16 *Provisions and Contingencies*).

Classification of an instrument as liability or equity

Equity is the residual interest in the **assets** of a **micro-entity** after deducting all its liabilities. Equity includes investments by the owners of the micro-entity, plus additions to those investments earned through profitable operations and retained for use in the micro-entity's operations, minus reductions to owners' investments as a result of unprofitable operations and distributions to owners. | 17.3

A financial instrument is classified as equity where the issuer can be required to settle an obligation in cash or by delivery of another **financial asset** (or otherwise to settle it in such a way that it would be a **financial liability**) only in the event of the liquidation of the issuer. | 17.4

A financial instrument is a financial liability of the issuer where the issuer does not have an unconditional right to avoid settling an obligation in cash or by delivery of another financial asset (or otherwise to settle it in such a way that it would be a financial liability), other than for the reason described in paragraph 17.4. | 17.5

Examples of instruments and their classification as equity or liabilities are set out below: | 17.6

(a) An instrument is classified as equity if the only payment holders of the instruments are entitled to receive is a pro rata share of the net assets of the micro-entity on liquidation.
(b) An instrument is classified as a liability if it obliges the micro-entity to make payments to the holder before liquidation, such as a mandatory dividend.
(c) A preference share that provides for mandatory redemption by the issuer for a fixed or determinable amount at a fixed or determinable future date, or gives the holder the right to require the issuer to redeem the instrument at or after a particular date for a fixed or determinable amount, is a financial liability.

Original issue of shares or other equity instruments

A micro-entity shall recognise the issue of shares or other equity instruments as equity when it issues those instruments and another party is obliged to provide cash or other resources to the micro-entity in exchange for the instruments. | 17.7

(a)   If the micro-entity receives the cash or other resources before the equity instruments are issued, and the micro-entity cannot be required to repay the cash or other resources received, the micro-entity shall recognise the corresponding increase in equity to the extent of consideration received.

(b)   To the extent that the equity instruments have been subscribed for but not issued (or called up), and the micro-entity has not yet received the cash or other resources, the micro-entity shall not recognise an increase in equity.

17.8   A micro-entity shall measure the equity instruments at the **fair value** of the cash or other resources received or receivable, net of direct costs of issuing the equity instruments.

17.9   A micro-entity shall account for the **transaction costs** of an equity transaction as a deduction from equity, net of any related **income tax** benefit.

Exercise of options, rights and warrants

17.10   A micro-entity shall apply the principles in paragraphs 17.7 to 17.9 to equity issued by means of exercise of options, rights, warrants and similar equity instruments.

Convertible debt and similar compound financial instruments

17.11   On issuing convertible debt, or a similar compound financial instrument, a micro-entity shall allocate the proceeds between the liability component and the equity component of the instrument. To make the allocation, the micro-entity shall first determine the amount of the liability component as the fair value of a similar liability that does not have a conversion feature or similar associated equity component. The micro-entity shall allocate the residual amount as the equity component. Transaction costs shall be allocated between the debt component and the equity component on the basis of their relative fair values.

17.12   The micro-entity shall not revise the allocation in a subsequent period.

17.13   In periods after the instruments were issued, the micro-entity shall account for the liability component as a financial instrument in accordance with Section 9. The example shown in the Appendix to Section 22 *Liabilities and Equity* of **FRS 102** illustrates the accounting for convertible debt by an issuer.

Treasury shares

17.14   Treasury shares are the equity instruments of a micro-entity that have been issued and subsequently reacquired by the micro-entity. A micro-entity shall deduct from equity the fair value of the consideration given for the treasury shares. The micro-entity shall not recognise a **gain** or loss in **profit or loss** on the purchase, sale, transfer or cancellation of treasury shares.

Distributions to owners

17.15   A micro-entity shall reduce its equity reserves for the amount of distributions to its owners (holders of its equity instruments).

Section 18 Revenue

Scope of this section

18.1   This section shall be applied in accounting for **revenue** arising from the following transactions and events:
(a)   the sale of goods (whether produced by the **micro-entity** for the purpose of sale or purchased for resale);
(b)   the rendering of services;
(c)   **construction contracts** in which the micro-entity is the contractor; and
(d)   the use by others of micro-entity **assets** yielding interest, royalties or dividends.

18.2   Revenue or other **income** arising from **lease** agreements is dealt with in Section 15 *Leases*.

Measurement of revenue

18.3   A micro-entity shall measure revenue at the amount receivable, taking into account any trade discounts, prompt settlement discounts and volume rebates allowed by the micro-entity.

18.4   A micro-entity shall include in revenue only the gross inflows of economic benefits received and receivable by the micro-entity on its own account. A micro-entity shall exclude from revenue all amounts collected on behalf of third parties such as sales taxes, goods and services taxes and value added taxes. In an agency relationship, a micro-entity (the **agent**) shall include in revenue only the amount of its commission. The amounts collected on behalf of the **principal** are not revenue of the micro-entity.

Deferred payment

If payment is deferred beyond normal credit terms, the amount of revenue recognised is equal to the cash price available on the transaction date. Any excess of the deferred payment amount over the cash price available on the transaction date is recognised as interest and accounted for in accordance with paragraph 9.14(a). **18.5**

Exchanges of goods or services

A micro-entity shall not recognise revenue: **18.6**

(a)   when goods or services are exchanged for goods or services that are of a similar nature and value; or

(b)   when goods or services are exchanged for dissimilar goods or services but the transaction lacks commercial substance.

A micro-entity shall recognise revenue when goods are sold or services are exchanged for dissimilar goods or services in a transaction that has commercial substance. In that case, the micro-entity shall measure the transaction: **18.7**

(a)   at the **fair value** of the goods or services received, adjusted by the amount of any cash transferred;

(b)   if the amount under (a) cannot be measured reliably, then at the fair value of the goods or services given up adjusted by the amount of any cash transferred; or

(c)   if the fair value of neither the goods or services received nor the goods or services given up can be measured reliably, then at the **carrying amount** of the goods or services given up adjusted by the amount of any cash transferred.

Identification of the revenue transaction

A micro-entity shall apply the **recognition** criteria to the separately identifiable components of a single transaction when necessary to reflect the substance of the transaction. For example, a micro-entity applies the recognition criteria to the separately identifiable components of a single transaction when the selling price of a product includes an identifiable amount for subsequent servicing. Conversely, a micro-entity applies the recognition criteria to two or more transactions together when they are linked in such a way that the commercial effect cannot be understood without reference to the series of transactions as a whole. **18.8**

Sale of goods

A micro-entity shall recognise revenue from the sale of goods when all the following conditions are satisfied: **18.9**

(a)   the micro-entity has transferred to the buyer the significant risks and rewards of ownership of the goods;

(b)   the micro-entity retains neither continuing managerial involvement to the degree usually associated with ownership nor effective control over the goods sold;

(c)   the amount of revenue can be measured reliably;

(d)   it is **probable** that the economic benefits associated with the transaction will flow to the micro-entity; and

(e)   the costs incurred or to be incurred in respect of the transaction can be measured reliably.

The assessment of when a micro-entity has transferred the significant risks and rewards of ownership to the buyer requires an examination of the circumstances of the transaction. In most cases, the transfer of the risks and rewards of ownership coincides with the transfer of the legal title or the passing of possession to the buyer. This is the case for most retail sales. In other cases, the transfer of risks and rewards of ownership occurs at a time different from the transfer of legal title or the passing of possession. **18.10**

A micro-entity does not recognise revenue if it retains significant risks and rewards of ownership. Examples of situations in which the micro-entity may retain the significant risks and rewards of ownership are: **18.11**

(a)   when the micro-entity retains an obligation for unsatisfactory performance not covered by normal warranties;

(b)   when the receipt of the revenue from a particular sale is contingent on the buyer selling the goods;

(c)   when the goods are shipped subject to installation and the installation is a significant part of the contract that has not yet been completed; and

(d)   when the buyer has the right to rescind the purchase for a reason specified in the sales contract, or at the buyer's sole discretion without any reason, and the micro-entity is uncertain about the probability of return.

18.12 If an entity retains only an insignificant risk of ownership, the transaction is a sale and the entity recognises the revenue. For example, a seller recognises revenue when it retains the legal title to the goods solely to protect the collectability of the amount due. Similarly, an entity recognises revenue when it offers a refund if the customer finds the goods faulty or is not satisfied for other reasons, and the entity can estimate the returns reliably. In such cases, the entity recognises a **provision** for returns in accordance with Section 16 *Provisions and Contingencies*.

Rendering of services

18.13 When the outcome of a transaction involving the rendering of services can be estimated reliably, a micro-entity shall recognise revenue associated with the transaction by reference to the stage of completion of the transaction at the end of the **reporting period** (sometimes referred to as the percentage of completion method). The outcome of a transaction can be estimated reliably when all the following conditions are satisfied:

(a)   the amount of revenue can be measured reliably;
(b)   it is probable that the economic benefits associated with the transaction will flow to the micro-entity;
(c)   the stage of completion of the transaction at the end of the reporting period can be measured reliably; and
(d)   the costs incurred for the transaction and the costs to complete the transaction can be measured reliably.

Paragraphs 18.18 to 18.24 provide guidance for applying the percentage of completion method.

18.14 When services are performed by an indeterminate number of acts over a specified period of time, a micro-entity recognises revenue on a straight-line basis over the specified period unless there is evidence that some other method better represents the stage of completion. When a specific act is much more significant than any other act, the micro-entity postpones recognition of revenue until the significant act is executed.

18.15 When the outcome of the transaction involving the rendering of services cannot be estimated reliably, a micro-entity shall recognise revenue only to the extent of the **expenses** recognised that are recoverable.

Construction contracts

18.16 When the outcome of a construction contract can be estimated reliably, a micro-entity shall recognise contract revenue and contract costs associated with the construction contract as revenue and expenses respectively by reference to the stage of completion of the contract activity at the end of the reporting period (often referred to as the percentage of completion method). Reliable estimation of the outcome requires reliable estimates of the stage of completion, future costs and collectability of billings. Paragraphs 18.18 to 18.24 provide guidance for applying the percentage of completion method.

18.17 The requirements of this section are usually applied separately to each construction contract. However, in some circumstances, it is necessary to apply this section to the separately identifiable components of a single contract or to a group of contracts together in order to reflect the substance of a contract or a group of contracts.

Percentage of completion method

18.18 This method is used to recognise revenue from rendering services (see paragraphs 18.13 to 18.15) and from construction contracts (see paragraphs 18.16 and 18.17). A micro-entity shall review and, when necessary, revise the estimates of revenue and costs as the service transaction or construction contract progresses.

18.19 A micro-entity shall determine the stage of completion of a transaction or contract using the method that measures most reliably the work performed. Possible methods include:

(a)   the proportion that costs incurred for work performed to date bear to the estimated total costs. Costs incurred for work performed to date do not include costs relating to future activity, such as for materials or prepayments;
(b)   surveys of work performed; and
(c)   completion of a physical proportion of the contract work or the completion of a proportion of the service contract.

Progress payments and advances received from customers often do not reflect the work performed.

18.20 A micro-entity shall recognise costs that relate to future activity on the transaction or contract, such as for materials or prepayments, as an asset if it is probable that the costs will be recovered.

18.21 A micro-entity shall recognise as an expense immediately any costs whose recovery is not probable.

18.22 When the outcome of a construction contract cannot be estimated reliably:

(a)   a micro-entity shall recognise revenue only to the extent of contract costs incurred that it is probable will be recoverable; and
(b)   the micro-entity shall recognise contract costs as an expense in the period in which they are incurred.

When it is probable that total contract costs will exceed total contract revenue on a construction contract, the expected **18.23** loss shall be recognised as an expense immediately, with a corresponding provision for an **onerous contract** (see Section 16 *Provisions and Contingencies*).

If the collectability of an amount already recognised as contract revenue is no longer probable, the micro-entity shall **18.24** recognise the uncollectible amount as an expense rather than as an adjustment of the amount of contract revenue.

Interest, royalties and dividends

A micro-entity shall recognise revenue arising from the use by others of micro-entity assets yielding interest, royalties and **18.25** dividends on the bases set out in paragraph 18.26 when:

(a) it is probable that the economic benefits associated with the transaction will flow to the micro-entity; and
(b) the amount of the revenue can be measured reliably.

A micro-entity shall recognise revenue on the following bases: **18.26**

(a) Interest income shall be recognised in accordance with Section 9 *Financial Instruments*.
(b) Royalties shall be recognised on an **accrual basis** in accordance with the substance of the relevant agreement.
(c) Dividends shall be recognised when the shareholder's right to receive payment is established.

Appendix to Section 18

Examples of revenue recognition under the principles in Section 18

This appendix accompanies, but is not part of, Section 18. It provides guidance for applying the requirements of Section 18 in recognising revenue.

The following examples focus on particular aspects of a transaction and are not a comprehensive discussion of all the **18A.1** relevant factors that might influence the recognition of revenue. The examples generally assume that the amount of revenue can be measured reliably, it is probable that the economic benefits will flow to the micro-entity and the costs incurred or to be incurred can be measured reliably.

Sale of goods

The law in different countries may cause the recognition criteria in Section 18 to be met at different times. In particular, **18A.2** the law may determine the point in time at which the micro-entity transfers the significant risks and rewards of ownership. Therefore, the examples in this appendix need to be read in the context of the laws relating to the sale of goods in the country in which the transaction takes place.

Example 1 'Bill and hold' sales, in which delivery is delayed at the buyer's request but the buyer takes title and accepts billing

The seller recognises revenue when the buyer takes title, provided: **18A.3**

(a) it is probable that delivery will be made;
(b) the item is on hand, identified and ready for delivery to the buyer at the time the sale is recognised;
(c) the buyer specifically acknowledges the deferred delivery instructions; and
(d) the usual payment terms apply.

Revenue is not recognised when there is simply an intention to acquire or manufacture the goods in time for delivery.

Example 2 Goods shipped subject to conditions: installation and inspection

The seller normally recognises revenue when the buyer accepts delivery, and installation and inspection are complete. **18A.4** However, revenue is recognised immediately upon the buyer's acceptance of delivery when:

(a) the installation process is simple, for example the installation of a factory-tested television receiver that requires only unpacking and connection of power and antennae; or
(b) the inspection is performed only for the purposes of final determination of contract prices, for example, shipments of iron ore, sugar or soya beans.

Example 3 Goods shipped subject to conditions: on approval when the buyer has negotiated a limited right of return

18A.5   If there is uncertainty about the possibility of return, the seller recognises revenue when the shipment has been formally accepted by the buyer or the goods have been delivered and the time period for rejection has elapsed.

Example 4 Goods shipped subject to conditions: consignment sales under which the recipient (buyer) undertakes to sell the goods on behalf of the shipper (seller)

18A.6   The shipper recognises revenue when the goods are sold by the recipient to a third party.

Example 5 Goods shipped subject to conditions: cash on delivery sales

18A.7   The seller recognises revenue when delivery is made and cash is received by the seller or its agent.

Example 6 Layaway sales under which the goods are delivered only when the buyer makes the final payment in a series of instalments

18A.8   The seller recognises revenue from such sales when the goods are delivered. However, when experience indicates that most such sales are consummated, revenue may be recognised when a significant deposit is received, provided the goods are on hand, identified and ready for delivery to the buyer.

Example 7 Orders when payment (or partial payment) is received in advance of delivery for goods not currently held in inventory, for example, the goods are still to be manufactured or will be delivered direct to the buyer from a third party

18A.9   The seller recognises revenue when the goods are delivered to the buyer.

Example 8 Sale and repurchase agreements (other than swap transactions) under which the seller concurrently agrees to repurchase the same goods at a later date, or when the seller has a call option to repurchase, or the buyer has a put option to require the repurchase, by the seller, of the goods

18A.10   For a sale and repurchase agreement on an asset other than a financial asset, the seller must analyse the terms of the agreement to ascertain whether, in substance, the risks and rewards of ownership have been transferred to the buyer. If they have been transferred, the seller recognises revenue. When the seller has retained the risks and rewards of ownership, even though legal title has been transferred, the transaction is a financing arrangement and does not give rise to revenue. For a sale and repurchase agreement on a financial asset, the derecognition provisions of Section 9 apply.

Example 9 Sales to intermediate parties, such as distributors, dealers or others for resale

18A.11   The seller generally recognises revenue from such sales when the risks and rewards of ownership have been transferred. However, when the buyer is acting, in substance, as an agent, the sale is treated as a consignment sale.

Example 10 Subscriptions to publications and similar items

18A.12   When the items involved are of similar value in each time period, the seller recognises revenue on a straight-line basis over the period in which the items are dispatched. When the items vary in value from period to period, the seller recognises revenue on the basis of the sales value of the item dispatched in relation to the total estimated sales value of all items covered by the subscription.

Example 11 Instalment sales, under which the consideration is receivable in instalments

18A.13   The seller recognises revenue based on the cash price a customer would pay at the date of sale. If the total amount paid through instalments is greater than the cash price payable at the date of sale, any excess is recognised as interest and accounted for in accordance with paragraph 9.14(a).

Example 12 Agreements for the construction of real estate

18A.14   A micro-entity that undertakes the construction of real estate, directly or through subcontractors, and enters into an agreement with one or more buyers before construction is complete, shall account for the agreement using the percentage of completion method, only if:

(a)   the buyer is able to specify the major structural elements of the design of the real estate before construction begins and/or specify major structural changes once construction is in progress (whether it exercises that ability or not); or

(b)   the buyer acquires and supplies construction materials and the micro-entity provides only construction services.

If the micro-entity is required to provide services together with construction materials in order to perform its contractual obligation to deliver real estate to the buyer, the agreement shall be accounted for as the sale of goods. In this case, the buyer does not obtain control or the significant risks and rewards of ownership of the work in progress in its current state as construction progresses. Rather, the transfer occurs only on delivery of the completed real estate to the buyer.   **18A.15**

Example 13 Sale with customer loyalty award

A micro-entity sells product A for CU100. Purchasers of product A get an award credit enabling them to buy product B   **18A.16**
for CU10. The normal selling price of product B is CU18. The micro-entity estimates that 40 per cent of the purchasers of product A will use their award to buy product B at CU10. The normal selling price of product A, after taking into account discounts that are usually offered but that are not available during this promotion, is CU95.

The fair value of the award credit is 40 per cent × [CU18 – CU10] = CU3.20. The micro-entity allocates the total revenue   **18A.17**
of CU100 between product A and the award credit by reference to their relative fair values of CU95 and CU3.20 respectively. Therefore:

(a)   Revenue for product A is CU100 × [CU95 / (CU95 + CU3.20)] = CU96.74
(b)   Revenue for product B is CU100 × [CU3.20 / (CU95 + CU3.20)] = CU3.26

Rendering of services

Example 14 Installation fees

The seller recognises installation fees as revenue by reference to the stage of completion of the installation, unless they   **18A.18**
are incidental to the sale of a product, in which case they are recognised when the goods are sold.

Example 15 Servicing fees included in the price of the product

When the selling price of a product includes an identifiable amount for subsequent servicing (eg after sales support and   **18A.19**
product enhancement on the sale of software), the seller defers that amount and recognises it as revenue over the period during which the service is performed. The amount deferred is that which will cover the expected costs of the services under the agreement, together with a reasonable profit on those services.

Example 16 Advertising commissions

Media commissions are recognised when the related advertisement or commercial appears before the public. Production   **18A.20**
commissions are recognised by reference to the stage of completion of the project.

Example 17 Admission fees

The seller recognises revenue from artistic performances, banquets and other special events when the event takes place.   **18A.21**
When a subscription to a number of events is sold, the seller allocates the fee to each event on a basis that reflects the extent to which services are performed at each event.

Example 18 Tuition fees

The seller recognises revenue over the period of instruction.   **18A.22**

Example 19 Initiation, entrance and membership fees

Revenue recognition depends on the nature of the services provided. If the fee permits only membership, and all other   **18A.23**
services or products are paid for separately, or if there is a separate annual subscription, the fee is recognised as revenue when no significant uncertainty about its collectability exists. If the fee entitles the member to services or publications to be provided during the membership period, or to purchase goods or services at prices lower than those charged to non-members, it is recognised on a basis that reflects the timing, nature and value of the benefits provided.

Franchise fees

Franchise fees may cover the supply of initial and subsequent services, equipment and other tangible assets, and know-   **18A.24**
how. Accordingly, franchise fees are recognised as revenue on a basis that reflects the purpose for which the fees were charged. The following methods of franchise fee recognition are appropriate.

Example 20 Franchise fees: Supplies of equipment and other tangible assets

18A.25   The franchisor recognises the fair value of the assets sold as revenue when the items are delivered or title passes.

Example 21 Franchise fees: Supplies of initial and subsequent services

18A.26   The franchisor recognises fees for the provision of continuing services, whether part of the initial fee or a separate fee, as revenue as the services are rendered. When the separate fee does not cover the cost of continuing services together with a reasonable profit, part of the initial fee, sufficient to cover the costs of continuing services and to provide a reasonable profit on those services, is deferred and recognised as revenue as the services are rendered.

18A.27   The franchise agreement may provide for the franchisor to supply equipment, inventories, or other tangible assets at a price lower than that charged to others or a price that does not provide a reasonable profit on those sales. In these circumstances, part of the initial fee, sufficient to cover estimated costs in excess of that price and to provide a reasonable profit on those sales, is deferred and recognised over the period the goods are likely to be sold to the franchisee. The balance of an initial fee is recognised as revenue when performance of all the initial services and other obligations required of the franchisor (such as assistance with site selection, staff training, financing and advertising) has been substantially accomplished.

18A.28   The initial services and other obligations under an area franchise agreement may depend on the number of individual outlets established in the area. In this case, the fees attributable to the initial services are recognised as revenue in proportion to the number of outlets for which the initial services have been substantially completed.

18A.29   If the initial fee is collectible over an extended period and there is a significant uncertainty that it will be collected in full, the fee is recognised as cash instalments are received.

Example 22 Franchise fees: Continuing franchise fees

18A.30   Fees charged for the use of continuing rights granted by the agreement, or for other services provided during the period of the agreement, are recognised as revenue as the services are provided or the rights used.

Example 23 Franchise fees: Agency transactions

18A.31   Transactions may take place between the franchisor and the franchisee that, in substance, involve the franchisor acting as agent for the franchisee. For example, the franchisor may order supplies and arrange for their delivery to the franchisee at no profit. Such transactions do not give rise to revenue.

Example 24 Fees from the development of customised software

18A.32   The software developer recognises fees from the development of customised software as revenue by reference to the stage of completion of the development, including completion of services provided for post-delivery service support.

Interest, royalties and dividends

Example 25 Licence fees and royalties

18A.33   The licensor recognises fees and royalties paid for the use of its assets (such as trademarks, patents, software, music copyright, record masters and motion picture films) in accordance with the substance of the agreement. As a practical matter, this may be on a straight-line basis over the life of the agreement, for example, when a licensee has the right to use specified technology for a specified period of time.

18A.34   An assignment of rights for a fixed fee or non-refundable guarantee under a non-cancellable contract that permits the licensee to exploit those rights freely and the licensor has no remaining obligations to perform is, in substance, a sale. An example is a licensing agreement for the use of software when the licensor has no obligations after delivery. Another example is the granting of rights to exhibit a motion picture film in markets in which the licensor has no control over the distributor and expects to receive no further revenues from the box office receipts. In such cases, revenue is recognised at the time of sale.

18A.35   In some cases, whether or not a licence fee or royalty will be received is contingent on the occurrence of a future event. In such cases, revenue is recognised only when it is probable that the fee or royalty will be received, which is normally when the event has occurred.

Section 19 Government Grants

Scope of this section

This section specifies the accounting for all **government grants**.   **19.1**

Government grants exclude those forms of government assistance that cannot reasonably have a value placed upon them   **19.2**
and transactions with government that cannot be distinguished from the normal trading transactions of the
micro-entity.

Recognition and measurement

Government grants, including non-monetary grants, shall not be recognised until there is reasonable assurance that: **19.3**

(a)   the micro-entity will comply with the conditions attaching to them; and
(b)   the grants will be received.

A micro-entity shall measure grants at the **fair value** of the **asset** received or receivable.   **19.4**

Where a grant becomes repayable it shall be recognised as a **liability** when the repayment meets the definition of a   **19.5**
liability.

A micro-entity shall classify government grants either as a grant relating to revenue or a grant relating to assets.   **19.6**

Government grants relating to revenue shall be recognised in income on a systematic basis over the periods in which the   **19.7**
micro-entity recognises the related costs for which the grant is intended to compensate.

A government grant that becomes receivable as compensation for **expenses** or losses already incurred or for the purpose   **19.8**
of giving immediate financial support to the entity with no future related costs shall be recognised as **income** in **profit
or loss** in the period in which it becomes receivable.

Government grants relating to assets shall be recognised in income on a systematic basis over the expected **useful life** of   **19.9**
the asset.

Where part of a government grant relating to an asset is deferred it shall be recognised as deferred income and not   **19.10**
deducted from the **carrying amount** of the asset.

Section 20 Borrowing Costs

Scope of this section

This section specifies the accounting for **borrowing costs**. Borrowing costs include: **20.1**

(a)   interest expense recognised in accordance with Section 9 *Financial Instruments*;
(b)   finance charges in respect of **finance leases** recognised in accordance with Section 15 *Leases*; and
(c)   exchange differences arising from foreign currency borrowings to the extent that they are regarded as an adjustment
       to interest costs.

Recognition

A **micro-entity** shall recognise all borrowing costs as an **expense** in **profit or loss** in the period in which they are   **20.2**
incurred.

Section 21 Share-based Payment

Scope of this section

This section specifies the accounting for all **share-based payment transactions** including: **21.1**

(a)   **equity-settled share-based payment transactions**;
(b)   **cash-settled share-based payment transactions**; and
(c)   transactions in which the **micro-entity** receives or acquires goods or services and the terms of the arrangement
       provide either the micro-entity or the supplier of those goods or services with a choice of whether the micro-entity
       settles the transaction in cash (or other **assets**) or by issuing equity instruments.

Appendix A

Equity-settled share-based payment transactions

21.2 A micro-entity shall not account for equity-settled share-based payments transactions until shares are issued, at which point the micro-entity shall apply the requirements of Section 17 *Liabilities and Equity*.

Cash-settled share-based payment transactions

21.3 A micro-entity shall recognise the goods or services received or acquired in a cash-settled share-based payment transaction when it obtains the goods or as the services are received and recognise a corresponding **liability**.

21.4 If the cash-settled share-based payments granted to employees **vest** immediately, the employee is not required to complete a specified period of service before becoming unconditionally entitled to those cash-settled share-based payments. In the absence of evidence to the contrary, the micro-entity shall presume that services rendered by the employee as consideration for the share-based payments have been received. In this case, on **grant date** the micro-entity shall recognise the services received in full, with a corresponding liability.

21.5 If the cash-settled share-based payments do not vest until the employee completes a specified period of service, the micro-entity shall presume that the services to be rendered by the employee as consideration for those cash-settled share-based payments will be received in the future, during the vesting period. The micro-entity shall account for those services as they are rendered by the employee during the vesting period, with a corresponding increase in the liability.

21.6 When the goods or services received or acquired in a cash-settled share-based payment transaction do not qualify for **recognition** as assets, the micro-entity shall recognise them as **expenses**.

21.7 A micro-entity shall measure the goods and services acquired and the liability incurred in accordance with the measurement requirements for a provision in Section 16 *Provisions and Contingencies*.

Share-based payment transactions with cash alternatives

21.8 Some share-based payment transactions give either the micro-entity or the counterparty a choice of settling the transaction in cash (or other assets) or by the transfer of equity instruments.

21.9 When the micro-entity has a choice of settlement of the transaction in cash (or other assets) or by the transfer of equity instruments, the micro-entity shall account for the whole transaction as set out in paragraph 21.2 unless:

(a) the choice of settlement in equity instruments has no commercial substance (eg because the micro-entity is legally prohibited from issuing shares); or

(b) the micro-entity has a past practice or a stated policy of settling in cash, or generally settles in cash whenever the counterparty asks for cash settlement.

In circumstances (a) and (b) the micro-entity shall account for the transaction as a wholly cash-settled transaction in accordance with paragraphs 21.3 to 21.7.

21.10 When the counterparty has a choice of settlement of the transaction in cash (or other assets) or by the transfer of equity instruments, the micro-entity shall account for the transaction as a wholly cash-settled share-based payment transaction in accordance with paragraphs 21.3 to 21.7 unless:

(a) the choice of settlement in cash (or other assets) has no commercial substance because the cash settlement amount (or value of the other assets) bears no relationship to, and is likely to be lower in value than, the **fair value** of the equity instruments.

In circumstance (a) the entity shall account for the whole transaction as set out in paragraph 21.2.

Section 22 Impairment of Assets

Objective and scope

22.1 An **impairment loss** occurs when the **carrying amount** of an **asset** exceeds its **recoverable amount**. This section shall be applied in accounting for the impairment of all assets (including **goodwill**), other than the following, for which other sections of this FRS establish impairment requirements:

(a) assets arising from **construction contracts** (see Section 18 *Revenue*);

(b) **financial assets** within the scope of Section 9 *Financial Instruments*; and

(c) **inventories** (see Section 10 *Inventories*).

Impairment of assets

General principles

If, and only if, the recoverable amount of an asset is less than its carrying amount, the **micro-entity** shall reduce the carrying amount of the asset to its recoverable amount.   **22.2**

If it is not possible to estimate the recoverable amount of the individual asset, a micro-entity shall estimate the recoverable amount of the **cash-generating unit** to which the asset belongs. This may be the case because measuring the recoverable amount requires forecasting cash flows, and sometimes individual assets do not generate cash flows by themselves. An impairment loss for a cash-generating unit shall be recognised and measured in accordance with the relevant requirements of Section 27 *Impairment of Assets* of **FRS 102**.   **22.3**

A micro-entity that has goodwill acquired in a **business combination** shall apply the additional impairment requirements applicable to goodwill in paragraphs 27.24 to 27.27 of FRS 102.   **22.4**

A micro-entity shall recognise an impairment loss immediately in **profit or loss**.   **22.5**

Indicators of impairment

A micro-entity shall assess at each **reporting date** whether there is any indication that an asset may be impaired. If any such indication exists, the micro-entity shall estimate the recoverable amount of the asset. If there is no indication of impairment, it is not necessary to estimate the recoverable amount.   **22.6**

In assessing whether there is any indication that an asset may be impaired, a micro-entity shall consider, as a minimum, the following indications: **22.7**

External sources of information

(a)   During the period, an asset's market value has declined significantly more than would be expected as a result of the passage of time or normal use.

(b)   Significant changes with an adverse effect on the micro-entity have taken place during the period, or will take place in the near future, in the technological, market, economic or legal environment in which the micro-entity operates or in the market to which an asset is dedicated.

(c)   Market interest rates or other market rates of return on investments have increased during the period, and those increases are likely to affect materially the discount rate used in calculating an asset's **value in use** and decrease the asset's **fair value less costs to sell**.

(d)   The carrying amount of the net assets of the micro-entity is more than the estimated **fair value** of the micro-entity as a whole (such an estimate may have been made, for example, in relation to the potential sale of part or all of the micro-entity).

Internal sources of information

Evidence is available of obsolescence or physical damage of an asset.

Significant changes with an adverse effect on the micro-entity have taken place during the period, or are expected to take place in the near future, in the extent to which, or manner in which, an asset is used or is expected to be used. These changes include the asset becoming idle, plans to discontinue or restructure the operation to which an asset belongs, plans to dispose of an asset before the previously expected date, and reassessing the **useful life** of an asset as finite rather than indefinite.

Evidence is available from internal reporting that indicates that the economic performance of an asset is, or will be, worse than expected. In this context economic performance includes operating results and cash flows.

If there is an indication that an asset may be impaired, this may indicate that the micro-entity should review the remaining useful life, the **depreciation (amortisation)** method or the **residual value** for the asset and adjust it in accordance with the section of this FRS applicable to the asset (eg Section 12 *Property, Plant and Equipment and Investment Property* and Section 13 *Intangible Assets other than Goodwill*), even if no impairment loss is recognised for the asset.   **22.8**

Measuring recoverable amount

The recoverable amount of an asset is the higher of its fair value less costs to sell and its value in use.   **22.9**

22.10 It is not always necessary to determine both an asset's fair value less costs to sell and its value in use. If either of these amounts exceeds the asset's carrying amount, the asset is not impaired and it is not necessary to estimate the other amount.

22.11 If there is no reason to believe that an asset's value in use materially exceeds its fair value less costs to sell, the asset's fair value less costs to sell may be used as its recoverable amount. This will often be the case for an asset that is held for disposal.

Fair value less costs to sell

22.12 Fair value less costs to sell is the amount obtainable from the sale of an asset in an arm's length transaction between knowledgeable, willing parties, less the costs of disposal. The best evidence of the fair value less costs to sell of an asset is a price in a binding sale agreement in an arm's length transaction or a market price in an **active market**. If there is no binding sale agreement or active market for an asset, fair value less costs to sell is based on the best information available to reflect the amount that a micro-entity could obtain, at the reporting date, from the disposal of the asset in an arm's length transaction between knowledgeable, willing parties, after deducting the costs of disposal. In determining this amount, a micro-entity considers the outcome of recent transactions for similar assets within the same industry.

22.13 When determining an asset's fair value less costs to sell, consideration shall be given to any restrictions imposed on that asset. Costs to sell shall also include the cost of obtaining relaxation of a restriction where necessary in order to enable the asset to be sold. If a restriction would also apply to any potential purchaser of an asset, the fair value of the asset may be lower than that of an asset whose use is not restricted.

Value in use

22.14 Value in use is the **present value** of the future cash flows expected to be derived from an asset. This present value calculation involves the following steps:

(a) estimating the future cash inflows and outflows to be derived from the continuing use of the asset and from its ultimate disposal; and
(b) applying the appropriate discount rate to those future cash flows.

22.15 In measuring value in use, estimates of future cash flows shall include:

(a) projections of cash inflows from the continuing use of the asset;
(b) projections of cash outflows that are necessarily incurred to generate the cash inflows from continuing use of the asset (including cash outflows to prepare the asset for use) and can be directly attributed, or allocated on a reasonable and consistent basis, to the asset; and
(c) net cash flows, if any, expected to be received (or paid) for the disposal of the asset at the end of its useful life in an arm's length transaction between knowledgeable, willing parties.

The micro-entity may wish to use any recent financial budgets or forecasts to estimate the cash flows, if available, and extrapolate the projections using a steady or declining growth rate for subsequent years, unless an increasing rate can be justified.

22.16 Estimates of future cash flows shall not include:

(a) cash inflows or outflows from **financing activities**; or
(b) income tax receipts or payments.

22.17 Future cash flows shall be estimated for the asset in its current condition. Estimates of future cash flows shall not include estimated future cash inflows or outflows that are expected to arise from:

(a) a future **restructuring** to which a micro-entity is not yet committed; or
(b) improving or enhancing the asset's performance.

22.18 The discount rate(s) used in the present value calculation shall be a pre-tax rate(s) that reflect(s) current market assessments of:

(a) the time value of money; and
(b) the risks specific to the asset for which the future cash flow estimates have not been adjusted.

The discount rate(s) used to measure an asset's value in use shall not reflect risks for which the future cash flow estimates have been adjusted, to avoid double-counting.

Reversal of an impairment loss

An impairment loss recognised for **goodwill** shall not be reversed in a subsequent period[1]. **22.19**

For all assets other than goodwill, if and only if the reasons for the impairment loss have ceased to apply, an impairment **22.20**
loss shall be reversed in a subsequent period. A micro-entity shall assess at each reporting date whether there is any
indication that an impairment loss recognised in prior periods may no longer exist or may have decreased. Indications that
an impairment loss may have decreased or may no longer exist are generally the opposite of those set out in
paragraph 22.7. If any such indication exists, the micro-entity shall determine whether all or part of the prior impairment
loss should be reversed.

Reversal where recoverable amount was estimated for an individual impaired asset

When the prior impairment loss was based on the recoverable amount of the individual impaired asset, the following **22.21**
requirements apply:

(a)   The micro-entity shall estimate the recoverable amount of the asset at the current reporting date.

(b)   If the estimated recoverable amount of the asset exceeds its carrying amount, the micro-entity shall increase the
      carrying amount to recoverable amount, subject to the limitation described in paragraph (c) below. That increase is
      a reversal of an impairment loss. The micro-entity shall recognise the reversal immediately in profit or loss.

(c)   The reversal of an impairment loss shall not increase the carrying amount of the asset above the carrying amount
      that would have been determined (net of amortisation or depreciation) had no impairment loss been recognised for
      the asset in prior years.

(d)   After a reversal of an impairment loss is recognised, the micro-entity shall adjust the depreciation (amortisation)
      charge for the asset in future periods to allocate the asset's revised carrying amount, less its residual value (if any),
      on a systematic basis over its remaining useful life.

Section 23 Employee Benefits

Scope of this section

Employee benefits are all forms of consideration given by a **micro-entity** in exchange for service rendered by employees, **23.1**
including directors and management. This section applies to all employee benefits, except for **share-based payment
transactions**, which are covered by Section 21 *Share-based Payment*. Employee benefits covered by this section will be
one of the following four types:

(a)   short-term employee benefits, which are employee benefits (other than **termination benefits**) that are expected to
      be settled wholly before 12 months after the end of the **reporting period** in which the employees render the related
      service;

(b)   **post-employment benefits**, which are employee benefits (other than termination benefits and short-term employee
      benefits) that are payable after the completion of employment;

(c)   other long-term employee benefits, which are all employee benefits, other than short-term employee benefits, post-
      employment benefits and termination benefits; or

(d)   termination benefits, which are employee benefits provided in exchange for the termination of an employee's
      employment as a result of either:

      (i)   a micro-entity's decision to terminate an employee's employment before the normal retirement date; or

      (ii)   an employee's decision to accept voluntary redundancy in exchange for those benefits.

General recognition principle for all employee benefits

A micro-entity shall recognise the cost of all employee benefits to which its employees have become entitled as a result **23.2**
of service rendered to the micro-entity during the reporting period:

(a)   As a **liability**, after deducting amounts that have been paid directly to the employees or as a contribution to an
      employee benefit fund[2]. If the amount paid exceeds the obligation arising from service before the **reporting date**,
      a micro-entity shall recognise that excess as an **asset** to the extent that the prepayment will lead to a reduction in
      future payments or a cash refund.

---

[1] *The prohibition of the reversal of goodwill impairment losses is subject to the introduction of the same requirement in company law. Prior to that
change being made this FRS requires the reversal of goodwill if the conditions set out in paragraph 22.20 are met.*

[2] *Contributions to an employee benefit fund that is an intermediate payment arrangement shall be accounted for in accordance with Section 7
Subsidiaries, Associates, Jointly Controlled Entities and Intermediate Payment Arrangements, and as a result if the employer is a sponsoring micro-
entity the assets and liabilities of the intermediary will be accounted for by the sponsoring micro-entity as an extension of its own business. In which
case the payment to the employee benefit fund does not extinguish the liability of the employer.*

(b)   As an **expense**, unless another section of this FRS requires the cost to be recognised as part of the cost of an asset such as **inventories** (for example in accordance with paragraph 10.8) or **property, plant and equipment** (in accordance with paragraph 12.9).

Short-term employee benefits

Examples

23.3   Short-term employee benefits include items such as the following, if expected to be settled wholly before 12 months after the end of the annual reporting period in which the employees render the related service:

(a)   wages, salaries and social security contributions;

(b)   paid annual leave and paid sick leave;

(c)   profit-sharing and bonuses; and

(d)   non-monetary benefits (such as medical care, housing, cars and free or subsidised goods or services) for current employees.

Measurement of short-term benefits generally

23.4   When an employee has rendered service to a micro-entity during the reporting period, the micro-entity shall measure the amounts recognised in accordance with paragraph 23.2 at the undiscounted amount of short-term employee benefits expected to be paid in exchange for that service.

Recognition and measurement: Short-term compensated absences

23.5   A micro-entity may compensate employees for absence for various reasons including annual leave and sick leave. Some short-term compensated absences accumulatethey can be carried forward and used in future periods if the employee does not use the current period's entitlement in full. Examples include annual leave and sick leave. A micro-entity shall recognise the expected cost of **accumulating compensated absences** when the employees render service that increases their entitlement to future compensated absences. The micro-entity shall measure the expected cost of accumulating compensated absences at the undiscounted additional amount that the micro-entity expects to pay as a result of the unused entitlement that has accumulated at the end of the reporting period. The micro-entity shall present this amount as falling due within one year at the reporting date.

23.6   A micro-entity shall recognise the cost of other (non-accumulating) compensated absences when the absences occur. The micro-entity shall measure the cost of non-accumulating compensated absences at the undiscounted amount of salaries and wages paid or payable for the period of absence.

Recognition: Profit-sharing and bonus plans

23.7   A micro-entity shall recognise the expected cost of profit-sharing and bonus payments only when:

(a)   the micro-entity has a present legal or **constructive obligation** to make such payments as a result of past events (this means that the micro-entity has no realistic alternative but to make the payments); and

(b)   a reliable estimate of the obligation can be made.

Post-employment benefits: Distinction between defined contribution plans and defined benefit plans

23.8   Post-employment benefits include, for example:

(a)   retirement benefits, such as pensions; and

(b)   other post-employment benefits, such as post-employment life insurance and post-employment medical care.

Arrangements whereby a micro-entity provides post-employment benefits are **post-employment benefit plans**. A micro-entity shall apply this section to all such arrangements whether or not they involve the establishment of a separate entity to receive contributions and to pay benefits. In some cases, these arrangements are imposed by law rather than by action of the micro-entity. In some cases, these arrangements arise from actions of the micro-entity even in the absence of a formal, documented plan.

23.9   Post-employment benefit plans are classified as either **defined contribution plans** or **defined benefit plans**, depending on their principal terms and conditions:

(a)   Defined contribution plans are post-employment benefit plans under which a micro-entity pays fixed contributions into a separate entity (a fund) and has no legal or constructive obligation to pay further contributions or to make direct benefit payments to employees if the fund does not hold sufficient assets to pay all employee benefits relating to employee service in the current and prior periods. The amount of the post-employment benefits received by the employee is determined by the amount of contributions paid by a micro-entity (and perhaps also the employee) to a post-employment benefit plan or to an insurer, together with investment returns arising from the contributions.

(b) Defined benefit plans are post-employment benefit plans other than defined contribution plans. Under defined benefit plans, the micro-entity's obligation is to provide the agreed benefits to current and former employees, and actuarial risk (that benefits will cost more or less than expected) and investment risk (that returns on assets set aside to fund the benefits will differ from expectations) are borne, in substance, by the micro-entity. If actuarial or investment experience is worse than expected, the micro-entity's obligation may be increased, and vice versa if actuarial or investment experience is better than expected.

Post-employment benefit plans

Recognition and measurement – requirements applicable to all plans

When contributions to a defined contribution or defined benefit plan are not expected to be settled wholly within 12 months after the end of the reporting period in which the employees render the related service, the liability recognised in accordance with paragraph 23.2(a) shall be measured at the **present value** of the contributions payable using the methodology for selecting a discount rate specified in paragraph 23.11. The unwinding of the discount shall be recognised as interest expense in **profit or loss** in the period in which it arises.   **23.10**

A micro-entity shall determine the rate used to discount the future payments by reference to market yields at the reporting date on high quality corporate bonds. In countries with no deep market in such bonds, the micro-entity shall use the market yields (at the reporting date) on government bonds. The currency and term of the corporate bonds or government bonds shall be consistent with the currency and estimated period of the future payments.   **23.11**

Recognition and measurement – requirements applicable to defined benefit plans

When a micro-entity participates in a defined benefit plan (which may include a **multi-employer plan** or **state plan**) and has entered into an agreement with the plan that determines how the micro-entity will fund a deficit (such as a schedule of contributions), the micro-entity shall recognise a liability for the contributions payable that arise from the agreement (to the extent that they relate to the deficit) and the resulting expense in profit or loss in accordance with paragraphs 23.2 and 23.10.   **23.12**

Where a micro-entity participates in a defined benefit plan that shares risks between entities under common control it shall recognise a cost equal to its contribution payable for the period. If a micro-entity is legally responsible for the plan and has entered into an agreement with the plan that determines how a deficit will be funded, the micro-entity shall recognise a liability for the contributions payable that arise from the agreement (to the extent that they relate to the deficit) and the resulting expense in profit or loss in accordance with paragraphs 23.2 and 23.10.   **23.13**

Other long-term employee benefits

Other long-term employee benefits include items such as the following, if not expected to be settled wholly before 12 months after the end of the annual reporting period in which the employees render the related service: **23.14**

(a) long-term paid absences such as long-service or sabbatical leave;
(b) other long-service benefits;
(c) long-term disability benefits;
(d) profit-sharing and bonuses; and
(e) deferred remuneration.

A micro-entity shall recognise a liability for other long-term employee benefits measured at the present value of the benefit obligation at the reporting date calculated using the methodology for selecting a discount rate in paragraph 23.11. The unwinding of the discount shall be recognised as interest expense in profit or loss in the period in which it arises.   **23.15**

Termination benefits

A micro-entity may be committed, by legislation, by contractual or other agreements with employees or their representatives or by a constructive obligation based on business practice, custom or a desire to act equitably, to make payments (or provide other benefits) to employees when it terminates their employment. Such payments are termination benefits.   **23.16**

Recognition

Because termination benefits do not provide a micro-entity with future economic benefits, a micro-entity shall recognise them as an expense in profit or loss immediately.   **23.17**

23.18 A micro-entity shall recognise termination benefits as a liability and an expense only when the micro-entity is demonstrably committed either:

(a)   to terminate the employment of an employee or group of employees before the normal retirement date; or

(b)   to provide termination benefits as a result of an offer made in order to encourage voluntary redundancy.

23.19 A micro-entity is demonstrably committed to a termination only when the micro-entity has a detailed formal plan for the termination[3] and is without realistic possibility of withdrawal from the plan.

Measurement

23.20 A micro-entity shall measure termination benefits at the best estimate of the expenditure that would be required to settle the obligation at the reporting date. In the case of an offer made to encourage voluntary redundancy, the measurement of termination benefits shall be based on the number of employees expected to accept the offer.

23.21 When termination benefits are due more than 12 months after the end of the reporting period, they shall be measured at their discounted present value using the methodology for selecting a discount rate specified in paragraph 23.11.

Disclosures in the notes

23.22 A micro entity shall disclose any commitment not recognised in the statement of financial position concerning pensions separately from other financial commitments, guarantees and contingencies (see paragraph 6A.2).

Section 24 Income Tax

Scope of this section

24.1 For the purpose of this FRS, **income tax** includes all domestic and foreign taxes that are based on **taxable profit**.

24.2 This section covers accounting for income tax. It requires a **micro-entity** to recognise the **current tax** consequences of transactions and other events that have been recognised in the **financial statements**. Current tax is tax payable (refundable) in respect of the taxable profit (tax loss) for the current period or past **reporting periods**. This section prohibits the recognition of **deferred tax** which represents the future tax consequences of transactions and events recognised in the financial statements of the current and previous periods.

24.3 This section also covers accounting for value added tax (VAT) and other similar sales taxes, which are not income taxes.

Current tax

24.4 A micro-entity shall recognise a current tax **liability** for tax payable on taxable profit for the current and past periods. If the amount of tax paid for the current and past periods exceeds the amount of tax payable for those periods, the micro-entity shall recognise the excess as a current tax **asset**.

24.5 A micro-entity shall recognise a current tax asset for the benefit of a tax loss that can be carried back to recover tax paid in a previous period.

24.6 A micro-entity shall measure a current tax liability (asset) at the amount of tax it expects to pay (recover) using the tax rates and laws that have been enacted or **substantively enacted** by the **reporting date**.

Deferred tax

24.7 A micro-entity shall not recognise deferred tax.

Measurement of current tax

24.8 A micro-entity shall not discount current tax assets and liabilities.

Withholding tax on dividends

24.9 When a micro-entity pays dividends to its shareholders, it may be required to pay a portion of the dividends to taxation authorities on behalf of shareholders. Outgoing dividends and similar amounts payable shall be recognised at an amount that includes any withholding tax but excludes other taxes, such as attributable tax credits.

---

[3]   *An example of the features of a detailed formal plan for restructuring, which may include termination benefits, is given in paragraph 16.15.*

Incoming dividends and similar income receivable shall be recognised at an amount that includes any withholding tax but excludes other taxes, such as attributable tax credits. Any withholding tax suffered shall be shown as part of the tax charge. **24.10**

Value Added Tax and other similar sales taxes

Turnover included in **profit or loss** shall exclude VAT and other similar sales taxes on taxable outputs and VAT imputed under the flat rate VAT scheme. **Expenses** shall exclude recoverable VAT and other similar recoverable sales taxes. Irrecoverable VAT allocable to **fixed assets** and to other items separately recognised shall be included in their cost where practicable and **material**. **24.11**

Presentation

Allocation in profit or loss

A micro-entity shall present changes in a current tax liability (asset) as **tax expense** (income). **24.12**

Offsetting

A micro-entity shall offset current tax assets and current tax liabilities, if and only if, it has a legally enforceable right to set off the amounts and it intends either to settle on a net basis or to realise the asset and settle the liability simultaneously. **24.13**

Section 25 Foreign Currency Translation

Scope of this section

A **micro-entity** may have transactions in foreign currencies. This section prescribes how to include foreign currency transactions in the financial statements of a micro-entity. Where a micro-entity has a foreign branch, the micro-entity should refer to the requirements of Section 30 *Foreign Currency Translation* of **FRS 102** to determine if the foreign branch has a different functional currency, and if so, should apply the requirements of Section 30 of FRS 102 to those transactions undertaken by the foreign branch. **25.1**

Reporting foreign currency transactions

Initial recognition

A foreign currency transaction is a transaction that is denominated or requires settlement in a foreign currency, including transactions arising when a micro-entity: **25.2**

(a) buys or sells goods or services whose price is denominated in a foreign currency;
(b) borrows or lends funds when the amounts payable or receivable are denominated in a foreign currency; or
(c) otherwise acquires or disposes of **assets**, or incurs or settles **liabilities**, denominated in a foreign currency.

A micro-entity shall record a foreign currency transaction by applying to the foreign currency amount the spot exchange rate at the date of the transaction unless: **25.3**

(a) the transaction is to be settled at a contracted rate, in which case that rate shall be used; or
(b) where a trading transaction is covered by a related or matching forward contract, in which case the rate of exchange specified in that contract shall be used.

The date of a transaction is the date on which the transaction first qualifies for **recognition** in accordance with this FRS. For practical reasons, a rate that approximates the actual rate at the date of the transaction is often used, for example, an average rate for a week or a month might be used for all transactions in each foreign currency occurring during that period. However, if exchange rates fluctuate significantly, the use of the average rate for a period is inappropriate. **25.4**

Reporting at the end of the subsequent reporting periods

At the end of each **reporting period**, unless it is applying a contracted rate in accordance with paragraph 25.3 a micro-entity shall: **25.5**

(a) translate foreign currency **monetary items** using the **closing rate**; and
(b) translate non-monetary items that are measured in terms of historical cost in a foreign currency using the exchange rate at the date of the transaction.

25.6 A micro-entity shall recognise, in **profit or loss** in the period in which they arise, exchange differences arising on the settlement of monetary items or on translating monetary items at rates different from those at which they were translated on initial recognition during the period or in previous periods.

Section 26 Events after the End of the Reporting Period

Scope of this section

26.1 This section defines events after the end of the **reporting period** and sets out principles for recognising and measuring those events.

Events after the end of the reporting period defined

26.2 Events after the end of the reporting period are those events, favourable and unfavourable, that occur between the end of the reporting period and the date when the financial statements are authorised for issue. There are two types of events:

(a) those that provide evidence of conditions that existed at the end of the reporting period (adjusting events after the end of the reporting period); and

(b) those that are indicative of conditions that arose after the end of the reporting period (non-adjusting events after the end of the reporting period).

26.3 Events after the end of the reporting period include all events up to the date when the **financial statements** are authorised for issue, even if those events occur after the public announcement of **profit or loss** or other selected financial information.

Recognition and measurement

Adjusting events after the end of the reporting period

26.4 A **micro-entity** shall adjust the amounts recognised in its **financial statements** to reflect adjusting events after the end of the reporting period.

26.5 The following are examples of adjusting events after the end of the reporting period that require a micro-entity to adjust the amounts recognised in its financial statements, or to recognise items that were not previously recognised:

(a) The settlement after the end of the reporting period of a court case that confirms that the micro-entity had a present obligation at the end of the reporting period. The micro-entity adjusts any previously recognised **provision** related to this court case in accordance with Section 16 *Provisions and Contingencies* or recognises a new provision. The micro-entity does not merely disclose a **contingent liability**. Rather, the settlement provides additional evidence to be considered in determining the provision that should be recognised at the end of the reporting period in accordance with Section 16.

(b) The receipt of information after the end of the reporting period indicating that an **asset** was impaired at the end of the reporting period, or that the amount of a previously recognised **impairment loss** for that asset needs to be adjusted. For example:

(i) the bankruptcy of a customer that occurs after the end of the reporting period usually confirms that a loss existed at the end of the reporting period on a trade receivable and that the micro-entity needs to adjust the **carrying amount** of the trade receivable; and

(ii) the sale of **inventories** after the end of the reporting period may give evidence about their selling price at the end of the reporting period for the purpose of assessing impairment at that date.

(c) The determination after the end of the reporting period of the cost of assets purchased, or the proceeds from assets sold, before the end of the reporting period.

(d) The determination after the end of the reporting period of the amount of profit-sharing or bonus payments, if the micro-entity had a legal or **constructive obligation** at the end of the reporting period to make such payments as a result of events before that date (see Section 23 *Employee Benefits*).

(e) The discovery of fraud or **errors** that show that the financial statements are incorrect.

Non-adjusting events after the end of the reporting period

26.6 A micro-entity shall not adjust the amounts recognised in its financial statements to reflect non-adjusting events after the end of the reporting period.

26.7 Examples of non-adjusting events after the end of the reporting period include:

(a) A decline in market value of investments between the end of the reporting period and the date when the financial statements are authorised for issue. The decline in market value does not normally relate to the condition of the investments at the end of the reporting period, but reflects circumstances that have arisen subsequently. Therefore, a micro-entity does not adjust the amounts recognised in its financial statements for the investments.

(b) An amount that becomes receivable as a result of a favourable judgement or settlement of a court case after the **reporting date** but before the financial statements are authorised for issue. This would be a **contingent asset** at the reporting date (see paragraph 16.18). However, agreement on the amount of damages for a judgement that was reached before the reporting date, but was not previously recognised because the amount could not be measured reliably, may constitute an adjusting event.

Going concern

A micro-entity shall not prepare its financial statements on a going concern basis if management determines after the end of the reporting period that it either intends to liquidate the micro-entity or to cease trading, or that it has no realistic alternative but to do so.   **26.8**

Deterioration in operating results and **financial position** after the reporting period may lead management to determine that they intend to liquidate the micro-entity or to cease trading or that they have no realistic alternative but to do so. If the going concern basis of accounting is no longer appropriate, the effect is so pervasive that this section requires a fundamental change in the basis of accounting.   **26.9**

Dividends

If a micro-entity declares dividends to holders of its equity instruments after the end of the reporting period, the micro-entity shall not recognise those dividends as a **liability** at the end of the reporting period because no obligation exists at that time.   **26.10**

Section 27 Specialised Activities

Scope of this section

This section sets out the financial reporting requirements for **micro-entities** involved in agriculture.   **27.1**

Agriculture

Recognition

A micro-entity that is engaged in **agricultural activity** shall recognise a **biological asset** or an item of **agricultural produce** when, and only when: **27.2**

(a) the micro-entity controls the **asset** as a result of past events;
(b) it is **probable** that future economic benefits associated with the asset will flow to the micro-entity; and
(c) the cost of the **asset** can be measured reliably.

Measurement

A micro-entity shall measure biological assets at cost less any accumulated **depreciation** and any accumulated **impairment losses**.   **27.3**

Agricultural produce harvested from a micro-entity's biological assets shall be measured at the point of harvest at the lower of cost and estimated selling price less costs to complete and sell.   **27.4**

Such measurement is the cost at that date when applying Section 10 *Inventories* or another applicable section of this FRS.

Disclosure in the notes

A micro-entity shall determine the amount of any financial commitments, guarantees and contingencies not recognised in the **statement of financial position** for the acquisition of a biological asset and disclose that amount within the total amount of financial commitments, guarantees and contingencies (see paragraph 6A.2).   **27.5**

A micro-entity shall disclose an indication of the nature and form of any biological asset or item of agricultural produce given as security in respect of its commitments, guarantees and contingencies (see paragraph 6A.3).   **27.6**

Appendix A

Section 28 Transition to this FRS

Scope of this section

28.1   This section applies to a **first-time adopter of this FRS**, regardless of its previous accounting framework.

28.2   Notwithstanding the requirements in paragraphs 28.3 and 28.4, a **micro-entity** that has applied this FRS in a previous **reporting period**, but whose most recent previous annual **financial statements** were prepared in accordance with a different accounting framework, must either apply this section or else apply this FRS retrospectively in accordance with Section 8 *Accounting Policies, Changes in Estimates and Errors* as if the micro-entity had never stopped applying this FRS.

First-time adoption

28.3   A first-time adopter of this FRS shall apply this section in its first financial statements that conform to this FRS.

28.4   A micro-entity's first financial statements that conform to this FRS are the first financial statements prepared in accordance with this FRS if, for example, the micro-entity:

(a)   did not present financial statements for previous periods; or

(b)   presented its most recent previous financial statements under previous UK and Republic of Ireland requirements or **FRS 102** and that are therefore not consistent with this FRS in all respects.

28.5   Paragraph 3.9 defines a complete set of financial statements for a micro-entity.

28.6   Paragraph 3.10 requires a micro-entity to disclose, in a complete set of financial statements, comparative information in respect of the preceding period for all amounts presented in the financial statements. Therefore, a micro-entity's **date of transition** to this FRS is the beginning of the earliest period for which the micro-entity presents full comparative information in accordance with this FRS in its first financial statements that comply with this FRS.

Procedures for preparing financial statements at the date of transition

28.7   Except as provided in paragraphs 28.9 to 28.11, a micro-entity shall, in its opening **statement of financial position** as of its date of transition to this FRS (ie the beginning of the earliest period presented):

(a)   recognise all **assets** and **liabilities** whose **recognition** is required by this FRS;

(b)   not recognise items as assets or liabilities if this FRS does not permit such recognition;

(c)   reclassify items that it recognised under its previous financial reporting framework as one type of asset, liability or component of **equity**, but are a different type of asset, liability or component of equity under this FRS; and

(d)   apply this FRS in **measuring** all recognised assets and liabilities.

This section does not require the opening statement of financial position to be presented.

28.8   The **accounting policies** that a micro-entity uses in its opening statement of financial position under this FRS may differ from those that it used for the same date using its previous financial reporting framework. The resulting adjustments arise from transactions, other events or conditions before the date of transition to this FRS. Therefore, a micro-entity shall recognise those adjustments directly in equity reserves at the date of transition to this FRS.

28.9   On first-time adoption of this FRS, a micro-entity shall not retrospectively change the accounting that it followed under its previous financial reporting framework for any of the following transactions:

(a)   *Derecognition of financial assets and financial liabilities*
Financial assets and **financial liabilities** derecognised under a micro-entity's previous accounting framework before the date of transition shall not be recognised upon adoption of this FRS. Conversely, for financial assets and liabilities that would have been derecognised under this FRS in a transaction that took place before the date of transition, but that were not derecognised under a micro-entity's previous accounting framework, a micro-entity may choose:

(i)   to derecognise them on adoption of this FRS; or

(ii)   to continue to recognise them until disposed of or settled.

(b)   *Accounting estimates.*

28.10   A micro-entity may use one or more of the following exemptions in preparing its first financial statements that conform to this FRS:

(a) *Business combinations and goodwill*

A first-time adopter is not required to apply Section 14 *Business Combinations and Goodwill* to **business combinations** that were effected before the date of transition to this FRS. However, if a first-time adopter restates any business combination to comply with Section 14, it shall restate all later business combinations. If a first-time adopter does not apply Section 14 retrospectively, the first-time adopter shall recognise and measure all its assets and liabilities acquired or assumed in a past business combination at the date of transition to this FRS in accordance with paragraphs 28.7 to 28.9 or, if applicable, with paragraphs 28.10(b) to (h) except that no adjustment shall be made to the **carrying amount** of **goodwill**.

(b) *Share-based payment transactions*

A first-time adopter is not required to apply Section 21 *Share-based Payment* to obligations arising from **share-based payment transactions** that were settled before the date of transition to this FRS.

(c) *Investment properties*

A first-time adopter is not required to retrospectively apply paragraph 12.15 to determine the depreciated cost of each of the major components of an **investment property** at the date of transition to this FRS. If this exemption is applied, a first-time adopter shall:

(i) Determine the total cost of the investment property including all of its components. Where no **depreciation** had been charged under the micro-entity's previous financial reporting framework, this can be calculated by reversing any revaluation **gains** or losses previously recorded in equity reserves.

(ii) The cost of land, if any, shall be separated from buildings.

(iii) Estimate the total depreciated cost of the investment property (excluding land) at the date of transition to this FRS, by recognising accumulated depreciation since the date of initial acquisition calculated on the basis of the **useful life** of the most significant component of the item of investment property (eg the main structural elements of the building).

(iv) A portion of the estimated total depreciated cost calculated in paragraph (iii) shall then be allocated to each of the other major components (ie excluding the most significant component identified above) to determine their depreciated cost. The allocation should be made on a reasonable and consistent basis. For example, a possible basis of allocation is to multiply the current cost to replace the component by the ratio of its remaining useful life to the expected useful life of a replacement component.

(v) Any amount of the total depreciated cost not allocated under paragraph (iv) shall be allocated to the most significant component of the investment property.

(d) *Compound financial instruments*

Paragraph 17.11 requires a micro-entity to split a **compound financial instrument** into its liability and equity components at the date of issue. A first-time adopter need not separate those two components if the liability component is not outstanding at the date of transition to this FRS.

(e) *Arrangements containing a lease*

A first-time adopter may elect to determine whether an arrangement existing at the date of transition to this FRS contains a **lease** (see paragraph 15.4) on the basis of facts and circumstances existing at that date, rather than when the arrangement was entered into.

(f) *Decommissioning liabilities included in the cost of property, plant and equipment or investment property*

Paragraph 12.9(c) states that the cost of an item of **property, plant and equipment** or **investment property** includes the initial estimate of the costs of dismantling and removing the item and restoring the site on which it is located, the obligation for which a micro-entity incurs either when the item is acquired or as a consequence of having used the item during a particular period for purposes other than to produce **inventories** during that period. A first-time adopter may elect to measure this component of the cost of an item of property, plant and equipment or investment property at the date of transition to this FRS, rather than on the date(s) when the obligation initially arose.

(g) *Dormant companies*

A company within the **Act's** definition of a dormant company may elect to retain its accounting policies for reported assets, liabilities and equity at the date of transition to this FRS until there is any change to those balances or the company undertakes any new transactions.

(h) *Lease incentives*

A first-time adopter is not required to apply paragraphs 15.15 and 15.25 to **lease incentives** provided the term of the lease commenced before the date of transition to this FRS. The first-time adopter shall continue to recognise any residual benefit or cost associated with these lease incentives on the same basis as that applied at the date of transition to this FRS.

If it is **impracticable** for a micro-entity to restate the opening statement of financial position at the date of transition for one or more of the adjustments required by paragraph 28.7, the micro-entity shall apply paragraphs 28.7 to 28.10 for such adjustments in the earliest period for which it is practicable to do so. **28.11**

Where applicable to the transactions, events or arrangements affected by applying these exemptions, a micro-entity may continue to use the exemptions that are applied at the date of transition to this FRS when preparing subsequent financial statements, until such time when the assets and liabilities associated with those transactions, events or arrangements are derecognised. **28.12**

Appendix A

APPROVAL BY THE FRC

Financial Reporting Standard 105 *The Financial Reporting Standard applicable to the Micro-entities Regime* was approved for issue by the Financial Reporting Council on 1 July 2015, following its consideration of the Accounting Council's Advice for this FRS.

THE ACCOUNTING COUNCIL'S ADVICE TO THE FRC TO ISSUE FRS 105

Introduction

1 This report provides an overview of the main issues that have been considered by the Accounting Council in advising the Financial Reporting Council (FRC) to issue FRS 105 *The Financial Reporting Standard applicable to the Micro-entities Regime*, incorporating the Council's advice following the publication of Financial Reporting Exposure Draft (FRED) 58 *Draft FRS 105 The Financial Reporting Standard applicable to the Micro-entities Regime* and FRED 50 *Draft FRC Abstract 1 Residential Management Companies' Financial Statements and Consequential Amendments to the FRSSE.*

2 The FRC, in accordance with the *Statutory Auditors (Amendment of Companies Act 2006 and Delegation of Functions etc) Order 2012* (SI 2012/1741), is a prescribed body for issuing accounting standards in the UK. The *Foreword to Accounting Standards* sets out the application of accounting standards in the Republic of Ireland.

3 In accordance with the *FRC Codes and Standards: procedures*, any proposal to issue, amend or withdraw a code or standard is put to the FRC Board with the full advice of the relevant Councils and/or the Codes & Standards Committee. Ordinarily, the FRC Board will only reject the advice put to it where:

(a) it is apparent that a significant group of stakeholders has not been adequately consulted;
(b) the necessary assessment of the impact of the proposal has not been completed, including an analysis of costs and benefits;
(c) insufficient consideration has been given to the timing or cost of implementation; or
(d) the cumulative impact of a number of proposals would make the adoption of an otherwise satisfactory proposal inappropriate.

4 The FRC has established the Accounting Council as the relevant Council to assist it in the setting of accounting standards.

Advice

5 The Accounting Council is advising the FRC to issue FRS 105 *The Financial Reporting Standard applicable to the Micro-entities Regime* to facilitate the effective adoption of the micro-entities regime introduced by company law. FRS 105 has been developed from the recognition and measurement requirements of FRS 102 *The Financial Reporting Standard applicable in the UK and Republic of Ireland*, adapted for compliance with the specific company law requirements applicable to the micro-entities regime and other appropriate simplifications.

6 The Accounting Council's Advice on FRS 102 is contained in that standard.

Background

7 The micro-entities regime was introduced in UK company law in 2013 with significantly reduced financial statements presentation and disclosure requirements. In order to reflect the legal requirements of the new micro-entities regime, the FRC amended the *Financial Reporting Standard for Smaller Entities* (FRSSE) in April 2014, but this was intended to be a temporary solution until the FRC developed a new standard for entities that prepare financial statements under the micro-entities regime.

8 In February 2015, the FRC published FRED 58 to consult on a new accounting standard for micro-entities.

9 In August 2013, the FRC issued FRED 50, a consultation on residential management companies' financial statements which is relevant in the context of the reporting by micro-entities.

10 The Accounting Council has considered the responses to FREDs 50 and 58 and took them into account when issuing its advice.

Objective

11 The FRC gives careful consideration to its objective and the intended effects when developing new accounting standards or requirements for the UK and Republic of Ireland. In developing accounting standards, including FRS 105, the

overriding objective of the FRC is to enable users of accounts to receive high-quality understandable financial reporting proportionate to the size and complexity of the entity and users' information needs.

In meeting this objective, the FRC aims to provide succinct financial reporting standards that: **12**

(a) have consistency with global accounting standards through the application of an IFRS-based solution unless an alternative clearly better meets the overriding objective;

(b) reflect up-to-date thinking and developments in the way businesses operate and the transactions they undertake;

(c) balance consistent principles for accounting by all UK and Republic of Ireland entities with practical solutions, based on size, complexity, public interest and users' information needs;

(d) promote efficiency within groups; and

(e) are cost-effective to apply.

Consistent recognition and measurement requirements with FRS 102

The Accounting Council is of the view that the reporting requirements for all small entities (including micro-entities) **13** should be based on FRS 102 because it improves consistency across the financial reporting framework in the UK and Republic of Ireland.

To that end, FRED 58 proposed that FRS 105 applies the recognition and measurement requirements of FRS 102, adapted **14** where necessary to reflect the legal requirements of the micro-entities regime and simplified further to reflect the size and nature of micro-entities.

Respondents to the consultation supported that FRS 105 should be developed from FRS 102 and the standard has been **15** finalised on that basis.

The Accounting Council notes that it would not otherwise have recommended some of the simplifications made in FRS **16** 105, including the omission of some of the disclosures required by FRS 102, if they had not been necessary to ensure legal compliance with the micro-entities regime. For example, the Accounting Council continues to believe that investment property should always, where practicable, be measured at fair value as this provides more relevant information to users of the financial statements on an investment property company's financial position and performance. However, company law prohibits the revaluation of any asset by micro-entities and instead requires that fixed assets are measured at cost less depreciation and impairment.

Amendments to FRS 102 to align FRS 105 with the legal requirements

Scope

FRS 105 is an accounting standard applicable to the preparation of the financial statements of a micro-entity which are **17** presumed in law to give a true and fair view in accordance with the micro-entities regime.

During its deliberations, the Accounting Council was requested to consider whether FRS 105 could be applied to financial **18** statements prepared for the purpose of submission to the tax authorities by unincorporated businesses and individuals that, if they were companies, would be eligible to apply the micro-entities regime.

The Accounting Council notes that the form and content of financial statements prepared for tax purposes is a matter for **19** the relevant tax authorities to determine and believes it is therefore not possible for the FRC to explicitly permit or prohibit the application of FRS 105 for such purpose. The Accounting Council notes that compliance with FRS 105 by businesses incorporated as companies that meet the conditions to apply the micros-entities regime will result in financial statements that in law are presumed to give a true and fair view.

The availability of the micro-entities regime is restricted to the smallest of companies and some types of entities are **20** excluded. For example, charities and financial institutions are ineligible to report under this regime. For that reason, in contrast to FRS 102, FRS 105 does not contain any specific requirements that only apply to these entities.

The micro-entities regime is not available to entities that are required or choose to prepare consolidated financial **21** statements. FRS 105 therefore does not contain accounting requirements that are relevant for the preparation of consolidated financial statements.

Presentation and disclosure

The micro-entities regime specifies certain minimum presentation and disclosure requirements. Financial statements **22** which include the prescribed minimum accounting items are presumed in law to give a true and fair view and no further disclosures need to be made. FRS 105 has been adapted to reflect the legal minimum presentation and disclosure requirements.

Recognition and measurement

23   The micro-entities regime prohibits the use of the Alternative Accounting Rules or the Fair Value Rules set out in company law and therefore micro-entities are not permitted to revalue or subsequently measure assets or liabilities at fair value. To take account of the legal restrictions on fair value measurement, FRS 105 does not allow the subsequent measurement of any asset or liability at fair value. This affects in particular financial instruments and investment properties which a micro-entity has to measure at depreciated cost.

Further simplifications over and above the legal requirements

24   The micro-entities regime is intended to be deregulatory and the Accounting Council believes it is appropriate to simplify some of the accounting requirements applicable under FRS 102. The Accounting Council considers that simplifications would be appropriate if:

(a)   the benefits of applying the accounting treatment in FRS 102 do not outweigh the burden for micro-entities and an alternative, more straightforward, treatment could be identified;

(b)   the lack of detail in the formats of the financial statements and/or supporting disclosures would limit the understanding of the financial information presented; and/or

(c)   transactions occur infrequently amongst micro-entities.

25   The Accounting Council notes that permitting accounting policy choices in FRS 105 would add complexity for preparers of a micro-entity's financial statements and could cause confusion to users due to the lack of detail in the formats of the financial statements and lack of supporting disclosures to explain the policy choice taken. As a result, the Accounting Council advises that FRS 105 should not contain accounting policy options, except on first-time adoption of FRS 105.

26   The Accounting Council advises that first-time adopters of FRS 105 should be given a choice on whether they apply the requirements of FRS 105 fully retrospectively or whether they apply one or more of the transitional exemptions. Although this introduces a degree of complexity for preparers and users, the Accounting Council believes transitional exemptions are important for a smooth transition and not allowing a choice would disadvantage micro-entities unnecessarily over entities that transition to FRS 102.

27   In all other cases where accounting policy options are provided in FRS 102 they should be removed in FRS 105. The Accounting Council advises that FRS 105 should mandate the most straightforward and easy to apply option.

28   The key areas where simplifications have been made are:

(a)   Prohibition of accounting for deferred taxation on the basis that this is a complex area of accounting and the lack of disclosure in a micro-entity's financial statements make it impossible to distinguish between current and deferred tax.

(b)   Prohibition of accounting for equity-settled share-based payments prior to the issue of the shares, because of the prohibition to use fair value measurements and lack of supporting disclosure in the financial statements.

(c)   A requirement that the contributions payable to any post-employment benefit plans are accounted for as an expense, subject to a requirement for defined benefit plans to recognise a liability for a schedule of contributions to the extent that it relates to the deficit. The simplification was made on the basis that very few micro-entities will have defined benefit pension schemes.

(d)   The distinction between functional and presentation currency is removed as it will be very rare for micro-entities to have a different functional and presentational currency.

(e)   Requirement to use contracted rates to translate foreign currency denominated assets and liabilities rather than spot rates. This will simplify the accounting when micro-entities enter into foreign currency forward contracts.

(f)   All borrowing and development costs must be expensed, because this is considered the simplest option of accounting for these costs.

(g)   Mandating the application of the accrual model to account for government grants because this is considered the simplest method of accounting for these transactions.

(h)   Simplifications in relation to the accounting for financial instruments as far as the allocation of interest and transaction costs is concerned. The effective interest rate method is considered too onerous to apply by micro-entities.

(i)   Removal of the requirement to impute a market-rate of interest in lending arrangements conducted at non-market rates because considering the nature and size of micro-entities the costs of mandating this requirement would exceed the benefits.

(j)   Simplified requirements for classifying financial instruments as equity or debt because most micro-entities will issue simple equity instruments.

(k) Prohibition of the recognition of separately identifiable intangible assets in a trade and asset acquisition because these are not required items in the financial statements formats.

(l) Removal of the requirements concerning accounting for hyperinflation because this is unlikely to be an issue for micro-entities.

(m) Removal of accounting requirements relating to specialised activities including extractive activities, service concessions, heritage assets and funding commitments because micro-entities will not typically enter into these transactions.

Feedback on the proposed simplification from respondents to FRED 58

Most respondents supported the proposed simplifications and the principles applied by the Accounting Council to assess whether a simplification is appropriate. It was noted that some stakeholders are of the view that the recognition of deferred tax should be permitted or required in FRS 105. However, after having considered these comments the Accounting Council retains its view that without additional disclosure the benefits of requiring micro-entities to account for deferred tax do not exceed the costs.   **29**

FRED 58 proposed that government grants should be accounted for using the performance model. The views of respondents on whether FRS 105 should require the performance or accrual model were divided. The evidence provided by respondents suggests that the accrual model may in practice be easier to apply than the performance model and the Accounting Council therefore advises that FRS 105 should mandate the accrual model.   **30**

Determining accounting policies where FRS 105 does not contain requirements

A micro-entity that enters into a transaction that is not specifically covered in FRS 105 is required to refer to the concepts and pervasive principles set out in Section 2 *Concepts and Pervasive Principles* of FRS 105 in determining its accounting policies. The Accounting Council notes that micro-entities are not required to refer to other accounting standards or authoritative guidance because these requirements may be inconsistent with the legal requirements of the micro-entities regime.   **31**

Transitional provisions – fair value/revaluation as deemed cost

The micro-entities regime requires micro-entities to apply the historical cost accounting rules, which require fixed assets to be included at purchase price or production cost. Therefore the Accounting Council advises that it would be inconsistent with the legal framework for micro-entities to provide in FRS 105 a transitional exemption to allow micro-entities to carry forward previous revaluations of property, plant and equipment or the fair value of investment properties or investments in shares as deemed cost.   **32**

FRS 105 provides a transitional exemption in respect of the determination of the depreciated historical cost of investment properties. Under the transitional exemption a micro-entity is permitted, for the purpose of estimating accumulated depreciation at the date of transition, to treat an investment property as if it were a single asset with a useful economic life equal to that of its most significant component, which is likely to be comprised of its main structural elements such as foundations, walls etc. This exempts a micro-entity from having to determine the historical cost of each component that has been replaced in the past and the depreciation that would have been charged since their initial recognition.   **33**

The Accounting Council notes that the micro-entities regime is optional and that if a micro-entity wishes to retain revalued amounts in its financial statement it could continue to apply the small company regime, rather than moving to the micro-entities regime.   **34**

Structure and language of FRS 105

FRS 105 should be as easily accessible and understandable as possible. A number of respondents to FRED 58 suggested that the accessibility of FRS 105 could be enhanced by departing from the section and paragraph numbering of FRS 102. The Accounting Council agrees and advises that FRS 105 should where possible maintain consistency with the language and terminology used in FRS 102, but use its own structure (ie section and paragraph numbering).   **35**

Residents' management companies

In considering the feedback received from the FRC's previous consultations, the Accounting Council noted that no clear consensus existed amongst respondents on the appropriate basis of accounting in the statutory financial statements of residents' management companies[4] where service charge monies are held on trust in accordance with section 42 of the   **36**

---

[4]   *An organisation which may be referred to in the lease, which is responsible for the provision of services, and manages and arranges maintenance of the property, but which does not necessarily have any legal interest in the property.*

Landlord and Tenant Act 1987. However, there was general agreement that no change should be made to FRS 105, or any other relevant financial reporting standard (including FRS 102), to address such a narrow and sector-specific issue.

37   The Accounting Council considered this issue carefully. It assessed the case for further intervention by reference to the FRC's published *Principles for the development of Codes, Standards and Guidance*[5] and, in particular, the extent to which the anticipated benefits from any changes to current practices would outweigh the costs incurred by the entities involved. It agreed with respondents that this matter does not merit a change in accounting standards, and therefore advises that no changes are made to FRS 105 (or FRS 102) that are specific to residents' management companies.

Effective date

38   FRS 105 is effective for accounting periods commencing on or after 1 January 2016, in line with the mandatory effective date of the consequential amendments to FRS 102 resulting from the UK's new small companies regime. Early application of FRS 105 is permitted.

39   See Appendix IV *Republic of Ireland (RoI) legal references* of FRS 105 for information on the applicability of the micro-entities regime in the Republic of Ireland.

Approval of this advice

40   This advice to the FRC was approved by the Accounting Council on 16 June 2015.

---

[5] *This can be found on the FRC's website at www.frc.org.uk/FRC-Documents/FRC/About-the-FRC/Principles-for-the-development-of-Codes.pdf.*

Appendix I: Glossary

This glossary is an integral part of this FRS.

accounting policies	The specific principles, bases, conventions, rules and practices applied by an entity in preparing and presenting **financial statements**.
accrual basis (of accounting)	The effects of transactions and other events are recognised when they occur (and not as cash or its equivalent is received or paid) and they are recorded in the accounting records and reported in the **financial statements** of the periods to which they relate.
accumulating compensated absences	Compensated absences that are carried forward and can be used in future periods if the current period's entitlement is not used in full.
Act	The Companies Act 2006
active market	A market in which all the following conditions exist: (a) the items traded in the market are homogeneous; (b) willing buyers and sellers can normally be found at any time; and (c) prices are available to the public.
agent	An entity is acting as an agent when it does not have exposure to the significant risks and rewards associated with the sale of goods or the rendering of services. One feature indicating that an entity is acting as an agent is that the amount the entity earns is predetermined, being either a fixed fee per transaction or a stated percentage of the amount billed to the customer.
agricultural activity	The management by an entity of the biological transformation of **biological assets** for sale, into **agricultural produce** or into additional biological assets.
agricultural produce	The harvested product of the entity's **biological assets**.
amortisation	The systematic allocation of the **depreciable amount** of an **asset** over its **useful life**.
asset	A resource controlled by the entity as a result of past events and from which future economic benefits are expected to flow to the entity.
associate	An entity, including an unincorporated entity such as a partnership, over which the investor has **significant influence** and that is neither a **subsidiary** nor an interest in a **joint venture**.
biological asset	A living animal or plant.
borrowing costs	Interest and other costs incurred by an entity in connection with the borrowing of funds.
business	An integrated set of activities and **assets** conducted and managed for the purpose of providing: (a) a return to investors; or (b) lower costs or other economic benefits directly and proportionately to policyholders or participants. A business generally consists of inputs, processes applied to those inputs, and resulting outputs that are, or will be, used to generate **revenues**. If **goodwill** is present in a transferred set of activities and assets, the transferred set shall be presumed to be a business.
business combination	The bringing together of separate entities or **businesses** into one reporting entity.
carrying amount	The amount at which an **asset** or **liability** is recognised in the **statement of financial position**.
cash-generating unit	The smallest identifiable group of **assets** that generates cash inflows that are largely independent of the cash inflows from other assets or groups of assets.
cash-settled share-based payment transaction	A **share-based payment transaction** in which the entity acquires goods or services by incurring a **liability** to transfer cash or other **assets** to the supplier of those goods or services for amounts that are based on the price (or value) of the entity's shares or other equity instruments of the entity or another group entity.
change in accounting estimate	An adjustment of the **carrying amount** of an **asset** or a **liability**, or the amount of the periodic consumption of an asset, that results from the assessment of the present status of, and expected future benefits and obligations associated with, assets and liabilities. Changes in accounting estimates result from new information or new developments and, accordingly, are not corrections of **errors**.

closing rate	The spot exchange rate at the end of the **reporting period.**
commencement of lease term	The date from which the lessee is entitled to exercise its right to use the leased asset. It is the date of initial **recognition** of the **lease** (ie the recognition of the **assets**, **liabilities**, **income** or **expenses** resulting from the lease, as appropriate).
compound financial instrument	A **financial instrument** that, from the issuer's perspective, contains both a **liability** and an **equity** element.
consolidated financial statements	The **financial statements** of a **parent** and its **subsidiaries** presented as those of a single economic entity.
construction contract	A contract specifically negotiated for the construction of an **asset** or a combination of assets that are closely interrelated or interdependent in terms of their design, technology and function or their ultimate purpose or use.
constructive obligation	An obligation that derives from an entity's actions where: (a) by an established pattern of past practice, published policies or a sufficiently specific current statement, the entity has indicated to other parties that it will accept certain responsibilities; and (b) as a result, the entity has created a valid expectation on the part of those other parties that it will discharge those responsibilities
contingent asset	A possible **asset** that arises from past events and whose existence will be confirmed only by the occurrence or non-occurrence of one or more uncertain future events not wholly within the control of the entity.
contingent liability	(a) a possible obligation that arises from past events and whose existence will be confirmed only by the occurrence or nonoccurrence of one or more uncertain future events not wholly within the control of the entity; or (b) a present obligation that arises from past events but is not recognised because: (i) it is not **probable** that an outflow of resources embodying economic benefits will be required to settle the obligation; or (ii) the amount of the obligation cannot be measured with sufficient reliability.
contingent rent	That portion of the lease payments that is not fixed in amount but is based on the future amount of a factor that changes other than with the passage of time (eg percentage of future sales, amount of future use, future price indices, and future market rates of interest).
control (of an entity)	The power to govern the financial and operating policies of an entity so as to obtain benefits from its activities.
current tax	The amount of **income tax** payable (refundable) in respect of the **taxable profit (tax loss)** for the current period or past **reporting periods**.
date of transition	The beginning of the earliest period for which an entity presents full comparative information in a given standard in its first financial statements that comply with that standard.
deferred tax	Income tax payable (recoverable) in respect of the **taxable profit (tax loss)** for future **reporting periods** as a result of past transactions or events.
defined benefit plans	**Post-employment benefit plans** other than **defined contribution plans**.
defined contribution plans	**Post-employment benefit plans** under which an entity pays fixed contributions into a separate entity (a fund) and has no legal or **constructive obligation** to pay further contributions or to make direct benefit payments to employees if the fund does not hold sufficient **assets** to pay all **employee benefits** relating to employee service in the current and prior periods.
depreciable amount	The cost of an **asset**, or other amount substituted for cost (in the **financial statements**), less its **residual value**.
depreciation	The systematic allocation of the **depreciable amount** of an **asset** over its **useful life**.
derecognition	The removal of a previously recognised **asset** or **liability** from an entity's **statement of financial position**.

derivative	Is a **financial instrument** with the following three characteristics:
	(a) its value changes in response to the change in a specified interest rate, financial instrument price, commodity price, foreign exchange rate, index of prices or rates, credit rating or credit index, or other variable (sometimes called the 'underlying'), provided in the case of a non-financial variable that the variable is not specific to a party to the contract;
	(b) it requires no initial net investment or an initial net investment that is smaller than would be required for other types of contracts that would be expected to have a similar response to changes in market factors; and
	(c) it is settled at a future date.
development	The application of **research** findings or other knowledge to a plan or design for the production of new or substantially improved materials, devices, products, processes, systems or services before the start of commercial production or use.
employee benefits	All forms of consideration given by an entity in exchange for service rendered by employees.
equity	The residual interest in the **assets** of the entity after deducting all its **liabilities**.
equity-settled share-based payment transaction	A **share-based payment transaction** in which the entity:
	(a) receives goods or services as consideration for its own equity instruments (including shares or **share options**); or
	(b) receives goods or services but has no obligation to settle the transaction with the supplier.
errors	Omissions from, and misstatements in, the entity's **financial statements** for one or more prior periods arising from a failure to use, or misuse of, reliable information that:
	(a) was available when financial statements for those periods were authorised for issue; and
	(b) could reasonably be expected to have been obtained and taken into account in the preparation and presentation of those financial statements.
expenses	Decreases in economic benefits during the **reporting period** in the form of outflows or depletions of **assets** or incurrences of **liabilities** that result in decreases in **equity**, other than those relating to distributions to equity investors.
fair value	The amount for which an **asset** could be exchanged, a **liability** settled, or an equity instrument granted could be exchanged, between knowledgeable, willing parties in an arm's length transaction. In the absence of any specific guidance provided in the relevant section of this FRS, the guidance in paragraph 2.31 shall be used in determining fair value.
fair value less costs to sell	The amount obtainable from the sale of an **asset** in an arm's length transaction between knowledgeable, willing parties, less the costs of disposal.
finance lease	A **lease** that transfers substantially all the risks and rewards incidental to ownership of an **asset**. Title may or may not eventually be transferred. A lease that is not a finance lease is an **operating lease**.
financial asset	Any **asset** that is:
	(a) cash;
	(b) an equity instrument of another entity;
	(c) a contractual right:
	(i) to receive cash or another financial asset from another entity; or
	(ii) to exchange financial assets or **financial liabilities** with another entity under conditions that are potentially favourable to the entity; or
	(d) a contract that will or may be settled in the entity's own equity instruments and:
	(i) under which the entity is or may be obliged to receive a variable number of the entity's own equity instruments; or
	(ii) that will or may be settled other than by the exchange of a fixed amount of cash or another financial asset for a fixed number of the entity's own equity instruments. For this purpose the entity's own equity instruments do not include instruments that are themselves contracts for the future receipt or delivery of the entity's own equity instruments.

financial guarantee contract	A contract that requires the issuer to make specified payments to reimburse the holder for a loss it incurs because a specified debtor fails to make payments when due in accordance with the original or modified terms of a debt instrument.
financial instrument	A contract that gives rise to a **financial asset** of one entity and a **financial liability** or equity instrument of another entity.

financial liability	Any **liability** that is:
	
	(a) a contractual obligation:
	
	     (i) to deliver cash or another **financial asset** to another entity; or
	
	     (ii) to exchange financial assets or financial liabilities with another entity under conditions that are potentially unfavourable to the entity, or
	
	(b) a contract that will or may be settled in the entity's own equity instruments and:
	
	     (i) under which the entity is or may be obliged to deliver a variable number of the entity's own equity instruments; or
	
	     (ii) will or may be settled other than by the exchange of a fixed amount of cash or another financial asset for a fixed number of the entity's own equity instruments. For this purpose the entity's own equity instruments do not include instruments that are themselves contracts for the future receipt or delivery of the entity's own equity instruments.

financial position	The relationship of the **assets**, **liabilities** and **equity** of an entity as reported in the **statement of financial position**.
financial statements	A structured presentation of the **financial position** and financial **performance** of an entity.
financing activities	Activities that result in changes in the size and composition of the contributed **equity** and borrowings of the entity.
first-time adopter of this FRS	An entity that presents its first annual **financial statements** that conform to this FRS, regardless of its previous accounting framework.
fixed assets	**Assets** of an entity which are intended for use on a continuing basis in the entity's activities.
FRS 102	FRS 102 *The Financial Reporting Standard applicable in the UK and Republic of Ireland*
gains	Increases in economic benefits that meet the definition of **income** but are not **revenue**.
goodwill	Future economic benefits arising from **assets** that are not capable of being individually identified and separately recognised.
government grant	Assistance by government in the form of a transfer of resources to an entity in return for past or future compliance with specified conditions relating to the **operating activities** of the entity. Government refers to government, government agencies and similar bodies whether local, national or international.
grant date	The date at which the entity and another party (including an employee) agree to a share-based payment arrangement, being when the entity and the counterparty have a shared understanding of the terms and conditions of the arrangement. At grant date the entity confers on the counterparty the right to cash, other **assets**, or equity instruments of the entity, provided the specified vesting conditions, if any, are met. If that agreement is subject to an approval process (for example, by shareholders), grant date is the date when that approval is obtained.
gross investment in a lease	The aggregate of: (a) the **minimum lease payments** receivable by the lessor under a **finance lease**; and (b) any unguaranteed **residual value** accruing to the lessor.
impairment loss	The amount by which the **carrying amount** of an **asset** exceeds: (a) in the case of **inventories**, its selling price less costs to complete and sell; (b) in the case of **financial assets** the amounts as set out in paragraph 9.18; or (c) in the case of any other asset, its **recoverable amount**.
impracticable	Applying a requirement is impracticable when the entity cannot apply it after making every reasonable effort to do so.
inception of the lease	The earlier of the date of the lease agreement and the date of commitment by the parties to the principal provisions of the **lease**.

income	Increases in economic benefits during the **reporting period** in the form of inflows or enhancements of **assets** or decreases of **liabilities** that result in increases in **equity**, other than those relating to contributions from equity investors.
income statement	**Financial statement** that presents all items of **income** and **expense** recognised in a **reporting period** (referred to as the profit and loss account in the **Act**).
income tax	All domestic and foreign taxes that are based on **taxable profits**. Income tax also includes taxes, such as withholding taxes, that are payable by a **subsidiary**, **associate** or **joint venture** on distributions to the reporting entity.
intangible asset	An identifiable non-monetary asset without physical substance. Such an **asset** is identifiable when: (a) it is separable, ie capable of being separated or divided from the entity and sold, transferred, licensed, rented or exchanged, either individually or together with a related contract, asset or **liability**; or (b) it arises from contractual or other legal rights, regardless of whether those rights are transferable or separable from the entity or from other rights and obligations.
interest rate implicit in the lease	The discount rate that, at the **inception of the lease**, causes the aggregate **present value** of: (a) the **minimum lease payments**; and (b) the unguaranteed **residual value** to be equal to the sum of: (i) the **fair value** of the leased **asset**; and (ii) any initial direct costs of the lessor.
inventories	**Assets**: (a) held for sale in the ordinary course of business; (b) in the process of production for such sale; or (c) in the form of materials or supplies to be consumed in the production process or in the rendering of services.
investment property	Property (land or a building, or part of a building, or both) held by the owner or by the lessee under a **finance lease** to earn rentals or for capital appreciation or both, rather than for: (a) use in the production or supply of goods or services or for administrative purposes; or (b) sale in the ordinary course of business.
joint control	The contractually agreed sharing of **control** over an economic activity. It exists only when the strategic financial and operating decisions relating to the activity require the unanimous consent of the parties sharing control (the **venturers**).
joint venture	A contractual arrangement whereby two or more parties undertake an economic activity that is subject to **joint control**. Joint ventures can take the form of jointly controlled operations, jointly controlled **assets**, or **jointly controlled entities**.
jointly controlled entity	A **joint venture** that involves the establishment of a corporation, partnership or other entity in which each **venturer** has an interest. The entity operates in the same way as other entities, except that a contractual arrangement between the venturers establishes **joint control** over the economic activity of the entity.
lease	An agreement whereby the lessor conveys to the lessee in return for a payment or series of payments the right to use an **asset** for an agreed period of time.
lease incentives	Incentives provided by the lessor to the lessee to enter into a new or renew an **operating lease**. Examples of such incentives include up-front cash payments to the lessee, the reimbursement or assumption by the lessor of costs of the lessee (such as relocation costs, leasehold improvements and costs associated with preexisting lease commitments of the lessee), or initial periods of the **lease** provided by the lessor rent-free or at a reduced rent.
lease term	The non-cancellable period for which the lessee has contracted to **lease** the **asset** together with any further terms for which the lessee has the option to continue to lease the asset, with or without further payment, when at the **inception of the lease** it is reasonably certain that the lessee will exercise the option.
lessee's incremental borrowing rate (of interest)	The rate of interest the lessee would have to pay on a similar **lease** or, if that is not determinable, the rate that, at the **inception of the lease**, the lessee would incur to borrow over a similar term, and with a similar security, the funds necessary to purchase the **asset**.
liability	A present obligation of the entity arising from past events, the settlement of which is expected to result in an outflow from the entity of resources embodying economic benefits.

material	Omissions or misstatements of items are material if they could, individually or collectively, influence the economic decisions of users taken on the basis of the **financial statements**. Materiality depends on the size and nature of the omission or misstatement judged in the surrounding circumstances. The size or nature of the item, or a combination of both, could be the determining factor.
measurement	The process of determining the monetary amounts at which the elements of the **financial statements** are to be recognised and carried in the **statement of financial position** and **income statement**.
micro-entity	Is an entity that meets all of the following conditions: (a) it is a company established under company law; (b) it qualifies as a micro-entity in accordance with section 384A of the **Act**; and (c) it is not excluded from being treated as a micro-entity under section 384B of the Act. Micro-entities are a subset of small companies as defined in the Act.
micro-entity minimum accounting items	The item of information required under the **micro-entities regime** to be contained in the **financial statements** of a **micro-entity**. These are set out in Sections 4 *Statement of Financial Position*, 5 *Income Statement* and 6 *Notes to the Financial Statements* of this FRS.
micro-entity provisions	Means any provisions of Part 15, Part 16 or regulations under Part 15 of the **Act** relating specifically to the individual accounts of an entity which qualifies as a **micro-entity**.
micro-entities regime	The legal requirements and exemptions relating to the preparation of the **financial statements** of **micro-entities** as set out in the **Act** and **Small Companies Regulations**.

minimum lease payments	The payments over the **lease term** that the lessee is or can be required to make, excluding **contingent rent**, costs for services and taxes to be paid by and reimbursed to the lessor, together with:
	
	(a) for a lessee, any amounts guaranteed by the lessee or by a party related to the lessee; or
	
	(b) for a lessor, any **residual value** guaranteed to the lessor by:
	
	    (i) the lessee;
	
	    (ii) a party related to the lessee; or
	
	    (iii) a third party unrelated to the lessor that is financially capable of discharging the obligations under the guarantee.
	
	However, if the lessee has an option to purchase the **asset** at a price that is expected to be sufficiently lower than **fair value** at the date the option becomes exercisable for it to be reasonably certain, at the **inception of the lease**, that the option will be exercised, the minimum lease payments comprise the minimum payments payable over the lease term to the expected date of exercise of this purchase option and the payment required to exercise it.

monetary items	Units of currency held and **assets** and **liabilities** to be received or paid in a fixed or determinable number of units of currency.
multi-employer (benefit) plans	**Defined contribution plans** (other than **state plans**) or **defined benefit plans** (other than state plans) that: (a) pool the **assets** contributed by various entities that are not under common control; and (b) use those assets to provide benefits to employees of more than one entity, on the basis that contribution and benefit levels are determined without regard to the identity of the entity that employs the employees concerned.
net investment in a lease	The **gross investment in a lease** discounted at the **interest rate implicit in the lease**.
non-exchange transaction	A transaction whereby an entity receives value from another entity without directly giving approximately equal value in exchange, or gives value to another entity without directly receiving approximately equal value in exchange.
notes (to the financial statements prepared under this FRS)	Notes contain information in addition to that presented in the **statement of financial position** and **income statement**. Notes are required to be presented at the foot of the statement of financial position.
onerous contract	A contract in which the unavoidable costs of meeting the obligations under the contract exceed the economic benefits expected to be received under it.

operating activities	The principal revenue-producing activities of the entity and other activities that are not investing or **financing activities**.
operating lease	A **lease** that does not transfer substantially all the risks and rewards incidental to ownership. A lease that is not an operating lease is a **finance lease**.
ordinary share	An equity instrument that is subordinate to all other classes of equity instrument.
owners	Holders of instruments classified as **equity**.
parent	An entity that has one or more **subsidiaries**.
performance	The relationship of the **income** and **expenses** of a **micro-entity**, as reported in the **income statement**.
post-employment benefits	**Employee benefits** (other than **termination benefits** and shortterm employee benefits) that are payable after the completion of employment.
post-employment benefit plans	Formal or informal arrangements under which an entity provides **post-employment benefits** for one or more employees.
present value	A current estimate of the present discounted value of the future net **cash flows** in the normal course of business.
principal	An entity is acting as a principal when it has exposure to the significant risks and rewards associated with the sale of goods or the rendering of services. Features that indicate that an entity is acting as a principal include: (a) the entity has the primary responsibility for providing the goods or services to the customer or for fulfilling the order, for example by being responsible for the acceptability of the products or services ordered or purchased by the customer; (b) the entity has **inventory** risk before or after the customer order, during shipping or on return; (c) the entity has latitude in establishing prices, either directly or indirectly, for example by providing additional goods or services; and (d) the entity bears the customer's credit risk for the amount receivable from the customer.
probable	More likely than not.
profit or loss	The total of **income** less **expenses**.
property, plant and equipment	Tangible assets that: (a) are held for use in the production or supply of goods or services, for rental to others, or for administrative purposes; and (b) are expected to be used during more than one period.
prospectively (applying a change in accounting policy)	Applying the new **accounting policy** to transactions, other events and conditions occurring after the date as at which the policy is changed.
provision	A **liability** of uncertain timing or amount.
prudence	The inclusion of a degree of caution in the exercise of the judgements needed in making the estimates required under conditions of uncertainty, such that **assets** or **income** are not overstated and **liabilities** or **expenses** are not understated.
recognition	The process of incorporating in the **statement of financial position** or **income statement** an item that meets the definition of an **asset, liability, equity, income** or **expense** and satisfies the following criteria: (a) it is **probable** that any future economic benefit associated with the item will flow to or from the **entity**; and (b) the item has a cost or value that can be measured with reliability.
recoverable amount	The higher of an **asset's** (or **cash-generating unit's**) **fair value less costs to sell** and its **value in use**.
reporting date	The end of the latest period covered by **financial statements**.
reporting period	The period covered by **financial statements**.
research	Original and planned investigation undertaken with the prospect of gaining new scientific or technical knowledge and understanding.

residual value (of an asset)	The estimated amount that an entity would currently obtain from disposal of an **asset**, after deducting the estimated costs of disposal, if the asset were already of the age and in the condition expected at the end of its **useful life**.
restructuring	A restructuring is a programme that is planned and controlled by management and materially changes either: (a) the scope of a business undertaken by an entity; or (b) the manner in which that business is conducted.
retrospective application (of an accounting policy)	Applying a new **accounting policy** to transactions, other events and conditions as if that policy had always been applied.
revenue	The gross inflow of economic benefits during the period arising in the course of the ordinary activities of an entity when those inflows result in increases in **equity**, other than increases relating to contributions from equity participants.
share-based payment transaction	A transaction in which the entity: (a) receives goods or services (including employee services) as consideration for its own equity instruments (including shares or **share options**); or (b) receives goods or services but has no obligation to settle the transaction with supplier; or (c) acquires goods or services by incurring **liabilities** to the supplier of those goods or services for amounts that are based on the price (or value) of the entity's shares or other equity instruments of the entity or another group entity.
share option	A contract that gives the holder the right, but not the obligation, to subscribe to the entity's shares at a fixed or determinable price for a specific period of time.
significant influence	Is the power to participate in the financial and operating policy decisions of the **associate** but is not **control** or **joint control** over those policies.
Small Companies Regulations	The Small Companies and Groups (Accounts and Directors' Report) Regulations 2008 (SI 2008/409)
state (employee benefit) plan	Employee benefit plans established by legislation to cover all entities (or all entities in a particular category, for example a specific industry) and operated by national or local government or by another body (for example an autonomous agency created specifically for this purpose) which is not subject to control or influence by the reporting entity.
statement of financial position	**Financial statement** that presents the relationship of an entity's **assets**, **liabilities** and **equity** as of a specific date (referred to as the balance sheet in the **Act**).
subsidiary	An entity, including an unincorporated entity such as a partnership, that is **controlled** by another entity (known as the **parent**).
substantively enacted	Tax rates shall be regarded as substantively enacted when the remaining stages of the enactment process historically have not affected the outcome and are unlikely to do so. A UK tax rate shall be regarded as having been substantively enacted if it is included in either: (a) a Bill that has been passed by the House of Commons and is awaiting only passage through the House of Lords and Royal Assent; or (b) a resolution having statutory effect that has been passed under the Provisional Collection of Taxes Act 1968. (Such a resolution could be used to collect taxes at a new rate before that rate has been enacted. In practice, corporation tax rates are now set a year ahead to avoid having to invoke the Provisional Collection of Taxes Act for the quarterly payment system.) A Republic of Ireland tax rate can be regarded as having been substantively enacted if it is included in a Bill that has been passed by the Dail.
tax expense	The aggregate amount included in **profit or loss** or **equity** for the **reporting period** in respect of **current tax**.
taxable profit (tax loss)	The profit (loss) for a **reporting period** upon which **income taxes** are payable or recoverable, determined in accordance with the rules established by the taxation authorities. Taxable profit equals taxable income less amounts deductible from taxable **income**.
termination benefits	**Employee benefits** provided in exchange for the termination of an employee's employment as a result of either: (a) an entity's decision to terminate an employee's employment before the normal retirement date; or (b) an employee's decision to accept voluntary redundancy in exchange for those benefits.

transaction costs (financial instruments)	Incremental costs that are directly attributable to the acquisition, issue or disposal of a **financial asset** or **financial liability**, or the issue or reacquisition of an entity's own equity instrument. An incremental cost is one that would not have been incurred if the entity had not acquired, issued or disposed of the financial asset or financial liability, or had not issued or reacquired its own equity instrument.
treasury shares	An entity's own equity instruments that are held by the entity.
turnover	The amounts derived from the provision of goods and services after deduction of: (a) trade discounts; (b) value added tax; and (c) any other taxes based on the amounts so derived.
useful life	The period over which an **asset** is expected to be available for use by an entity or the number of production or similar units expected to be obtained from the asset by an entity.
value in use	The **present value** of the future cash flows expected to be derived from an **asset** or **cash-generating unit**.
venturer	A party to a **joint venture** that has **joint control** over that joint venture.
vest	Become an entitlement. Under a share-based payment arrangement, a counterparty's right to receive cash, other **assets** or equity instruments of the entity vests when the counterparty's entitlement is no longer conditional on the satisfaction of any vesting conditions.

Appendix II: Table of equivalence for UK Companies Act terminology

The following table compares company law terminology with broadly equivalent terminology used in this FRS. In some cases there are minor differences between the broadly equivalent definitions, which are also summarised below.

Company law terminology	FRS 105 terminology
Accounting reference date	Reporting date
Accounts	Financial statements
Balance sheet	Statement of financial position
Capital and reserves	Equity
Cash at bank and in hand	Cash
Debtors	Trade receivables
Diminution in value [of assets]	Impairment
Financial year	Reporting period
Net realisable value [of any current asset]	Estimated selling price less costs to complete and sell
Profit and loss account	Income statement
Stocks	Inventories
Tangible assets	Includes: property, plant and equipment and investment property
Trade creditors	Trade payables

Appendix III: Note on legal requirements

Introduction

This appendix provides an overview of how the requirements of FRS 105 address UK company law requirements. It is therefore written from the perspective of a company to which *The Small Companies and Groups (Accounts and Directors' Report) Regulations 2008* (SI 2008/409) amended by *The Small Companies (Micro-Entities' Accounts) Regulations 2013* (SI 2013/3008) and *The Companies, Partnerships and Groups (Accounts and Reports) Regulations 2015* (SI 2015/980) apply.

A3.1

The Small Companies (Micro-Entities' Accounts) Regulations 2013 were made in November 2013 and apply to the financial statements of micro-entities for accounting periods ending on or after 30 September 2013 for companies filing their accounts on or after 1 December 2013.

A3.2

The definition of a micro-entity is contained in sections 384A and 384B of the Companies Act 2006 (Act). The qualifying conditions are met by a company in a year in which it does not exceed two or more of the following criteria:

A3.3

(a)	Turnover	£632,000
(b)	Balance sheet total	£316,000
(c)	Number of employees	10

For any company, other than a newly incorporated company, to qualify as a micro-entity, the qualifying conditions must be met for two consecutive years. A company will cease to qualify as a micro-entity if it fails to meet the qualifying conditions for two consecutive years. However, if a company which qualified as a micro-entity in one period no longer meets the criteria for a micro-entity in the next period, the company may continue to claim the exemptions available in the next period. If that company then reverts back to being a micro-entity by meeting the criteria, the exemptions will continue uninterrupted.

A3.4

Certain companies are excluded by section 384B of the Act from being treated as micro-entities, including those excluded from the small companies regime for reasons of public interest (as set out in section 384), certain financial institutions, charities, those voluntarily preparing group accounts and those included in group accounts. The Act should be referred to for a full list of excluded companies.

A3.5

Entities that are not companies, such as limited liability partnerships (LLPs), do not meet the definition of a micro-entity.

A3.6

Applicable accounting framework

Accounts prepared in accordance with FRS 105 are classified as 'Companies Act individual accounts' for the purposes of section 395 of the Act and are therefore required to comply with the applicable provisions of Parts 15 and 16 of the Act and with the Regulations referred to in paragraph A3.1.

A3.7

Fair value at initial recognition

The Small Companies (Micro-Entities' Accounts) Regulations 2013 state that micro-entities are not permitted to apply the Alternative Accounting Rules or the Fair Value Rules as set out in company law. Therefore micro-entities are only permitted to apply the Historical Cost Accounting Rules.

A3.8

FRS 105 states that certain types of assets and liabilities must be measured at fair value at initial recognition, for example inventories acquired through a non-exchange transaction. This does not breach the prohibition against fair value accounting as the use of a fair value is a method of estimating cost at initial recognition.

A3.9

True and fair view

FRS 105 is an accounting standard and all accounting standards issued by the Financial Reporting Council are applicable to the preparation of financial statements that are intended to give a true and fair view. Financial statements of a micro-entity that include the minimum accounting items specified by *The Small Companies (Micro-Entities' Accounts) Regulations 2013* are presumed in law to give a true and fair view.

A3.10

Distributable profits

A3.11   The determination of profits available for distribution is a complex area where accounting and company law interface. In determining profits available for distribution any entity may refer to Technical Release 02/10 *Guidance on realised and distributable profits under the Companies Act 2006* issued by the Institute of Chartered Accountants in England and Wales and the Institute of Chartered Accountants of Scotland, or any successor document, to determine profits available for distribution.

Appendix IV: Republic of Ireland (RoI) legal references

At the time of issuing FRS 105, the micro-entities legislation is not available for application in the Republic of Ireland. However, the Irish Department of Jobs, Enterprise and Innovation has consulted on the possible enactment of this legislation in its *Consultation on the transposition of the EU Accounting Directive 2013/34/EU.*   **A4.1**

If legislation giving effect to the micro-entities option is enacted in Ireland, FRS 105 will be available for application in line with the effective date of the relevant legislation and will be updated to include Republic of Ireland legal references.   **A4.2**

COPYRIGHT NOTICE

Further copies, £20.00 (post-free) can be obtained from:
FRC Publications
Lexis House
30 Farringdon Street
London
EC4A 4HH
Tel: **0845 370 1234**
Email: **customer.services@lexisnexis.co.uk**
Or order online at: **www.frcpublications.com**

Appendix B

SI 2008/409 – Small Companies and Groups (Accounts and Directors' Report) Regulations 2008

Part 1 – Introduction

Part 2 – Form and content of individual accounts

Part 3 – Directors' report

Part 4 – Form and content of group accounts

Part 5 – Interpretation

Schedule 1 – Companies Act individual accounts

Schedule 2 – Information about related undertakings where company not preparing group accounts (Companies Act or IAS individual accounts)

Schedule 3 – Information about directors' benefits: remuneration (Companies Act or IAS accounts)

Schedule 4 – Companies Act abbreviated accounts for delivery to registrar of companies

Schedule 5 – Matters to be dealt with in directors' report

Schedule 6 – Group accounts

Schedule 7 – Interpretation of term "provisions"

Schedule 8 – General interpretation

Small Companies and Groups (Accounts and Directors' Report) Regulations 2008

(SI 2008/409 as amended by SI 2015/980 The Companies, Partnerships and Groups (Accounts and Reports) Regulations 2015)

Made on 19 February 2008 by the Secretary of State, in exercise of the powers conferred by s.396(3), 404(3), 409(1) to (3), 412(1) to (3), 416(4), 444(3)(a) and (b), 677(3)(a), 712(2)(b)(i), 836(1)(b)(i) and 1292(1)(a) and (c) of the Companies Act 2006. Operative from 6 April 2008.

PART 1 – INTRODUCTION
CITATION AND INTERPRETATION

1(1) These Regulations may be cited as the Small Companies and Groups (Accounts and Directors' Report) Regulations 2008.

1(2) In these Regulations "**the 2006 Act**" means the Companies Act 2006.

Commencement and application

2(1) These Regulations come into force on 6th April 2008.

2(2) They apply in relation to financial years beginning on or after 6th April 2008.

2(3) They apply to companies which are subject to the small companies regime under Part 15 of the 2006 Act (see section 381 of that Act).

PART 2 – FORM AND CONTENT OF INDIVIDUAL ACCOUNTS
COMPANIES ACT INDIVIDUAL ACCOUNTS

3(1) Subject to the following provisions of this regulation and regulation 5A, Companies Act individual accounts under section 396 of the 2006 Act (Companies Act: individual accounts) must comply with the provisions of Schedule 1 to these Regulations as to the form and content of the balance sheet and profit and loss account, and additional information to be provided by way of notes to the accounts.

3(1A) Sections C (alternative accounting rules) and D (fair value accounting) in Part 2 of Schedule 1 to these Regulations do not apply to a company which qualifies as a micro-entity in relation to a financial year (see sections 384A and 384B of the 2006 Act) and whose accounts for that year are prepared in accordance with the exemption permitted by–

    (a) regulation 5A, or
    (b) paragraph 1(1A) of Section A in Part 1 of Schedule 1 to these Regulations.

3(2) [Omitted by SI 2015/980, reg. 14(2).]

3(3) Accounts are treated as having complied with any provision of Schedule 1 to these Regulations if they comply instead with the corresponding provision of Schedule 1 to the Large and Medium-Sized Companies and Groups (Accounts and Reports) Regulations 2008.

History – In reg. 3(1), "Subject to the following provisions of this regulation and regulation 5A," inserted; and reg. 3(1A) inserted by SI 2013/3008, reg. 9(1) and (2), with effect from 1 December 2013 in respect of (a) financial years ending on or after 30 September 2013; and (b) companies, which deliver the accounts required by s. 444 to the registrar on or after 1 December 2013.

Reg. 3(2) omitted by SI 2015/980, reg. 14(2), with effect in relation to–

    (a) financial years beginning on or after 1 January 2016, and

    (b) a financial year of a company beginning on or after 1 January 2015, but before 1 January 2016, if the directors of the company so decide.

Former reg. 3(2) read as follows:

3(2) The profit and loss account of a company that falls within section 408 of the 2006 Act (individual profit and loss account where group accounts prepared) need not contain the information specified in paragraphs 59 to 61 of Schedule 1 to these Regulations (information supplementing the profit and loss account).

Information about related undertakings (Companies Act or IAS individual accounts)

  4 [Omitted by SI 2015/980, reg. 14(3).]

History – Reg. 4 omitted by SI 2015/980, reg. 14(3), with effect in relation to–

    (a) financial years beginning on or after 1 January 2016, and

    (b) a financial year of a company beginning on or after 1 January 2015, but before 1 January 2016, if the directors of the company so decide.

Former reg. 4 read as follows:

4(1) Subject to regulation 5A, Companies Act or IAS individual accounts must comply with the provisions of Schedule 2 to these Regulations as to information about related undertakings to be given in notes to the company's accounts.

4(2) Information otherwise required to be given by Schedule 2 to these Regulations need not be disclosed with respect to an undertaking that–

    (a) is established under the law of a country outside the United Kingdom, or

    (b) carries on business outside the United Kingdom, if the conditions specified in section 409(4) of the 2006 Act are met (see section 409(5) of the 2006 Act for disclosure required where advantage taken of this exemption).

This paragraph does not apply in relation to the information required by paragraphs 4 and 8 of Schedule 2 to these Regulations.

History – In reg. 4(1), "Subject to regulation 5A," inserted by SI 2013/3008, reg. 9(1) and (3), with effect from 1 December 2013 in respect of (a) financial years ending on or after 30 September 2013; and (b) companies, which deliver the accounts required by s. 444 to the registrar on or after 1 December 2013.

Information about directors' benefits: remuneration (Companies Act or IAS individual accounts)

  5 [Omitted by SI 2015/980, reg. 14(4).]

History – Reg. 5 omitted by SI 2015/980, reg. 14(4), with effect in relation to–

    (a) financial years beginning on or after 1 January 2016, and

    (b) a financial year of a company beginning on or after 1 January 2015, but before 1 January 2016, if the directors of the company so decide.

Former reg. 5 read as follows:

5(5) Subject to regulation 5A, Companies Act or IAS individual accounts must comply with the provisions of Schedule 3 to these Regulations as to information about directors' remuneration to be given in notes to the company's accounts.

History – In reg. 5, "Subject to regulation 5A," inserted by SI 2013/3008, reg. 9(1) and (4), with effect from 1 December 2013 in respect of (a) financial years ending on or after 30 September 2013; and (b) companies, which deliver the accounts required by s. 444 to the registrar on or after 1 December 2013.

Companies Act individual accounts: micro-entities – notes to the accounts

5A Nothing in Schedule 1, 2 or 3 to these Regulations requires the Companies Act individual accounts of a company for a financial year in which the company qualifies as a micro-entity (see sections 384A and 384B of the 2006 Act) to contain any information by way of notes to the accounts, except that the company is required to disclose by way of notes to the accounts the information required by paragraph 57 in Part 3 of Schedule 1.

History – Reg. 5A inserted by SI 2013/3008, reg. 9(1) and (5), with effect from 1 December 2013 in respect of (a) financial years ending on or after 30 September 2013; and (b) companies, which deliver the accounts required by s. 444 to the registrar on or after 1 December 2013.

Accounts for delivery to registrar of companies (Companies Act individual accounts)

6 [Omitted by SI 2015/980, reg. 14(5).]

History – Reg. 6 omitted by SI 2015/980, reg. 14(5), with effect in relation to–

(a) financial years beginning on or after 1 January 2016, and
(b) a financial year of a company beginning on or after 1 January 2015, but before 1 January 2016, if the directors of the company so decide.

Former reg. 6 read as follows:

6(1) Except where section 444(3B) of the 2006 Act applies, the directors of a company for which they are preparing Companies Act individual accounts may deliver to the registrar of companies under section 444 of the 2006 Act (filing obligations of companies subject to small companies regime) a copy of a balance sheet which complies with Schedule 4 to these Regulations rather than Schedule 1.

6(2) Companies Act individual accounts delivered to the registrar need not give the information required by–

(a) paragraph 4 of Schedule 2 to these Regulations (shares of company held by subsidiary undertakings), or
(b) Schedule 3 to these Regulations (directors' benefits).

History – In reg. 6(1), "Except where section 444(3B) of the 2006 Act applies, the directors" substituted for "The directors" by SI 2013/3008, reg. 9(1) and (6), with effect from 1 December 2013 in respect of (a) financial years ending on or after 30 September 2013; and (b) companies, which deliver the accounts required by s. 444 to the registrar on or after 1 December 2013.

PART 3 – DIRECTORS' REPORT
DIRECTORS' REPORT

7 The report which the directors of a company are required to prepare under section 415 of the 2006 Act (duty to prepare directors' report) must disclose the matters specified in Schedule 5 to these Regulations.

PART 4 – FORM AND CONTENT OF GROUP ACCOUNTS
COMPANIES ACT GROUP ACCOUNTS

8(1) Where the directors of a parent company which–

(a) is subject to the small companies regime, and

(b) has prepared Companies Act individual accounts in accordance with regulation 3, prepare Companies Act group accounts under section 398 of the 2006 Act (option to prepare group accounts), those accounts must comply with the provisions of Schedule 6 to these Regulations as to the form and content of the consolidated balance sheet and consolidated profit and loss account, and additional information to be provided by way of notes to the accounts.

8(2) Accounts are treated as having complied with any provision of Schedule 6 if they comply instead with the corresponding provision of Schedule 6 to the Large and Medium-Sized Companies and Groups (Accounts and Reports) Regulations 2008.

History – In reg. 8, the words "Part 1 of" omitted by SI 2015/980, reg. 15(2), with effect in relation to–

(a) financial years beginning on or after 1 January 2016, and

(b) a financial year of a company beginning on or after 1 January 2015, but before 1 January 2016, if the directors of the company so decide.

Information about directors' benefits: remuneration (Companies Act or IAS group accounts)

9 [Omitted by SI 2015/980, reg. 15(3).]

History – Reg. 9 omitted by SI 2015/980, reg. 15(3), with effect in relation to–

(a) financial years beginning on or after 1 January 2016, and

(b) a financial year of a company beginning on or after 1 January 2015, but before 1 January 2016, if the directors of the company so decide.

Former reg. 9 read as follows:

9(9) Companies Act or IAS group accounts must comply with the provisions of Schedule 3 to these Regulations as to information about directors' remuneration to be given in notes to the company's accounts.

Information about related undertakings (Companies Act or IAS group accounts)

10(1) Companies Act or IAS group accounts must comply with the provisions of Part 2 of Schedule 6 to these Regulations as to information about related undertakings to be given in notes to the company's accounts.

10(2) Information otherwise required to be given by Part 2 of Schedule 6 need not be disclosed with respect to an undertaking that–

(a) is established under the law of a country outside the United Kingdom, or

(b) carries on business outside the United Kingdom, if the conditions specified in section 409(4) of the 2006 Act are met (see section 409(5) of the 2006 Act for disclosure required where advantage taken of this exemption).

This paragraph does not apply in relation to the information required by paragraphs 26 and 35 of Schedule 6 to these Regulations.

Accounts for delivery to registrar of companies (companies act group accounts)

11 Companies Act group accounts delivered to the registrar of companies under section 444 of the 2006 Act need not give the information required by–

    (a) omitted by SI 2015/980, reg. 15(4),

    (b) paragraph 25 of Schedule 6 to these Regulations (shares of company held by subsidiary undertakings).

History – Reg. 11(a) omitted by SI 2015/980, reg. 15(4), with effect in relation to–

    (a) financial years beginning on or after 1 January 2016, and

    (b) a financial year of a company beginning on or after 1 January 2015, but before 1 January 2016, if the directors of the company so decide.

Former reg. 11(a) read as follows:

    (a) Schedule 3 to these Regulations (directors' benefits), or

PART 5 – INTERPRETATION
DEFINITION OF "PROVISIONS"

12 Schedule 7 to these Regulations defines "**provisions**" for the purpose of these Regulations and for the purposes of–

    (a) section 677(3)(a) (Companies Act accounts: relevant provisions for purposes of financial assistance) in Part 18 of the 2006 Act,

    (b) section 712(2)(b)(i) (Companies Act accounts: relevant provisions to determine available profits for redemption or purchase by private company out of capital) in that Part,

    (c) section 836(1)(b)(i) (Companies Act accounts: relevant provisions for distribution purposes) in Part 23 of that Act, and

    (d) section 841(2)(a) (Companies Act accounts: provisions to be treated as realised losses) in that Part.

Notes – Paragraph (d) inserted by SI 2009/1581, reg. 11(1) and (2): 27 June 2009 applying in relation to financial years beginning on or after 6 April 2008 which have not ended before 27 June 2009.

General interpretation

13 Schedule 8 to these Regulations contains general definitions for the purposes of these Regulations.

SCHEDULES   Regulation 3(1)

SCHEDULE 1 COMPANIES ACT INDIVIDUAL ACCOUNTS

PART 1 – GENERAL RULES AND FORMATS
SECTION A GENERAL RULES

1(1) Subject to the following provisions of this Schedule–

    (a) every balance sheet of a company must show the items listed in either of the balance sheet formats in Section B of this Part, and

    (b) every profit and loss account must show the items listed in either of the profit and loss account formats in Section B.

1(1A) But, subject to the following provisions of this Schedule, in relation to a company which qualifies as a micro-entity in relation to a financial year (see sections 384A and 384B of the 2006 Act)–

(a) the only items which must be shown on the company's balance sheet for that year are those listed in either of the balance sheet formats in Section C of this Part, and

(b) the only items which must be shown on the company's profit and loss account for that year are those listed in the profit and loss account format in Section C.

1(2) References in this Schedule to the items listed in any of the formats in Section B and Section C are to those items read together with any of the notes following the formats which apply to those items.

1(3) Subject to paragraph 1A the items must be shown in the order and under the headings and sub-headings given in the particular format used, but–

(a) the notes to the formats may permit alternative positions for any particular items, and

(b) the heading or sub-heading for any item does not have to be distinguished by any letter or number assigned to that item in the format used.

History – In para. 1(1)(b), the word "either" substituted for the words "any one" by SI 2015/980, reg. 16(2)(a), with effect in relation to–

(a) financial years beginning on or after 1 January 2016, and

(b) a financial year of a company beginning on or after 1 January 2015, but before 1 January 2016, if the directors of the company so decide.

In para. 1(3), the words "Subject to paragraph 1A" inserted by SI 2015/980, reg. 16(2)(b), with effect in relation to–

(a) financial years beginning on or after 1 January 2016, and

(b) a financial year of a company beginning on or after 1 January 2015, but before 1 January 2016, if the directors of the company so decide.

1A(1) Where appropriate to the circumstances of a company's business, the company's directors may, with reference to one of the formats in Section B, draw up an abridged balance sheet showing only those items in that format preceded by letters and roman numerals, provided that–

(a) in the case of format 1, note (5) of the notes to the formats is complied with,

(b) in the case of format 2, notes (5) and (10) of those notes are complied with, and

(c) all of the members of the company have consented to the drawing up of the abridged balance sheet.

1A(2) Where appropriate to the circumstances of a company's business, the company's directors may, with reference to one of the formats in Section B, draw up an abridged profit and loss account, combining under one item called "Gross profit or loss"–

(a) items 1, 2, 3 and 6 in the case of format 1, and

(b) items 1 to 5 in the case of format 2

provided that, in either case, all of the members of the company have consented to the drawing up of the abridged profit and loss account.

1A(3) Such consent as is referred to in sub-paragraphs (1) and (2) may only be given as regards the preparation of, as appropriate, the balance sheet or profit and loss account in respect of the preceding financial year.

1A(4) Sub-paragraphs (1) and (2) do not apply in relation to the preparation of, as appropriate, a company's balance sheet or profit and loss account for a particular financial year if the company was a charity at any time within that year.

History – Para. 1A inserted by SI 2015/980, reg. 16(2)(c), with effect in relation to–

  (a) financial years beginning on or after 1 January 2016, and
  (b) a financial year of a company beginning on or after 1 January 2015, but before 1 January 2016, if the directors of the company so decide.

1B(1) The company's directors may adapt one of the balance sheet formats in Section B so to distinguish between current and non-current items in a different way, provided that–

  (a) the information given is at least equivalent to that which would have been required by the use of such format had it not been thus adapted, and
  (b) the presentation of those items is in accordance with generally accepted accounting principles or practice.

1B(2) The company's directors may, otherwise than pursuant to paragraph 1A(2), adapt one of the profit and loss account formats in Section B, provided that–

  (a) the information given is at least equivalent to that which would have been required by the use of such format had it not been thus adapted, and
  (b) the presentation is in accordance with generally accepted accounting principles or practice.

History – Para. 1B inserted by SI 2015/980, reg. 16(2)(c), with effect in relation to–

  (a) financial years beginning on or after 1 January 2016, and
  (b) a financial year of a company beginning on or after 1 January 2015, but before 1 January 2016, if the directors of the company so decide.

1C So far as is practicable, the following provisions of Section A of this Part of this Schedule apply to the balance sheet or profit or loss account of a company notwithstanding any such abridgment or adaptation pursuant to paragraph 1A or 1B.

History – Para. 1C inserted by SI 2015/980, reg. 16(2)(c), with effect in relation to–

  (a) financial years beginning on or after 1 January 2016, and
  (b) a financial year of a company beginning on or after 1 January 2015, but before 1 January 2016, if the directors of the company so decide.

2(1) Where in accordance with paragraph 1(1) a company's balance sheet or profit and loss account for any financial year has been prepared by reference to one of the formats in Section B, the company's directors must use the same format in preparing Companies Act individual accounts for subsequent financial years, unless in their opinion there are special reasons for a change.

2(2) Particulars of any such change must be given in a note to the accounts in which the new format is first used, and the reasons for the change must be explained.

2A Where in accordance with paragraph 1(1A) a company's balance sheet or profit and loss account for any financial year has been prepared by reference to one of the formats in Section C, the company's directors must use the same format in preparing Companies Act individual accounts for subsequent financial years, unless in their opinion there are special reasons for a change.

3(1) Any item required to be shown in a company's balance sheet or profit and loss account may be shown in greater detail than required by the particular format used.

3(2) The balance sheet or profit and loss account may include an item representing or covering the amount of any asset or liability, income or expenditure not otherwise covered by any of the items listed in the format used, save that none of the following may be treated as assets in any balance sheet–

    (a) preliminary expenses,
    (b) expenses of, and commission on, any issue of shares or debentures,
    (c) costs of research.

4(1) Where the special nature of the company's business requires it, the company's directors must adapt the arrangement, headings and sub-headings otherwise required in respect of items given an Arabic number in the balance sheet or profit and loss account format used.

4(2) The directors may combine items to which Arabic numbers are given in any of the formats set out in Section B if–

    (a) their individual amounts are not material to assessing the state of affairs or profit or loss of the company for the financial year in question, or
    (b) the combination facilitates that assessment.

4(3) Where sub-paragraph (2)(b) applies, the individual amounts of any items which have been combined must be disclosed in a note to the accounts.

5(1) Subject to sub-paragraph (2), the directors must not include a heading or sub-heading corresponding to an item in the balance sheet or profit and loss account format used if there is no amount to be shown for that item for the financial year to which the balance sheet or profit and loss account relates.

5(2) Where an amount can be shown for the item in question for the immediately preceding financial year that amount must be shown under the heading or sub-heading required by the format for that item.

6 Every profit and loss account other than one prepared by reference to the format in Section C must show the amount of a company's profit or loss before taxation.

History – In para. 6, the words "on ordinary activities" omitted by SI 2015/980, reg. 16(2)(d), with effect in relation to–

    (a) financial years beginning on or after 1 January 2016, and
    (b) a financial year of a company beginning on or after 1 January 2015, but before 1 January 2016, if the directors of the company so decide.

7(1) For every item shown in the balance sheet or profit and loss account the corresponding amount for the immediately preceding financial year must also be shown.

7(2) Where that corresponding amount is not comparable with the amount to be shown for the item in question in respect of the financial year to which the balance sheet or profit and loss account relates, the former amount may be adjusted, and particulars of the non-comparability and of any adjustment must be disclosed in a note to the accounts.

8 Amounts in respect of items representing assets or income may not be set off against amounts in respect of items representing liabilities or expenditure (as the case may be), or vice versa.

9 The company's directors must, in determining how amounts are presented within items in the profit and loss account and balance sheet, have regard to the substance of the reported transaction or arrangement, in accordance with generally accepted accounting principles or practice.

History – The following amendments were made by SI 2013/3008, reg. 10(1) and (2), with effect from 1 December 2013 in respect of (a) financial years ending on or after 30 September 2013; and (b) companies, which deliver the accounts required by s. 444 to the registrar on or after 1 December 2013:

*   Paragraph 1(1A) inserted.
*   In para. 1(2), "and Section C" inserted.

- In para. 2(1), "paragraph 1(1)" substituted for "paragraph 1".
- Paragraph 2A inserted.
- In para. 6, "other than one prepared by reference to the format in Section C" inserted.

9A Where an asset or liability relates to more than one item in the balance sheet, the relationship of such asset or liability to the relevant items must be disclosed either under those items or in the notes to the accounts.

History – Para. 9A inserted by SI 2015/980, reg. 16(2)(e), with effect in relation to–

(a) financial years beginning on or after 1 January 2016, and
(b) a financial year of a company beginning on or after 1 January 2015, but before 1 January 2016, if the directors of the company so decide.

SECTION B – THE REQUIRED FORMATS FOR THE ACCOUNTS OF COMPANIES OTHER THAN MICRO-ENTITIES
Balance sheet formats – Format 1

A.   Called up share capital not paid *(1)*

B.   Fixed assets

   I.   Intangible assets

      1.   Goodwill *(2)*
      2.   Other intangible assets *(3)*

   II.   Tangible assets

      1.   Land and buildings
      2.   Plant and machinery etc.

   III.   Investments

      1.   Shares in group undertakings and participating interests
      2.   Loans to group undertakings and undertakings in which the company has a participating interest
      3.   Other investments other than loans
      4.   Other investments *(4)*

C.   Current assets

   I.   Stocks

      1.   Stocks
      2.   Payments on account

   II.   Debtors *(5)*

      1.   Trade debtors
      2.   Amounts owed by group undertakings and undertakings in which the company has a participating interest
      3.   Other debtors *(1)*

   III.   Investments

      1.   Shares in group undertakings
      2.   Other investments *(4)*

   IV.   Cash at bank and in hand

D. Prepayments and accrued income *(6)*

E. Creditors: amounts falling due within one year

    1. Bank loans and overdrafts
    2. Trade creditors
    3. Amounts owed to group undertakings and undertakings in which the company has a participating interest
    4. Other creditors *(7)*

F. Net current assets (liabilities) *(8)*

G. Total assets less current liabilities

H. Creditors: amounts falling due after more than one year

    1. Bank loans and overdrafts
    2. Trade creditors
    3. Amounts owed to group undertakings and undertakings in which the company has a participating interest
    4. Other creditors *(7)*

I. Provisions for liabilities

J. Accruals and deferred income *(7)*

K. Capital and reserves

    I.   Called up share capital *(9)*
    II.   Share premium account
    III. Revaluation reserve
    IV.   Other reserves
    V.   Profit and loss account

Balance sheet formats – Format 2

ASSETS

A. Called up share capital not paid *(1)*

B. Fixed assets

    I. Intangible assets

        1. Goodwill *(2)*
        2. Other intangible assets *(3)*

    II. Tangible assets

        1. Land and buildings
        2. Plant and machinery etc.

    III. Investments

        1. Shares in group undertakings and participating interests
        2. Loans to group undertakings and undertakings in which the company has a participating interest
        3. Other investments other than loans
        4. Other investments *(4)*

C.   Current assets

    I.   Stocks

       1.   Stocks
       2.   Payments on account

    II.   Debtors *(5)*

       1.   Trade debtors
       2.   Amounts owed by group undertakings and undertakings in which the company has a participating interest
       3.   Other debtors *(1)*

    III.   Investments

       1.   Shares in group undertakings
       2.   Other investments *(4)*

    IV.   Cash at bank and in hand

D.   Prepayments and accrued income *(6)*

CAPITAL, RESERVES AND LIABILITIES

A.   Capital and reserves

    I.   Called up share capital *(9)*
    II.   Share premium account
    III.   Revaluation reserve
    IV.   Other reserves
    V.   Profit and loss account

B.   Provisions for liabilities

C.   Creditors *(10)*

       1.   Bank loans and overdrafts
       2.   Trade creditors
       3.   Amounts owed to group undertakings and undertakings in which the company has a participating interest
       4.   Other creditors *(7)*

D.   Accruals and deferred income *(7)*

Notes on the balance sheet formats

(1)   *Called up share capital not paid*

(Formats 1 and 2, items A and C.II.3.)
This item may either be shown at item A or included under item C.II.3 in Format 1 or 2.

(2)   *Goodwill*

(Formats 1 and 2, item B.I.1.)
Amounts representing goodwill must only be included to the extent that the goodwill was acquired for valuable consideration.

(3) *Other intangible assets*

(Formats 1 and 2, item B.I.2.)
Amounts in respect of concessions, patents, licences, trade marks and similar rights and assets must only be included in a company's balance sheet under this item if either–

    (a) the assets were acquired for valuable consideration and are not required to be shown under goodwill, or

    (b) the assets in question were created by the company itself.

(4) *Others: Other investments*

(Formats 1 and 2, items B.III.4 and C.III.2.)
Where amounts in respect of own shares held are included under either of these items, the nominal value of such shares must be shown separately.

(5) *Debtors*

(Formats 1 and 2, items C.II.1 to 3.)
The amount falling due after more than one year must be shown separately for each item included under debtors and, in the case of format 2, the aggregate amount falling due after more than one year must also be shown.

(6) *Prepayments and accrued income*

(Formats 1 and 2, item D.)
This item may alternatively be included under item C.II.3 in Format 1 or 2.

(7) *Other creditors*

(Format 1, items E.4, H.4 and J and Format 2, items C.4 and D.)
There must be shown separately–

    (a) the amount of any convertible loans, and

    (b) the amount for creditors in respect of taxation and social security.

Payments received on account of orders must be included in so far as they are not shown as deductions from stocks.

In Format 1, accruals and deferred income may be shown under item J or included under item E.4 or H.4, or both (as the case may require). In Format 2, accruals and deferred income may be shown under item D or within item C.4 under Liabilities.

(8) *Net current assets (liabilities)*

(Format 1, item F.)
In determining the amount to be shown under this item any prepayments and accrued income must be taken into account wherever shown.

(9) *Called up share capital*

(Format 1, item K.I and Format 2, Liabilities item A.I.)
The amount of allotted share capital and the amount of called up share capital which has been paid up must be shown separately.

(10) *Creditors*

(Format 2, Liabilities items C.1 to 4.)
Amounts falling due within one year and after one year must be shown separately for each of these items and for the aggregate of all of these items.

Profit and loss account formats – Format 1

(see note (14) below)

1. Turnover

2. Cost of sales *(11)*

3. Gross profit or loss

4. Distribution costs *(11)*

5. Administrative expenses *(11)*

6. Other operating income

7. Income from shares in group undertakings

8. Income from participating interests

9. Income from other fixed asset investments *(12)*

10. Other interest receivable and similar income *(12)*

11. Amounts written off investments

12. Interest payable and similar expenses *(13)*

13. Tax on profit or loss

14. Profit or loss after taxation

15. Omitted

16. Omitted

17. Omitted

18. Omitted

19. Other taxes not shown under the above items

20. Profit or loss for the financial year

Profit and loss account formats – Format 2

1. Turnover

2. Change in stocks of finished goods and in work in progress

3. Own work capitalised

4. Other operating income

5. (a) Raw materials and consumables
    (b) Other external charges

6. Staff costs

    (a) wages and salaries
    (b) social security costs
    (c) other pension costs

7. (a) Depreciation and other amounts written off tangible and intangible fixed assets
    (b) Amounts written off current assets, to the extent that they exceed write-offs which are normal in the undertaking concerned

8. Other operating expenses

9. Income from shares in group undertakings

10. Income from participating interests

11. Income from other fixed asset investments *(12)*

12. Other interest receivable and similar income *(12)*

13. Amounts written off investments

14. Interest payable and similar expenses *(13)*

15. Tax on profit or loss

16. Profit or loss after taxation

17. Omitted

18. Omitted

19. Omitted

20. Omitted

21. Other taxes not shown under the above items

22. Profit or loss for the financial year

Notes on the profit and loss account formats

(11) *Cost of sales: distribution costs: administrative expenses*

(Format 1, items 2, 4 and 5.)
These items must be stated after taking into account any necessary provisions for depreciation or diminution in value of assets.

(12) *Income from other fixed asset investments: other interest receivable and similar income*

(Format 1, items 9 and 10; Format 2, items 11 and 12.)
Income and interest derived from group undertakings must be shown separately from income and interest derived from other sources.

(13) *Interest payable and similar expenses*

(Format 1, item 12; Format 2, item 14.)
The amount payable to group undertakings must be shown separately.

History – New heading for section B substituted by SI 2013/3008, reg. 10(1) and (3), with effect from 1 December 2013 in respect of (a) financial years ending on or after 30 September 2013; and (b) companies, which deliver the accounts required by s. 444 to the registrar on or after 1 December 2013. Before substitution, the heading was "SECTION B – THE REQUIRED FORMATS FOR ACCOUNTS".

In section B, the following amendments were made by SI 2015/980, reg. 16(3), with effect in relation to– (a) financial years beginning on or after 1 January 2016, and (b) a financial year of a company beginning on or after 1 January 2015, but before 1 January 2016, if the directors of the company so decide:

- the heading "CAPITAL, RESERVES AND LIABILITIES" substituted for the word "LIABILITIES".
- in note (5) of "Notes on the balance sheet formats", the words "and, in the case of format 2, the aggregate amount falling due after more than one year must also be shown" substituted for the words "unless the aggregate amount of debtors falling due after more than one year is disclosed in the notes to the accounts".
- in note (10), the words "unless the aggregate amount of creditors falling due within one year and the aggregate amount of creditors falling due after more than one year is disclosed in the notes to the accounts" omitted.
- in profit and loss account format 1–

  - at item 12, the word "expenses" substitute for "charges";
  - at item 13, the words "on ordinary activities" omitted;
  - at item 14, the words "on ordinary activities" omitted;
  - items 15–18 omit.

- in profit and loss account format 2–

  - item 7(b) substituted;
  - at item 8, the word "expenses" substitute for "charges";
  - at item 14, the word "expenses" substitute for "charges";
  - at item 15, the words "on ordinary activities" omitted;
  - at item 16, the words "on ordinary activities" omitted;
  - items 17–20 omitted.

- profit and loss account format 3 omitted.
- profit and loss account format 4 omitted.
- in note (11) of "Notes on the profit and loss account formats", the words "and Format 3, items A 1, 2 and 3" omitted.
- in note (12), the words "Format 3, items B 5 and 6 and Format 4, items B 7 and 8" omitted.
- in note (13) title, the word "expenses" substitute for "charges"; and the words "Format 3, item A 5 and Format 4, item A 7" omitted.
- note (14) omitted.

SECTION C – THE REQUIRED FORMATS FOR THE ACCOUNTS OF MICRO-ENTITIES

Balance Sheet Formats

Format 1

(A) Called up share capital not paid

(B) Fixed assets

(C) Current assets

(D) Prepayments and accrued income

(E) Creditors: amounts falling due within one year

(F) Net current assets (liabilities)

(G) Total assets less current liabilities

(H) Creditors: amounts falling due after more than one year

(I) Provisions for liabilities

(J) Accruals and deferred income

(K) Capital and reserves

Format 2

ASSETS

(A) Called up share capital not paid

(B) Fixed assets

(C) Current Assets

(D) Prepayments and accrued income

CAPITAL, RESERVES AND LIABILITIES

(A) Capital and reserves

(B) Provisions

(C) Creditors (1)

(D) Accruals and deferred income

Notes on the balance sheet formats

(1) *Creditors*

(Format 2, item C under Liabilities)
Aggregate amounts falling due within one year and after one year must be shown separately.

Profit and loss account format

(A) Turnover

(B) Other income

(C) Cost of raw materials and consumables

(D) Staff costs

(E) Depreciation and other amounts written off assets

(F) Other charges

(G) Tax

(H) Profit or loss

History – Section C inserted by SI 2013/3008, reg. 10(1) and (4), with effect from 1 December 2013 in respect of (a) financial years ending on or after 30 September 2013; and (b) companies, which deliver the accounts required by s. 444 to the registrar on or after 1 December 2013.

In section C, the heading "CAPITAL, RESERVES AND LIABILITIES" substituted for "LIABILITIES" by SI 2015/980, reg. 16(4), with effect in relation to–

(a) financial years beginning on or after 1 January 2016, and
(b) a financial year of a company beginning on or after 1 January 2015, but before 1 January 2016, if the directors of the company so decide.

PART 2 – ACCOUNTING PRINCIPLES AND RULES
SECTION A – ACCOUNTING PRINCIPLES

Preliminary

10(1) The amounts to be included in respect of all items shown in a company's accounts must be determined in accordance with the principles set out in this Section.

10(2) But if it appears to the company's directors that there are special reasons for departing from any of those principles in preparing the company's accounts in respect of any financial year they may do so, in which case particulars of the departure, the reasons for it and its effect must be given in a note to the accounts.

Accounting principles

11 The company is presumed to be carrying on business as a going concern.

12 Accounting policies and measurement bases must be applied consistently within the same accounts and from one financial year to the next.

History – In para. 12, the words "and measurement bases" inserted by SI 2015/980, reg. 17(2)(a), with effect in relation to–

(a) financial years beginning on or after 1 January 2016, and
(b) a financial year of a company beginning on or after 1 January 2015, but before 1 January 2016, if the directors of the company so decide.

13 The amount of any item must be determined on a prudent basis, and in particular–

(a) only profits realised at the balance sheet date must be included in the profit and loss account,
(b) all liabilities which have arisen in respect of the financial year to which the accounts relate or a previous financial year must be taken into account, including those which only become apparent between the balance sheet date and the date on which it is signed on behalf of the board of directors in accordance with section 414 of the 2006 Act (approval and signing of accounts) and
(c) all provisions for diminution of value must be recognised, whether the result of the financial year is a profit or a loss.

History – Para. 13(c), (and the word "and" preceding it) inserted; the word "and" in para. (a) omitted by SI 2015/980, reg. 17(2)(b), with effect in relation to–

    (a) financial years beginning on or after 1 January 2016, and

    (b) a financial year of a company beginning on or after 1 January 2015, but before 1 January 2016, if the directors of the company so decide.

14 All income and charges relating to the financial year to which the accounts relate must be taken into account, without regard to the date of receipt or payment.

15 In determining the aggregate amount of any item, the amount of each individual asset or liability that falls to be taken into account must be determined separately.

15A The opening balance sheet for each financial year shall correspond to the closing balance sheet for the preceding financial year.

History – Para. 15A inserted by SI 2015/980, reg. 17(2)(c), with effect in relation to–

    (a) financial years beginning on or after 1 January 2016, and

    (b) a financial year of a company beginning on or after 1 January 2015, but before 1 January 2016, if the directors of the company so decide.

SECTION B – HISTORICAL COST ACCOUNTING RULES

Preliminary

16 Subject to Sections C and D of this Part of this Schedule, the amounts to be included in respect of all items shown in a company's accounts must be determined in accordance with the rules set out in this Section.

Fixed assets

General rules

17(1) The amount to be included in respect of any fixed asset must be its purchase price or production cost.

17(2) This is subject to any provision for depreciation or diminution in value made in accordance with paragraphs 18 to 20.

Rules for depreciation and diminution in value

18 In the case of any fixed asset which has a limited useful economic life, the amount of–

    (a) its purchase price or production cost, or

    (b) where it is estimated that any such asset will have a residual value at the end of the period of its useful economic life, its purchase price or production cost less that estimated residual value, must be reduced by provisions for depreciation calculated to write off that amount systematically over the period of the asset's useful economic life.

19(1) Where a fixed asset investment of a description falling to be included under item B.III of either of the balance sheet formats set out in Section B of Part 1 of this Schedule has diminished in value, provisions for diminution in value may be made in respect of it and the amount to be included in respect of it may be reduced accordingly.

19(2) Provisions for diminution in value must be made in respect of any fixed asset which has diminished in value if the reduction in its value is expected to be permanent (whether its useful economic life is limited or not), and the amount to be included in respect of it must be reduced accordingly.

19(3) Provisions made under sub-paragraph (1) or (2) must be charged to the profit and loss account and disclosed separately in a note to the accounts if not shown separately in the profit and loss account.

History – In para. 19(1), "Section B of" inserted by SI 2013/3008, reg. 11(a), with effect from 1 December 2013 in respect of (a) financial years ending on or after 30 September 2013; and (b) companies, which deliver the accounts required by s. 444 to the registrar on or after 1 December 2013.

Para. 19(3) substituted by SI 2015/980, reg. 17(3)(a), with effect in relation to–

  (a) financial years beginning on or after 1 January 2016, and
  (b) a financial year of a company beginning on or after 1 January 2015, but before 1 January 2016, if the directors of the company so decide.

Former para. 19(3) read as follows:

(3) Any provisions made under sub-paragraph (1) or (2) which are not shown in the profit and loss account must be disclosed (either separately or in aggregate) in a note to the accounts.

20(1) Where the reasons for which any provision was made in accordance with paragraph 19 have ceased to apply to any extent, that provision must be written back to the extent that it is no longer necessary.

20(2) Any amounts written back under sub-paragraph (1) must be recognised in the profit and loss account and disclosed separately in a note to the accounts if not shown separately in the profit and loss account.

History – Para. 20(2) substituted by SI 2015/980, reg. 17(3)(b), with effect in relation to–

  (a) financial years beginning on or after 1 January 2016, and
  (b) a financial year of a company beginning on or after 1 January 2015, but before 1 January 2016, if the directors of the company so decide.

Former para. 20(2) read as follows:

(2) Any amounts written back in accordance with sub-paragraph (1) which are not shown in the profit and loss account must be disclosed (either separately or in aggregate) in a note to the accounts.

Intangible Assets

21(1) Where this is in accordance with generally accepted accounting principles or practice, development costs may be included in "other intangible assets" under "fixed assets" in the balance sheet formats set out in Section B of Part 1 of this Schedule.

21(2) If any amount is included in a company's balance sheet in respect of development costs, the note on accounting policies (see paragraph 44 of this Schedule) must include the following information–

  (a) the period over which the amount of those costs originally capitalised is being or is to be written off, and
  (b) the reasons for capitalising the development costs in question.

History – Para. 21 and the heading preceding it substituted by SI 2015/980, reg. 17(3)(c), with effect in relation to–

    (a) financial years beginning on or after 1 January 2016, and

    (b) a financial year of a company beginning on or after 1 January 2015, but before 1 January 2016, if the directors of the company so decide.

Former para. 21 read as follows:

Development costs

21(1) Development costs may only in special circumstances be included in "other intangible assets" under "fixed assets" in the balance sheet formats set out in Section B of Part 1 of this Schedule.

21(2) If any amount is included in a company's balance sheet in respect of development costs the following information must be given in a note to the accounts–

    (a) the period over which the amount of those costs originally capitalised is being or is to be written off, and

    (b) the reasons for capitalising the development costs in question.

History – Para. 21(1) substituted by SI 2013/3008, reg. 11(b), with effect from 1 December 2013 in respect of (a) financial years ending on or after 30 September 2013; and (b) companies, which deliver the accounts required by s. 444 to the registrar on or after 1 December 2013. Before substitution, the paragraph read:

(1) Notwithstanding that an item in respect of "development costs" is included under "fixed assets" in the balance sheet formats set out in Part 1 of this Schedule, an amount may only be included in a company's balance sheet in respect of development costs in special circumstances.

22(1) Intangible assets must be written off over the useful economic life of the intangible asset.

22(2) Where in exceptional cases the useful life of intangible assets cannot be reliably estimated, such assets must be written off over a period chosen by the directors of the company.

22(3) The period referred to in sub-paragraph (2) must not exceed ten years.

22(4) There must be disclosed in a note to the accounts the period referred to in sub-paragraph (2) and the reasons for choosing that period.

History – Para. 22 substituted by SI 2015/980, reg. 17(3)(c), with effect in relation to–

    (a) financial years beginning on or after 1 January 2016, and

    (b) a financial year of a company beginning on or after 1 January 2015, but before 1 January 2016, if the directors of the company so decide.

Former para. 22 read as follows:

22(1) The application of paragraphs 17 to 20 in relation to goodwill (in any case where goodwill is treated as an asset) is subject to the following.

22(2) Subject to sub-paragraph (3), the amount of the consideration for any goodwill acquired by a company must be reduced by provisions for depreciation calculated to write off that amount systematically over a period chosen by the directors of the company.

22(3) The period chosen must not exceed the useful economic life of the goodwill in question.

22(4) In any case where any goodwill acquired by a company is shown or included as an asset in the company's balance sheet there must be disclosed in a note to the accounts–

    (a) the period chosen for writing off the consideration for that goodwill, and
    (b) the reasons for choosing that period.

Current assets

23 Subject to paragraph 24, the amount to be included in respect of any current asset must be its purchase price or production cost.

24(1) If the net realisable value of any current asset is lower than its purchase price or production cost, the amount to be included in respect of that asset must be the net realisable value.

24(2) Where the reasons for which any provision for diminution in value was made in accordance with sub-paragraph (1) have ceased to apply to any extent, that provision must be written back to the extent that it is no longer necessary.

MISCELLANEOUS AND SUPPLEMENTARY PROVISIONS

Excess of money owed over value received as an asset item

25(1) Where the amount repayable on any debt owed by a company is greater than the value of the consideration received in the transaction giving rise to the debt, the amount of the difference may be treated as an asset.

25(2) Where any such amount is so treated–

    (a) it must be written off by reasonable amounts each year and must be completely written off before repayment of the debt, and
    (b) if the current amount is not shown as a separate item in the company's balance sheet, it must be disclosed in a note to the accounts.

Assets included at a fixed amount

26(1) Subject to sub-paragraph (2), the following may be included at a fixed quantity and value in the balance sheet formats set out in Section B of Part 1 of this Schedule–

    (a) assets which fall to be included amongst the fixed assets of a company under the item "intangible assets", and
    (b) raw materials and consumables within the item "stocks".

26(2) Sub-paragraph (1) applies to assets of a kind which are constantly being replaced where–

    (a) their overall value is not material to assessing the company's state of affairs, and
    (b) their quantity, value and composition are not subject to material variation.

History – Paragraph 26(1) substituted by SI 2013/3008, reg. 11(c), with effect from 1 December 2013 in respect of (a) financial years ending on or after 30 September 2013; and (b) companies, which deliver the accounts required by s. 444 to the registrar on or after 1 December 2013. Before substitution, the paragraph read:

26(1) Subject to sub-paragraph (2), assets which fall to be included–

    (a) amongst the fixed assets of a company under the item "tangible assets", or
    (b) amongst the current assets of a company under the item "raw materials and consumables", may be included at a fixed quantity and value.

Determination of purchase price or production cost

27(1) The purchase price of an asset is to be determined by adding to the actual price paid any expenses incidental to its acquisition and then subtracting any incidental reductions in the cost of acquisition.

27(2) The production cost of an asset is to be determined by adding to the purchase price of the raw materials and consumables used the amount of the costs incurred by the company which are directly attributable to the production of that asset.

27(3) In addition, there may be included in the production cost of an asset–

    (a) a reasonable proportion of the costs incurred by the company which are only indirectly attributable to the production of that asset, but only to the extent that they relate to the period of production, and

    (b) interest on capital borrowed to finance the production of that asset, to the extent that it accrues in respect of the period of production, provided, however, in a case within paragraph (b), that the inclusion of the interest in determining the cost of that asset and the amount of the interest so included is disclosed in a note to the accounts.

27(4) In the case of current assets distribution costs may not be included in production costs.

History – In para. 27(1), the words "and then subtracting any incidental reductions in the cost of acquisition" inserted by SI 2015/980, reg. 17(3)(d), with effect in relation to–

    (a) financial years beginning on or after 1 January 2016, and

    (b) a financial year of a company beginning on or after 1 January 2015, but before 1 January 2016, if the directors of the company so decide.

28(1) The purchase price or production cost of–

    (a) any assets which, by virtue of regulation 3(1) and Section B of Part 1 of this Schedule, fall to be included under any item shown in a company's balance sheet under the general item "stocks", and

    (b) any assets which are fungible assets (including investments), may be determined by the application of any of the methods mentioned in sub-paragraph (2) in relation to any such assets of the same class, provided that the method chosen is one which appears to the directors to be appropriate in the circumstances of the company.

28(2) Those methods are–

    (a) the method known as "first in, first out" (FIFO),

    (b) the method known as "last in, first out" (LIFO),

    (c) a weighted average price, and

    (d) any other method reflecting generally accepted best practice.

28(3) For the purposes of this paragraph, assets of any description must be regarded as fungible if assets of that description are substantially indistinguishable one from another.

History – In para. 28(1), ", by virtue of regulation 3(1) and Section B of Part 1 of this Schedule," inserted by SI 2013/3008, reg. 11(d), with effect from 1 December 2013 in respect of (a) financial years ending on or after 30 September 2013; and (b) companies, which deliver the accounts required by s. 444 to the registrar on or after 1 December 2013.

In para. 28(2)(d), the words "reflecting generally accepted best practice" substituted for the words "similar to any of the methods mentioned above" by SI 2015/980, reg. 17(3)(e), with effect in relation to–

    (a) financial years beginning on or after 1 January 2016, and

    (b) a financial year of a company beginning on or after 1 January 2015, but before 1 January 2016, if the directors of the company so decide.

Substitution of original stated amount where price or cost unknown

29(1) This paragraph applies where–

(a) there is no record of the purchase price or production cost of any asset of a company or of any price, expenses or costs relevant for determining its purchase price or production cost in accordance with paragraph 27, or

(b) any such record cannot be obtained without unreasonable expense or delay.

29(2) In such a case, the purchase price or production cost of the asset must be taken, for the purposes of paragraphs 17 to 24, to be the value ascribed to it in the earliest available record of its value made on or after its acquisition or production by the company.

Equity method in respect of participating interests

29A(1) Participating interests may be accounted for using the equity method.

29A(2) If participating interests are accounted for using the equity method–

(a) the proportion of profit or loss attributable to a participating interest and recognised in the profit and loss account may be that proportion which corresponds to the amount of any dividends, and

(b) where the profit attributable to a participating interest and recognised in the profit and loss account exceeds the amount of any dividends, the difference must be placed in a reserve which cannot be distributed to shareholders.

29A(3) The reference to "dividends" in sub-paragraph (2) includes dividends already paid and those whose payment can be claimed.

History – Para. 29A and the heading preceding it inserted by SI 2015/980, reg. 17(3)(f), with effect in relation to–

(a) financial years beginning on or after 1 January 2016, and

(b) a financial year of a company beginning on or after 1 January 2015, but before 1 January 2016, if the directors of the company so decide.

SECTION C – ALTERNATIVE ACCOUNTING RULES

Preliminary

30(1) The rules set out in Section B are referred to below in this Schedule as the historical cost accounting rules.

30(2) Those rules, with the omission of paragraphs 16, 22 and 26 to 29, are referred to below in this Part of this Schedule as the depreciation rules; and references below in this Schedule to the historical cost accounting rules do not include the depreciation rules as they apply by virtue of paragraph 33.

31 Subject to paragraphs 33 to 35, the amounts to be included in respect of assets of any description mentioned in paragraph 32 may be determined on any basis so mentioned.

Alternative accounting rules

32(1) Intangible fixed assets, other than goodwill, may be included at their current cost.

32(2) Tangible fixed assets may be included at a market value determined as at the date of their last valuation or at their current cost.

32(3) Investments of any description falling to be included under item B III of either of the balance sheet formats set out Part 1 of this Schedule may be included either–

    (a)   at a market value determined as at the date of their last valuation, or

    (b)   at a value determined on any basis which appears to the directors to be appropriate in the circumstances of the company.

But in the latter case particulars of the method of valuation adopted and of the reasons for adopting it must be disclosed in a note to the accounts.

32(4) Omitted by SI 2015/980, reg. 17(4)(a).

32(5) Omitted by SI 2015/980, reg. 17(4)(a).

History – Para. 32(4) and (5) omitted by SI 2015/980, reg. 17(4)(a), with effect in relation to–

    (a)   financial years beginning on or after 1 January 2016, and

    (b)   a financial year of a company beginning on or after 1 January 2015, but before 1 January 2016, if the directors of the company so decide.

Former para. 32(4) and (5) read as follows:

32(4) Investments of any description falling to be included under item C III of either of the balance sheet formats set out in Part 1 of this Schedule may be included at their current cost.

32(5) Stocks may be included at their current cost.

Application of the depreciation rules

33(1) Where the value of any asset of a company is determined on any basis mentioned in paragraph 32, that value must be, or (as the case may require) be the starting point for determining, the amount to be included in respect of that asset in the company's accounts, instead of its purchase price or production cost or any value previously so determined for that asset.

The depreciation rules apply accordingly in relation to any such asset with the substitution for any reference to its purchase price or production cost of a reference to the value most recently determined for that asset on any basis mentioned in paragraph 32.

33(2) The amount of any provision for depreciation required in the case of any fixed asset by paragraphs 18 to 20 as they apply by virtue of sub-paragraph (1) is referred to below in this paragraph as the adjusted amount, and the amount of any provision which would be required by any of those paragraphs in the case of that asset according to the historical cost accounting rules is referred to as the historical cost amount.

33(3) Where sub-paragraph (1) applies in the case of any fixed asset the amount of any provision for depreciation in respect of that asset–

    (a)   included in any item shown in the profit and loss account in respect of amounts written off assets of the description in question, or

    (b)   taken into account in stating any item so shown which is required by note (11) of the notes on the profit and loss account formats set out in Part 1 of this Schedule to be stated after taking into account any necessary provision for depreciation or diminution in value of assets included under it, may be the historical cost amount instead of the adjusted amount, provided that the amount of any difference between the two is shown separately in the profit and loss account or in a note to the accounts.

Additional information to be provided in case of departure from historical cost accounting rules

34(1) This paragraph applies where the amounts to be included in respect of assets covered by any items shown in a company's accounts have been determined on any basis mentioned in paragraph 32.

34(2) The items affected and the basis of valuation adopted in determining the amounts of the assets in question in the case of each such item must be disclosed in the note on accounting policies (see paragraph 44 of this Schedule).

34(3) In the case of each balance sheet item affected, the comparable amounts determined according to the historical cost accounting rules must be shown in a note to the accounts.

34(4) In sub-paragraph (3), references in relation to any item to the comparable amounts determined as there mentioned are references to–

(a) the aggregate amount which would be required to be shown in respect of that item if the amounts to be included in respect of all the assets covered by that item were determined according to the historical cost accounting rules, and

(b) the aggregate amount of the cumulative provisions for depreciation or diminution in value which would be permitted or required in determining those amounts according to those rules.

History – In para. 34(2), the words "the note on accounting policies (see paragraph 44 of this Schedule)" substituted for the words "a note to the accounts" by SI 2015/980, reg. 17(4)(b), with effect in relation to–

(a) financial years beginning on or after 1 January 2016, and

(b) a financial year of a company beginning on or after 1 January 2015, but before 1 January 2016, if the directors of the company so decide.

Para. 34(3) substituted by SI 2015/980, reg. 17(4)(c), with effect in relation to–

(a) financial years beginning on or after 1 January 2016, and

(b) a financial year of a company beginning on or after 1 January 2015, but before 1 January 2016, if the directors of the company so decide.

Former para. 34(3) read as follows:

34(3) In the case of each balance sheet item affected (except stocks) either–

(a) the comparable amounts determined according to the historical cost accounting rules, or

(b) the differences between those amounts and the corresponding amounts actually shown in the balance sheet in respect of that item, must be shown separately in the balance sheet or in a note to the accounts.

Revaluation reserve

35(1) With respect to any determination of the value of an asset of a company on any basis mentioned in paragraph 32, the amount of any profit or loss arising from that determination (after allowing, where appropriate, for any provisions for depreciation or diminution in value made otherwise than by reference to the value so determined and any adjustments of any such provisions made in the light of that determination) must be credited or (as the case may be) debited to a separate reserve ("the revaluation reserve").

35(2) The amount of the revaluation reserve must be shown in the company's balance sheet under a separate sub-heading in the position given for the item "revaluation reserve" under "Capital and reserves" in Format 1 or 2 of the balance sheet formats set out in Part 1 of this Schedule.

35(3) An amount may be transferred–

  (a) from the revaluation reserve–

    (i)   to the profit and loss account, if the amount was previously charged to that account or represents realised profit, or
    (ii) on capitalisation,

  (b) to or from the revaluation reserve in respect of the taxation relating to any profit or loss credited or debited to the reserve.

The revaluation reserve must be reduced to the extent that the amounts transferred to it are no longer necessary for the purposes of the valuation method used.

35(4) In sub-paragraph (3)(a)(ii) "capitalisation", in relation to an amount standing to the credit of the revaluation reserve, means applying it in wholly or partly paying up unissued shares in the company to be allotted to members of the company as fully or partly paid shares.

35(5) The revaluation reserve must not be reduced except as mentioned in this paragraph.

35(6) The treatment for taxation purposes of amounts credited or debited to the revaluation reserve must be disclosed in a note to the accounts.

History – In para. 35(2), the words 'under "Capital and reserves"' inserted; and the words "but need not be shown under that name" omitted by SI 2015/980, reg. 17(4)(d), with effect in relation to–

  (a) financial years beginning on or after 1 January 2016, and
  (b) a financial year of a company beginning on or after 1 January 2015, but before 1 January 2016, if the directors of the company so decide.

SECTION D – FAIR VALUE ACCOUNTING

Inclusion of financial instruments at fair value

36(1) Subject to sub-paragraphs (2) to (5), financial instruments (including derivatives) may be included at fair value.

36(2) Sub-paragraph (1) does not apply to financial instruments that constitute liabilities unless–

  (a) they are held as part of a trading portfolio,
  (b) they are derivatives, or
  (c) they are financial instruments falling within sub-paragraph (4).

36(3) Unless they are financial instruments falling within sub-paragraph (4), sub-paragraph (1) does not apply to–

  (a) financial instruments (other than derivatives) held to maturity,
  (b) loans and receivables originated by the company and not held for trading purposes,
  (c) interests in subsidiary undertakings, associated undertakings and joint ventures,
  (d) equity instruments issued by the company,
  (e) contracts for contingent consideration in a business combination, or
  (f) other financial instruments with such special characteristics that the instruments, according to generally accepted accounting principles or practice, should be accounted for differently from other financial instruments.

36(4) Financial instruments which under international accounting standards may be included in accounts at fair value, may be so included, provided that the disclosures required by such accounting standards are made.

36(5) If the fair value of a financial instrument cannot be determined reliably in accordance with paragraph 37, sub-paragraph (1) does not apply to that financial instrument.

36(6) In this paragraph–

"associated undertaking" has the meaning given by paragraph 19 of Schedule 6 to these Regulations;
"joint venture" has the meaning given by paragraph 18 of that Schedule.

History – Para. 36(4) substituted by SI 2015/980, reg. 17(5)(a), with effect in relation to–

(a) financial years beginning on or after 1 January 2016, and
(b) a financial year of a company beginning on or after 1 January 2015, but before 1 January 2016, if the directors of the company so decide.

Former para. 36(4) read as follows:

36(4) Financial instruments that, under international accounting standards adopted by the European Commission on or before 5th September 2006 in accordance with the IAS Regulation, may be included in accounts at fair value, may be so included, provided that the disclosures required by such accounting standards are made.

Determination of fair value

37(1) The fair value of a financial instrument is its value determined in accordance with this paragraph.

37(2) If a reliable market can readily be identified for the financial instrument, its fair value is to be determined by reference to its market value.

37(3) If a reliable market cannot readily be identified for the financial instrument but can be identified for its components or for a similar instrument, its fair value is determined by reference to the market value of its components or of the similar instrument.

37(4) If neither sub-paragraph (2) nor (3) applies, the fair value of the financial instrument is a value resulting from generally accepted valuation models and techniques.

37(5) Any valuation models and techniques used for the purposes of sub-paragraph (4) must ensure a reasonable approximation of the market value.

Hedged items

38 A company may include any assets and liabilities, or identified portions of such assets or liabilities, that qualify as hedged items under a fair value hedge accounting system at the amount required under that system.

Other assets that may be included at fair value

39(1) This paragraph applies to–

(a) stocks
(b) investment property, and
(c) living animals and plants.

39(2) Such stocks, investment property, and living animals and plants may be included at fair value, provided that, as the case maybe, all such stocks, investment property, and living animals and plants are so included where their fair value can reliably be determined.

39(3) In this paragraph, "fair value" means fair value determined in accordance with generally accepted accounting principles or practice.

History – Para. 39 substituted by SI 2015/980, reg. 17(5)(b), with effect in relation to–

    (a) financial years beginning on or after 1 January 2016, and
    (b) a financial year of a company beginning on or after 1 January 2015, but before 1 January 2016, if the directors of the company so decide.

Former para. 39 read as follows:

39(1) This paragraph applies to–

    (a) investment property, and
    (b) living animals and plants, that, under international accounting standards, may be included in accounts at fair value.

39(2) Such investment property and such living animals and plants may be included at fair value, provided that all such investment property or, as the case may be, all such living animals and plants are so included where their fair value can reliably be determined.

39(3) In this paragraph, "fair value" means fair value determined in accordance with relevant international accounting standards.

Accounting for changes in value

40(1) This paragraph applies where a financial instrument is valued in accordance with paragraph 36 or 38 or an asset is valued in accordance with paragraph 39.

40(2) Notwithstanding paragraph 13 in this Part of this Schedule, and subject to sub-paragraphs (3) and (4), a change in the value of the financial instrument or of the investment property or living animal or plant must be included in the profit and loss account.

40(3) Where–

    (a) the financial instrument accounted for is a hedging instrument under a hedge accounting system that allows some or all of the change in value not to be shown in the profit and loss account, or
    (b) the change in value relates to an exchange difference arising on a monetary item that forms part of a company's net investment in a foreign entity, the amount of the change in value must be credited to or (as the case may be) debited from a separate reserve ("the fair value reserve").

40(4) Where the instrument accounted for–

    (a) is an available for sale financial asset, and
    (b) is not a derivative, the change in value may be credited to or (as the case may be) debited from the fair value reserve.

The fair value reserve

41(1) The fair value reserve must be adjusted to the extent that the amounts shown in it are no longer necessary for the purposes of paragraph 40(3) or (4).

41(2) Omitted by SI 2015/980, reg. 17(5)(c).

History – Para. 41(2) omitted by SI 2015/980, reg. 17(5)(c), with effect in relation to–

    (a) financial years beginning on or after 1 January 2016, and
    (b) a financial year of a company beginning on or after 1 January 2015, but before 1 January 2016, if the directors of the company so decide.

Former para. 41(2) read as follows:

41(2) The treatment for taxation purposes of amounts credited or debited to the fair value reserve must be disclosed in a note to the accounts.

PART 3 – NOTES TO THE ACCOUNTS
PRELIMINARY

42(1) Any information required in the case of a company by the following provisions of this Part of this Schedule must be given by way of a note to the accounts.

42(2) These notes must be presented in the order in which, where relevant, the items to which they relate are presented in the balance sheet and in the profit and loss account.

History – Para. 42 substituted by SI 2015/980, reg. 18(2), with effect in relation to–

    (a) financial years beginning on or after 1 January 2016, and
    (b) a financial year of a company beginning on or after 1 January 2015, but before 1 January 2016, if the directors of the company so decide.

Former para. 42 read as follows:

42 Any information required in the case of any company by the following provisions of this Part of this Schedule must (if not given in the company's accounts) be given by way of a note to those accounts.

Reserves and dividends

43 Omitted by SI 2015/980, reg. 18(3).

History – Para. 43 omitted by SI 2015/980, reg. 18(3), with effect in relation to–

    (a) financial years beginning on or after 1 January 2016, and
    (b) a financial year of a company beginning on or after 1 January 2015, but before 1 January 2016, if the directors of the company so decide.

Former para. 43 read as follows:

43 There must be stated–

    (a) any amount set aside or proposed to be set aside to, or withdrawn or proposed to be withdrawn from, reserves,
    (b) the aggregate amount of dividends paid in the financial year (other than those for which a liability existed at the immediately preceding balance sheet date),
    (c) the aggregate amount of dividends that the company is liable to pay at the balance sheet date, and
    (d) the aggregate amount of dividends that are proposed before the date of approval of the accounts, and not otherwise disclosed under paragraph (b) or (c).

Disclosure of accounting policies

44 The accounting policies adopted by the company in determining the amounts to be included in respect of items shown in the balance sheet and in determining the profit or loss of the company must be stated (including such policies with respect to the depreciation and diminution in value of assets).

Information supplementing the balance sheet

45 Paragraphs 48 to 57 require information which either supplements the information given with respect to any particular items shown in the balance sheet or is otherwise relevant to assessing the company's state of affairs in the light of the information so given.

History – In para. 45, "48 to 57" substituted for "46 to 58" by SI 2015/980, reg. 18(4), with effect in relation to–

   (a) financial years beginning on or after 1 January 2016, and
   (b) a financial year of a company beginning on or after 1 January 2015, but before 1 January 2016, if the directors of the company so decide.

Share capital

46 Omitted by SI 2015/980, reg. 18(5).

History – Para. 46 omitted by SI 2015/980, reg. 18(5), with effect in relation to–

   (a) financial years beginning on or after 1 January 2016, and
   (b) a financial year of a company beginning on or after 1 January 2015, but before 1 January 2016, if the directors of the company so decide.

Former para. 46 read as follows:

46(1) Where shares of more than one class have been allotted, the number and aggregate nominal value of shares of each class allotted must be given.

46(2) In the case of any part of the allotted share capital that consists of redeemable shares, the following information must be given–

   (a) the earliest and latest dates on which the company has power to redeem those shares,
   (b) whether those shares must be redeemed in any event or are liable to be redeemed at the option of the company or of the shareholder, and
   (c) whether any (and, if so, what) premium is payable on redemption.

47 Omitted by SI 2015/980, reg. 18(6).

History – Para. 47 omitted by SI 2015/980, reg. 18(6), with effect in relation to–

   (a) financial years beginning on or after 1 January 2016, and
   (b) a financial year of a company beginning on or after 1 January 2015, but before 1 January 2016, if the directors of the company so decide.

Former para. 47 read as follows:

47 If the company has allotted any shares during the financial year, the following information must be given–

   (a) the classes of shares allotted, and
   (b) as respects each class of shares, the number allotted, their aggregate nominal value, and the consideration received by the company for the allotment.

Fixed assets

48(1) In respect of each item which is or would but for paragraph 4(2)(b) be shown under the general item "fixed assets" in the company's balance sheet the following information must be given–

    (a) the appropriate amounts in respect of that item as at the date of the beginning of the financial year and as at the balance sheet date respectively,

    (b) the effect on any amount shown in the balance sheet in respect of that item of–

        (i) any revision of the amount in respect of any assets included under that item made during that year on any basis mentioned in paragraph 32,

        (ii) acquisitions during that year of any assets,

        (iii) disposals during that year of any assets, and

        (iv) any transfers of assets of the company to and from that item during that year.

48(2) The reference in sub-paragraph (1)(a) to the appropriate amounts in respect of any item as at any date there mentioned is a reference to amounts representing the aggregate amounts determined, as at that date, in respect of assets falling to be included under that item on either of the following bases, that is to say–

    (a) on the basis of purchase price or production cost (determined in accordance with paragraphs 27 and 28), or

    (b) on any basis mentioned in paragraph 32, (leaving out of account in either case any provisions for depreciation or diminution in value).

48(3) In respect of each item within sub-paragraph (1) there must also be stated–

    (a) the cumulative amount of provisions for depreciation or diminution in value of assets included under that item as at each date mentioned in sub-paragraph (1)(a),

    (b) the amount of any such provisions made in respect of the financial year,

    (c) the amount of any adjustments made in respect of any such provisions during that year in consequence of the disposal of any assets, and

    (d) the amount of any other adjustments made in respect of any such provisions during that year.

49 Where any fixed assets of the company (other than listed investments) are included under any item shown in the company's balance sheet at an amount determined on any basis mentioned in paragraph 32, the following information must be given–

    (a) the years (so far as they are known to the directors) in which the assets were severally valued and the several values, and

    (b) in the case of assets that have been valued during the financial year, the names of the persons who valued them or particulars of their qualifications for doing so and (whichever is stated) the bases of valuation used by them.

Investments

50 Omitted by SI 2015/980, reg. 18(7).

History – Para. 50 omitted by SI 2015/980, reg. 18(7), with effect in relation to–

    (a) financial years beginning on or after 1 January 2016, and

    (b) a financial year of a company beginning on or after 1 January 2015, but before 1 January 2016, if the directors of the company so decide.

Former para. 50 read as follows:

50(1) In respect of the amount of each item which is or would but for paragraph 4(2)(b) be shown in the company's balance sheet under the general item "investments" (whether as fixed assets or as current assets) there must be stated how much of that amount is ascribable to listed investments.

50(2) Where the amount of any listed investments is stated for any item in accordance with subparagraph (1), the following amounts must also be stated–

    (a) the aggregate market value of those investments where it differs from the amount so stated, and

    (b) both the market value and the stock exchange value of any investments of which the former value is, for the purposes of the accounts, taken as being higher than the latter.

Information about fair value of assets and liabilities

51(1) This paragraph applies where financial instruments or other assets have been valued in accordance with, as appropriate, paragraph 36, 38 or 39.

51(2) There must be stated–

    (a) the significant assumptions underlying the valuation models and techniques used to determine the fair values,

    (b) for each category of financial instrument or other asset, the fair value of the assets in that category and the changes in value–

        (i) included directly in the profit and loss account, or

        (ii) credited to or (as the case may be) debited from the fair value reserve, in respect of those assets, and

    (c) for each class of derivatives, the extent and nature of the instruments, including significant terms and conditions that may affect the amount, timing and certainty of future cash flows.

51(3) Where any amount is transferred to or from the fair value reserve during the financial year, there must be stated in tabular form–

    (a) the amount of the reserve as at the date of the beginning of the financial year and as at the balance sheet date respectively, and

    (b) the amount transferred to or from the reserve during that year.

History – Para. 51 substituted by SI 2015/980, reg. 18(8), with effect in relation to–

    (a) financial years beginning on or after 1 January 2016, and

    (b) a financial year of a company beginning on or after 1 January 2015, but before 1 January 2016, if the directors of the company so decide.

Former para. 51 read as follows:

51(1) This paragraph applies where financial instruments have been valued in accordance with paragraph 36 or 38.

51(2) There must be stated–

    (a) the significant assumptions underlying the valuation models and techniques used where the fair value of the instruments has been determined in accordance with paragraph 37(4),

    (b) for each category of financial instrument, the fair value of the instruments in that category and the changes in value–

        (i) included in the profit and loss account, or

        (ii) credited to or (as the case may be) debited from the fair value reserve, in respect of those instruments, and

(c) for each class of derivatives, the extent and nature of the instruments, including significant terms and conditions that may affect the amount, timing and certainty of future cash flows.

51(3) Where any amount is transferred to or from the fair value reserve during the financial year, there must be stated in tabular form–

(a) the amount of the reserve as at the date of the beginning of the financial year and as at the balance sheet date respectively,
(b) the amount transferred to or from the reserve during that year, and
(c) the source and application respectively of the amounts so transferred.

52 Omitted by SI 2015/980, reg. 18(9).

History – Para. 52 omitted by SI 2015/980, reg. 18(9), with effect in relation to–

(a) financial years beginning on or after 1 January 2016, and
(b) a financial year of a company beginning on or after 1 January 2015, but before 1 January 2016, if the directors of the company so decide.

Former para. 52 read as follows:

52(1) This paragraph applies if–

(a) the company has financial fixed assets that could be included at fair value by virtue of paragraph 36,
(b) the amount at which those items are included under any item in the company's accounts is in excess of their fair value, and
(c) the company has not made provision for diminution in value of those assets in accordance with paragraph 19(1) of this Schedule.

52(2) There must be stated–

(a) the amount at which either the individual assets or appropriate groupings of those individual assets are included in the company's accounts,
(b) the fair value of those assets or groupings, and
(c) the reasons for not making a provision for diminution in value of those assets, including the nature of the evidence that provides the basis for the belief that the amount at which they are stated in the accounts will be recovered.

Information where investment property and living animals and plants included at fair value

53 Omitted by SI 2015/980, reg. 18(10).

History – Para. 53 omitted by SI 2015/980, reg. 18(10), with effect in relation to–

(a) financial years beginning on or after 1 January 2016, and
(b) a financial year of a company beginning on or after 1 January 2015, but before 1 January 2016, if the directors of the company so decide.

Former para. 53 read as follows:

53(1) This paragraph applies where the amounts to be included in a company's accounts in respect of investment property or living animals and plants have been determined in accordance with paragraph 39.

53(2) The balance sheet items affected and the basis of valuation adopted in determining the amounts of the assets in question in the case of each such item must be disclosed in a note to the accounts.

53(3) In the case of investment property, for each balance sheet item affected there must be shown, either separately in the balance sheet or in a note to the accounts–

    (a)   the comparable amounts determined according to the historical cost accounting rules, or

    (b)   the differences between those amounts and the corresponding amounts actually shown in the balance sheet in respect of that item.

53(4) In sub-paragraph (3), references in relation to any item to the comparable amounts determined in accordance with that sub-paragraph are to–

    (a)   the aggregate amount which would be required to be shown in respect of that item if the amounts to be included in respect of all the assets covered by that item were determined according to the historical cost accounting rules, and

    (b)   the aggregate amount of the cumulative provisions for depreciation or diminution in value which would be permitted or required in determining those amounts according to those rules.

Information about revalued fixed assets

54(1) This paragraph applies where fixed assets are measured at revalued amounts.

54(2) Where this paragraph applies, the following information must be given in tabular form–

    (a)   movements in the revaluation reserve in the financial year, with an explanation of the tax treatment of items therein, and

    (b)   the carrying amount in the balance sheet that would have been recognised had the fixed assets not been revalued.

History – Para. 54 and the heading preceding it substituted by SI 2015/980, reg. 18(11), with effect in relation to–

    (a)   financial years beginning on or after 1 January 2016, and

    (b)   a financial year of a company beginning on or after 1 January 2015, but before 1 January 2016, if the directors of the company so decide.

Former para. 54 read as follows:

Reserves and provisions

54(1) This paragraph applies where any amount is transferred–

    (a)   to or from any reserves, or

    (b)   to any provisions for liabilities, or

    (c)   from any provision for liabilities otherwise than for the purpose for which the provision was established, and the reserves or provisions are or would but for paragraph 4(2)(b) be shown as separate items in the company's balance sheet.

54(2) The following information must be given in respect of the aggregate of reserves or provisions included in the same item–

    (a)   the amount of the reserves or provisions as at the date of the beginning of the financial year and as at the balance sheet date respectively,

    (b)   any amounts transferred to or from the reserves or provisions during that year, and

    (c)   the source and application respectively of any amounts so transferred.

54(3) Particulars must be given of each provision included in the item "other provisions" in the company's balance sheet in any case where the amount of that provision is material.

Details of indebtedness

55(1) For the aggregate of all items shown under "creditors" in the company's balance sheet there must be stated the aggregate of the following amounts–

(a) the amount of any debts included under "creditors" which are payable or repayable otherwise than by instalments and fall due for payment or repayment after the end of the period of five years beginning with the day next following the end of the financial year, and

(b) in the case of any debts so included which are payable or repayable by instalments, the amount of any instalments which fall due for payment after the end of that period.

55(2) In respect of each item shown under "creditors" in the company's balance sheet there must be stated the aggregate amount of any debts included under that item in respect of which any security has been given by the company with an indication of the nature and form of any such security.

55(3) References above in this paragraph to an item shown under "creditors" in the company's balance sheet include references, where amounts falling due to creditors within one year and after more than one year are distinguished in the balance sheet–

(a) in a case within sub-paragraph (1), to an item shown under the latter of those categories,

(b) in a case within sub-paragraph (2), to an item shown under either of those categories. References to items shown under "creditors" include references to items which would but for paragraph 4(2)(b) be shown under that heading.

History – In para. 55(2), the words "with an indication of the nature and form of any such security" inserted by SI 2015/980, reg. 18(12), with effect in relation to–

(a) financial years beginning on or after 1 January 2016, and

(b) a financial year of a company beginning on or after 1 January 2015, but before 1 January 2016, if the directors of the company so decide.

56 Omitted by SI 2015/980, reg. 18(13).

History – Para. 56 omitted by SI 2015/980, reg. 18(13), with effect in relation to–

(a) financial years beginning on or after 1 January 2016, and

(b) a financial year of a company beginning on or after 1 January 2015, but before 1 January 2016, if the directors of the company so decide.

Former para. 56 read as follows:

56 If any fixed cumulative dividends on the company's shares are in arrear, there must be stated–

(a) the amount of the arrears, and

(b) the period for which the dividends or, if there is more than one class, each class of them are in arrear.

Guarantees and other financial commitments

57(1) The total amount of any financial commitments, guarantees and contingencies that are not included in the balance sheet must be stated.

57(2) An indication of the nature and form of any valuable security given by the company in respect of commitments, guarantees and contingencies within sub-paragraph (1) must be given.

57(3) The total amount of any commitments within sub-paragraph (1) concerning pensions must be separately disclosed.

57(4) The total amount of any commitments within sub-paragraph (1) which are undertaken on behalf of or for the benefit of–

(a)   any parent undertaking, fellow subsidiary undertaking or any subsidiary undertaking of the company, or
(b)   any undertaking in which the company has a participating interest
      must be separately stated and those within paragraph (a) must also be stated separately from those within paragraph (b).

History – Para. 57 substituted by SI 2015/980, reg. 18(14), with effect in relation to–

(a)   financial years beginning on or after 1 January 2016, and
(b)   a financial year of a company beginning on or after 1 January 2015, but before 1 January 2016, if the directors of the company so decide.

Former para. 57 read as follows:

57(1) Particulars must be given of any charge on the assets of the company to secure the liabilities of any other person, including, where practicable, the amount secured.

57(2) The following information must be given with respect to any other contingent liability not provided for–

(a)   the amount or estimated amount of that liability,
(b)   its legal nature, and
(c)   whether any valuable security has been provided by the company in connection with that liability and if so, what.

57(3) There must be stated, where practicable, the aggregate amount or estimated amount of contracts for capital expenditure, so far as not provided for.

57(4) Particulars must be given of–

(a)   any pension commitments included under any provision shown in the company's balance sheet, and
(b)   any such commitments for which no provision has been made, and where any such commitment relates wholly or partly to pensions payable to past directors of the company separate particulars must be given of that commitment so far as it relates to such pensions.

57(5) Particulars must also be given of any other financial commitments that–

(a)   have not been provided for, and
(b)   are relevant to assessing the company's state of affairs.

57(6) Commitments within any of sub-paragraphs (1) to (5) which are undertaken on behalf of or for the benefit of–

(a)   any parent undertaking or fellow subsidiary undertaking, or
(b)   any subsidiary undertaking of the company, must be stated separately from the other commitments within that sub-paragraph, and commitments within paragraph (a) must also be stated separately from those within paragraph (b).

Miscellaneous matters

58   Omitted by SI 2015/980, reg. 18(15).

History – Para. 58 omitted by SI 2015/980, reg. 18(15), with effect in relation to–

(a)   financial years beginning on or after 1 January 2016, and

(b) a financial year of a company beginning on or after 1 January 2015, but before 1 January 2016, if the directors of the company so decide.

Former para. 58 read as follows:

58 Particulars must be given of any case where the purchase price or production cost of any asset is for the first time determined under paragraph 29.

Information supplementing the profit and loss account

59 Omitted by SI 2015/980, reg. 18(16).

History – Para. 59 omitted by SI 2015/980, reg. 18(16), with effect in relation to–

(a) financial years beginning on or after 1 January 2016, and
(b) a financial year of a company beginning on or after 1 January 2015, but before 1 January 2016, if the directors of the company so decide.

Former para. 59 read as follows:

59 Paragraphs 60 and 61 require information which either supplements the information given with respect to any particular items shown in the profit and loss account or otherwise provides particulars of income or expenditure of the company or of circumstances affecting the items shown in the profit and loss account (see regulation 3(2) for exemption for companies falling within section 408 of the 2006 Act).

Particulars of turnover

60 Omitted by SI 2015/980, reg. 18(17).

History – Para. 60 omitted by SI 2015/980, reg. 18(17), with effect in relation to–

(a) financial years beginning on or after 1 January 2016, and
(b) a financial year of a company beginning on or after 1 January 2015, but before 1 January 2016, if the directors of the company so decide.

Former para. 60 read as follows:

60(1) If the company has supplied geographical markets outside the United Kingdom during the financial year in question, there must be stated the percentage of its turnover that, in the opinion of the directors, is attributable to those markets.

60(2) In analysing for the purposes of this paragraph the source of turnover, the directors of the company must have regard to the manner in which the company's activities are organised.

Miscellaneous matters

61(1) Where any amount relating to any preceding financial year is included in any item in the profit and loss account, the effect must be stated.

61(2) The amount and nature of any individual items of income or expenditure of exceptional size or incidence must be stated.

History – Para. 61(2) substituted for sub-para. (2) and (3) by SI 2015/980, reg. 18(18), with effect in relation to–

    (a) financial years beginning on or after 1 January 2016, and
    (b) a financial year of a company beginning on or after 1 January 2015, but before 1 January 2016, if the directors of the company so decide.

Sums denominated in foreign currencies

62 Omitted by SI 2015/980, reg. 18(19).

History – Para. 62 omitted by SI 2015/980, reg. 18(19), with effect in relation to–

    (a) financial years beginning on or after 1 January 2016, and
    (b) a financial year of a company beginning on or after 1 January 2015, but before 1 January 2016, if the directors of the company so decide.

Former para. 62 read as follows:

62 Where sums originally denominated in foreign currencies have been brought into account under any items shown in the balance sheet or profit and loss account, the basis on which those sums have been translated into sterling (or the currency in which the accounts are drawn up) must be stated.

Dormant companies acting as agents

63 Omitted by SI 2015/980, reg. 18(20).

History – Para. 63 omitted by SI 2015/980, reg. 18(20), with effect in relation to–

    (a) financial years beginning on or after 1 January 2016, and
    (b) a financial year of a company beginning on or after 1 January 2015, but before 1 January 2016, if the directors of the company so decide.

Former para. 63 read as follows:

63 Where the directors of a company take advantage of the exemption conferred by section 480 of the 2006 Act (dormant companies: exemption from audit), and the company has during the financial year in question acted as an agent for any person, the fact that it has so acted must be stated.

Post balance sheet events

64 The nature and financial effect of material events arising after the balance sheet date which are not reflected in the profit and loss account or balance sheet must be stated.

History – Para. 64 inserted by SI 2015/980, reg. 18(21), with effect in relation to–

    (a) financial years beginning on or after 1 January 2016, and
    (b) a financial year of a company beginning on or after 1 January 2015, but before 1 January 2016, if the directors of the company so decide.

Parent undertaking information

65 Where the company is a subsidiary undertaking, the following information must be given in respect of the parent undertaking of the smallest group of undertakings for which group accounts are drawn up of which the company is a member–

(a) the name of the parent undertaking which draws up the group accounts,

(b) the address of the undertaking's registered office (whether in or outside the United Kingdom), or

(c) if it is unincorporated, the address of its principal place of business.

History – Para. 65 inserted by SI 2015/980, reg. 18(21), with effect in relation to–

(a) financial years beginning on or after 1 January 2016, and

(b) a financial year of a company beginning on or after 1 January 2015, but before 1 January 2016, if the directors of the company so decide.

Related party transactions

66(1) Particulars may be given of transactions which the company has entered into with related parties, and must be given if such transactions are material and have not been concluded under normal market conditions with–

(a) owners holding a participating interest in the company;

(b) companies in which the company itself has a participating interest; and

(c) the company's directors.

66(2) Particulars of the transactions required to be disclosed under sub-paragraph (1) must include–

(a) the amount of such transactions,

(b) the nature of the related party relationship, and

(c) other information about the transactions necessary for an understanding of the financial position of the company.

66(3) Information about individual transactions may be aggregated according to their nature, except where separate information is necessary of an understanding of the effects of the related party transactions on the financial position of the company.

66(4) Particulars need not be given of transactions entered into between two or more members of a group, provided that any subsidiary undertaking which is a party to the transaction is wholly-owned by such a member.

66(5) In this paragraph, "related party" has the same meaning as in international accounting standards.

History – Para. 66 inserted by SI 2015/980, reg. 18(21), with effect in relation to–

(a) financial years beginning on or after 1 January 2016, and

(b) a financial year of a company beginning on or after 1 January 2015, but before 1 January 2016, if the directors of the company so decide.

SCHEDULE 2
Regulation 4

INFORMATION ABOUT RELATED UNDERTAKINGS WHERE COMPANY NOT PREPARING GROUP ACCOUNTS (COMPANIES ACT OR IAS INDIVIDUAL ACCOUNTS)

History – Sch. 2 omitted by SI 2015/980, reg. 19, with effect in relation to–

(a) financial years beginning on or after 1 January 2016, and

(b) a financial year of a company beginning on or after 1 January 2015, but before 1 January 2016, if the directors of the company so decide.

Former Sch. 2 read as follows:

SCHEDULE 2 Regulation 4

INFORMATION ABOUT RELATED UNDERTAKINGS WHERE COMPANY NOT PREPARING GROUP ACCOUNTS (COMPANIES ACT OR IAS INDIVIDUAL ACCOUNTS)

PART 1 – REQUIRED DISCLOSURES

Subsidiary undertakings

1(1) The following information must be given where at the end of the financial year the company has subsidiary undertakings.

1(2) The name of each subsidiary undertaking must be stated.

1(3) There must be stated with respect to each subsidiary undertaking–

   (a) if it is incorporated outside the United Kingdom, the country in which it is incorporated,

   (b) if it is unincorporated, the address of its principal place of business.

Holdings in subsidiary undertakings

2(1) There must be stated in relation to shares of each class held by the company in a subsidiary undertaking–

   (a) the identity of the class, and

   (b) the proportion of the nominal value of the shares of that class represented by those shares.

2(2) The shares held by or on behalf of the company itself must be distinguished from those attributed to the company which are held by or on behalf of a subsidiary undertaking.

Financial information about subsidiary undertakings

3(1) There must be disclosed with respect to each subsidiary undertaking–

   (a) the aggregate amount of its capital and reserves as at the end of its relevant financial year, and

   (b) its profit or loss for that year.

3(2) That information need not be given if the company would (if it were not subject to the small companies regime) be exempt by virtue of section 400 or 401 of the 2006 Act (parent company included in accounts of larger group) from the requirement to prepare group accounts.

3(3) That information need not be given if the company's investment in the subsidiary undertaking is included in the company's accounts by way of the equity method of valuation.

3(4) That information need not be given if–

   (a) the subsidiary undertaking is not required by any provision of the 2006 Act to deliver a copy of its balance sheet for its relevant financial year and does not otherwise publish that balance sheet in the United Kingdom or elsewhere, and

   (b) the company's holding is less than 50% of the nominal value of the shares in the undertaking.

179

3(5) Information otherwise required by this paragraph need not be given if it is not material.

3(6) For the purposes of this paragraph the "relevant financial year" of a subsidiary undertaking is–

(a) if its financial year ends with that of the company, that year, and
(b) if not, its financial year ending last before the end of the company's financial year.

Shares of company held by subsidiary undertakings

4(1) The number, description and amount of the shares in the company held by or on behalf of its subsidiary undertakings must be disclosed.

4(2) Sub-paragraph (1) does not apply in relation to shares in the case of which the subsidiary undertaking is concerned as personal representative or, subject as follows, as trustee.

4(3) The exception for shares in relation to which the subsidiary undertaking is concerned as trustee does not apply if the company, or any subsidiary undertaking of the company, is beneficially interested under the trust, otherwise than by way of security only for the purposes of a transaction entered into by it in the ordinary course of a business which includes the lending of money.

4(4) Part 2 of this Schedule has effect for the interpretation of the reference in sub-paragraph (3) to a beneficial interest under a trust.

Significant holdings in undertakings other than subsidiary undertakings

5(1) The information required by paragraphs 6 and 7 must be given where at the end of the financial year the company has a significant holding in an undertaking which is not a subsidiary undertaking of the company.

5(2) A holding is significant for this purpose if–

(a) it amounts to 20% or more of the nominal value of any class of shares in the undertaking, or
(b) the amount of the holding (as stated or included in the company's accounts) exceeds 20% of the amount (as so stated) of the company's assets.

6(1) The name of the undertaking must be stated.

6(2) There must be stated–

(a) if the undertaking is incorporated outside the United Kingdom, the country in which it is incorporated,
(b) if it is unincorporated, the address of its principal place of business.

6(3) There must also be stated–

(a) the identity of each class of shares in the undertaking held by the company, and
(b) the proportion of the nominal value of the shares of that class represented by those shares.

7(1) There must also be stated–

(a) the aggregate amount of the capital and reserves of the undertaking as at the end of its relevant financial year, and
(b) its profit or loss for that year.

7(2) That information need not be given if–

(a) the company would (if it were not subject to the small companies regime) be exempt by virtue of section 400 or 401 of the 2006 Act (parent company included in accounts of larger group) from the requirement to prepare group accounts, and

(b) the investment of the company in all undertakings in which it has such a holding as is mentioned in sub-paragraph (1) is shown, in aggregate, in the notes to the accounts by way of the equity method of valuation.

7(3) That information need not be given in respect of an undertaking if–

(a) the undertaking is not required by any provision of the 2006 Act to deliver to the registrar a copy of its balance sheet for its relevant financial year and does not otherwise publish that balance sheet in the United Kingdom or elsewhere, and

(b) the company's holding is less than 50% of the nominal value of the shares in the undertaking.

7(4) Information otherwise required by this paragraph need not be given if it is not material.

7(5) For the purposes of this paragraph the "relevant financial year" of an undertaking is–

(a) if its financial year ends with that of the company, that year, and

(b) if not, its financial year ending last before the end of the company's financial year.

Membership of certain undertakings

8(1) The information required by this paragraph must be given where at the end of the financial year the company is a member of a qualifying undertaking.

8(2) There must be stated–

(a) the name and legal form of the undertaking, and

(b) the address of the undertaking's registered office (whether in or outside the United (Kingdom) or, if it does not have such an office, its head office (whether in or outside the United Kingdom).

8(3) Where the undertaking is a qualifying partnership there must also be stated either–

(a) that a copy of the latest accounts of the undertaking has been or is to be appended to the copy of the company's accounts sent to the registrar under section 444 of the 2006 Act, or

(b) the name of at least one body corporate (which may be the company) in whose group accounts the undertaking has been or is to be dealt with on a consolidated basis.

8(4) Information otherwise required by sub-paragraph (2) need not be given if it is not material.

8(5) Information otherwise required by sub-paragraph (3)(b) need not be given if the notes to the company's accounts disclose that advantage has been taken of the exemption conferred by regulation 7 of the Partnerships (Accounts) Regulations 2008.

8(6) In sub-paragraph (1) "member", in relation to a qualifying undertaking which is a qualifying partnership, has the same meaning as in the Partnerships (Accounts) Regulations 2008.

8(7) In this paragraph–

"dealt with on a consolidated basis" and "qualifying partnership" have the same meanings as in the Partnerships (Accounts) Regulations 2008;
"qualifying undertaking" means–

(a) a qualifying partnership, or

(b) an unlimited company each of whose members is–

   (i)   a limited company,

   (ii)   another unlimited company each of whose members is a limited company,

   (iii) a Scottish partnership which is not a limited partnership, each of whose members is a limited company, or

   (iv)   a Scottish partnership which is a limited partnership, each of whose general partners is a limited company.

8(8) In sub-paragraph (7) the references to a limited company, another unlimited company, a Scottish partnership which is not a limited partnership or a Scottish partnership which is a limited partnership include a comparable undertaking incorporated in or formed under the law of a country or territory outside the United Kingdom.

8(9) In sub-paragraph (7) "general partner" means–

(a) in relation to a Scottish partnership which is a limited partnership, a person who is a general partner within the meaning of the Limited Partnerships Act 1907, and

(b) in relation to an undertaking incorporated in or formed under the law of any country or territory outside the United Kingdom and which is comparable to a Scottish partnership which is a limited partnership, a person comparable to such a general partner.

8(10) In sub-paragraphs (7), (8) and (9) "limited partnership" means a partnership registered under the Limited Partnerships Act 1907.

History – In para. 8(5), "Partnerships (Accounts) Regulations 2008" substituted for "Partnerships and Unlimited Companies (Accounts) Regulations 1993" by SI 2008/569, reg. 17(1)(a), with effect from 6 April 2008.

Para. 8(6) substituted and 8(7)–(10) inserted by SI 2013/2005, reg. 5, with effect from 1 September 2013 applying in relation to a financial year of a company beginning on or after 1 October 2013. The version of para. 8 applying to financial years beginning before 1 October 2013 read as follows:

(1) The information required by this paragraph must be given where at the end of the financial year the company is a member of a qualifying undertaking.

(2) There must be stated–

(a) the name and legal form of the undertaking, and

(b) the address of the undertaking's registered office (whether in or outside the United (Kingdom) or, if it does not have such an office, its head office (whether in or outside the United Kingdom).

(3) Where the undertaking is a qualifying partnership there must also be stated either–

(a) that a copy of the latest accounts of the undertaking has been or is to be appended to the copy of the company's accounts sent to the registrar under section 444 of the 2006 Act, or

(b) the name of at least one body corporate (which may be the company) in whose group accounts the undertaking has been or is to be dealt with on a consolidated basis.

(4) Information otherwise required by sub-paragraph (2) need not be given if it is not material.

(5) Information otherwise required by sub-paragraph (3)(b) need not be given if the notes to the company's accounts disclose that advantage has been taken of the exemption conferred by regulation 7 of the Partnerships (Accounts) Regulations 2008.

(6) In this paragraph–

"dealt with on a consolidated basis", **"member"** and **"qualifying partnership"** have the same meanings as in the Partnerships (Accounts) Regulations 2008;
"qualifying undertaking" means–

    (a) a qualifying partnership, or

    (b) an unlimited company each of whose members is–

        (i) a limited company,

        (ii) another unlimited company each of whose members is a limited company, or

        (iii) a Scottish partnership each of whose members is a limited company, and references in this paragraph to a limited company, another unlimited company or a Scottish partnership include a comparable undertaking incorporated in or formed under the law of a country or territory outside the United Kingdom.

Parent undertaking drawing up accounts for larger group

9(1) Where the company is a subsidiary undertaking, the following information must be given with respect to the parent undertaking of–

    (a) the largest group of undertakings for which group accounts are drawn up and of which the company is a member, and

    (b) the smallest such group of undertakings.

9(2) The name of the parent undertaking must be stated.

9(3) There must be stated–

    (a) if the undertaking is incorporated outside the United Kingdom, the country in which it is incorporated,

    (b) if it is unincorporated, the address of its principal place of business.

9(4) If copies of the group accounts referred to in sub-paragraph (1) are available to the public, there must also be stated the addresses from which copies of the accounts can be obtained.

Identification of ultimate parent company

10(1) Where the company is a subsidiary undertaking, the following information must be given with respect to the company (if any) regarded by the directors as being the company's ultimate parent company.

10(2) The name of that company must be stated.

10(3) If that company is incorporated outside the United Kingdom, the country in which it is incorporated must be stated (if known to the directors).

10(4) In this paragraph "company" includes any body corporate.

Construction of references to shares held by company

11(1) References in this Part of this Schedule to shares held by a company are to be construed as follows.

11(2) For the purposes of paragraphs 2 and 3 (information about subsidiary undertakings)–

    (a) there must be attributed to the company any shares held by a subsidiary undertaking, or by a person acting on behalf of the company or a subsidiary undertaking; but

(b) there must be treated as not held by the company any shares held on behalf of a person other than the company or a subsidiary undertaking.

11(3) For the purposes of paragraphs 5 to 7 (information about undertakings other than subsidiary undertakings)–

(a) there must be attributed to the company shares held on its behalf by any person; but
(b) there must be treated as not held by a company shares held on behalf of a person other than the company.

11(4) For the purposes of any of those provisions, shares held by way of security must be treated as held by the person providing the security–

(a) where apart from the right to exercise them for the purpose of preserving the value of the security, or of realising it, the rights attached to the shares are exercisable only in accordance with his instructions, and
(b) where the shares are held in connection with the granting of loans as part of normal business activities and apart from the right to exercise them for the purpose of preserving the value of the security, or of realising it, the rights attached to the shares are exercisable only in his interests.

PART 2 – INTERPRETATION OF REFERENCES TO "BENEFICIAL INTEREST"

Introduction

12(1) References in this Schedule to a beneficial interest are to be interpreted in accordance with the following provisions.

12(2) This Part of this Schedule applies in relation to debentures as it applies in relation to shares.

Residual interests under pension and employees' share schemes

13(1) Where shares in an undertaking are held on trust for the purposes of a pension scheme or an employees' share scheme, there must be disregarded any residual interest of the undertaking or any of its subsidiary undertakings (the "residual beneficiary") that has not vested in possession.

13(2) A "residual interest" means a right to receive any of the trust property in the event of–

(a) all the liabilities arising under the scheme having been satisfied or provided for, or
(b) the residual beneficiary ceasing to participate in the scheme, or
(c) the trust property at any time exceeding what is necessary for satisfying the liabilities arising or expected to arise under the scheme.

13(3) In sub-paragraph (2)–

(a) references to a right include a right dependent on the exercise of a discretion vested by the scheme in the trustee or any other person, and
(b) references to liabilities arising under a scheme include liabilities that have resulted or may result from the exercise of any such discretion.

13(4) For the purposes of this paragraph a residual interest vests in possession–

(a) in a case within sub-paragraph (2)(a), on the occurrence of the event there mentioned, whether or not the amount of the property receivable pursuant to the right mentioned in that sub-paragraph is then ascertained,

(b) in a case within sub-paragraph (2)(b) or (c), when the residual beneficiary becomes entitled to require the trustee to transfer to it any of the property receivable pursuant to that right.

Employer's charges and other rights of recovery

14(1) Where shares in an undertaking are held on trust there must be disregarded–

(a) if the trust is for the purposes of a pension scheme, any such rights as are mentioned in sub-paragraph (2),

(b) if the trust is for the purposes of an employees' share scheme, any such rights as are mentioned in paragraph (a) of that sub-paragraph, being rights of the undertaking or any of its subsidiary undertakings.

14(2) The rights referred to are–

(a) any charge or lien on, or set-off against, any benefit or other right or interest under the scheme for the purpose of enabling the employer or former employer of a member of the scheme to obtain the discharge of a monetary obligation due to him from the member,

(b) any right to receive from the trustee of the scheme, or as trustee of the scheme to retain, an amount that can be recovered or retained under section 61 of the Pension Schemes Act 1993 or section 57 of the Pension Schemes (Northern Ireland) Act 1993 (deduction of contributions equivalent premium from refund of scheme contributions) or otherwise, as reimbursement or partial reimbursement for any contributions equivalent premium paid in connection with the scheme under Chapter 3 of Part 3 of that Act.

Trustee's right to expenses, remuneration, indemnity etc.

15(1) Where an undertaking is a trustee, there must be disregarded any rights which the undertaking has in its capacity as trustee.

15(2) This includes in particular–

(a) any right to recover its expenses or be remunerated out of the trust property, and

(b) any right to be indemnified out of that property for any liability incurred by reason of any act or omission of the undertaking in the performance of its duties as trustee.

Meaning of "pension scheme"

16(1) In this Part of this Schedule "pension scheme" means any scheme for the provision of benefits consisting of or including relevant benefits for or in respect of employees or former employees.

16(2) For this purpose "relevant benefits" means any pension, lump sum, gratuity or other like benefit given or to be given on retirement or on death or in anticipation of retirement or, in connection with past service, after retirement or death.

Application of provisions to directors

17 In paragraphs 14(2) and 16, "employee" and "employer" are to be read as if a director of an undertaking were employed by it.

SCHEDULE 3

Regulations 5 and 9

INFORMATION ABOUT DIRECTORS' BENEFITS: REMUNERATION (COMPANIES ACT OR IAS ACCOUNTS)

History – Sch. 3 omitted by SI 2015/980, reg. 20, with effect in relation to–

(a) financial years beginning on or after 1 January 2016, and
(b) a financial year of a company beginning on or after 1 January 2015, but before 1 January 2016, if the directors of the company so decide.

Former Sch. 3 read as follows:

SCHEDULE 3

Regulations 5 and 9

INFORMATION ABOUT DIRECTORS' BENEFITS: REMUNERATION (COMPANIES ACT OR IAS ACCOUNTS)

PART 1 – INFORMATION REQUIRED TO BE DISCLOSED

Total amount of directors' remuneration etc.

1(1) There must be shown the overall total of the following amounts–

(a) the amount of remuneration paid to or receivable by directors in respect of qualifying services;

(b) the amount of money paid to or receivable by directors, and the net value of assets (other than money, share options or shares) received or receivable by directors, under long term incentive schemes in respect of qualifying services; and

(c) the value of any company contributions–

   (i) paid, or treated as paid, to a pension scheme in respect of directors' qualifying services, and

   (ii) by reference to which the rate or amount of any money purchase benefits that may become payable will be calculated.

1(2) There must be shown the number of directors (if any) to whom retirement benefits are accruing in respect of qualifying services–

(a) under money purchase schemes, and
(b) under defined benefit schemes.

Compensation to directors for loss of office

2(1) There must be shown the aggregate amount of any payments made to directors or past directors for loss of office.

2(2) "Payment for loss of office" has the same meaning as in section 215 of the 2006 Act.

Sums paid to third parties in respect of directors' services

3(1) There must be shown the aggregate amount of any consideration paid to or receivable by third parties for making available the services of any person–

(a) as a director of the company, or
(b) while director of the company–

    (i) as director of any of its subsidiary undertakings, or
    (ii) otherwise in connection with the management of the affairs of the company or any of its subsidiary undertakings.

3(2) In sub-paragraph (1)–

(a) the reference to consideration includes benefits otherwise than in cash, and
(b) in relation to such consideration the reference to its amount is to the estimated money value of the benefit.

The nature of any such consideration must be disclosed.

3(3) For the purposes of this paragraph a "third party" means a person other than–

(a) the director himself or a person connected with him or body corporate controlled by him, or
(b) the company or any of its subsidiary undertakings.

PART 2 – SUPPLEMENTARY PROVISIONS

General nature of obligations

4(1) This Schedule requires information to be given only so far as it is contained in the company's books and papers or the company has the right to obtain it from the persons concerned.

4(2) For the purposes of this Schedule any information is treated as shown if it is capable of being readily ascertained from other information which is shown.

Provisions as to amounts to be shown

5(1) The following provisions apply with respect to the amounts to be shown under this Schedule.

5(2) The amount in each case includes all relevant sums, whether paid by or receivable from the company, any of the company's subsidiary undertakings or any other person.

5(3) References to amounts paid to or receivable by a person include amounts paid to or receivable by a person connected with him or a body corporate controlled by him (but not so as to require an amount to be counted twice).

5(4) Except as otherwise provided, the amounts to be shown for any financial year are–

(a) the sums receivable in respect of that year (whenever paid) or,
(b) in the case of sums not receivable in respect of a period, the sums paid during that year.

5(5) Sums paid by way of expenses allowance that are charged to United Kingdom income tax after the end of the relevant financial year must be shown in a note to the first accounts in which it is practicable to show them and must be distinguished from the amounts to be shown apart from this provision.

5(6) Where it is necessary to do so for the purpose of making any distinction required in complying with this Schedule, the directors may apportion payments between the matters in respect of which they have been paid or are receivable in such manner as they think appropriate.

Exclusion of sums liable to be accounted for to company etc.

6(1) The amounts to be shown under this Schedule do not include any sums that are to be accounted for–

  (a) to the company or any of its subsidiary undertakings, or
  (b) by virtue of sections 219 and 222(3) of the 2006 Act (payments in connection with share transfers: duty to account), to persons who sold their shares as a result of the offer made.

6(2) Where–

  (a) any such sums are not shown in a note to the accounts for the relevant financial year on the ground that the person receiving them is liable to account for them, and
  (b) the liability is afterwards wholly or partly released or is not enforced within a period of two years, those sums, to the extent to which the liability is released or not enforced, must be shown in a note to the first accounts in which it is practicable to show them and must be distinguished from the amounts to be shown apart from this provision.

Meaning of "remuneration"

7(1) In this Schedule "**remuneration**" of a director includes–

  (a) salary, fees and bonuses, sums paid by way of expenses allowance (so far as they are chargeable to United Kingdom income tax), and
  (b) subject to sub-paragraph (2), the estimated money value of any other benefits received by him otherwise than in cash.

7(2) The expression does not include–

  (a) the value of any share options granted to a director or the amount of any gains made on the exercise of any such options,
  (b) any company contributions paid, or treated as paid, in respect of him under any pension scheme or any benefits to which he is entitled under any such scheme, or
  (c) any money or other assets paid to or received or receivable by him under any long term incentive scheme.

Meaning of "long term incentive scheme"

8(1) In this Schedule "**long term incentive scheme**" means an agreement or arrangement–

  (a) under which money or other assets may become receivable by a director, and
  (b) which includes one or more qualifying conditions with respect to service or performance which cannot be fulfilled within a single financial year.

8(2) For this purpose the following must be disregarded–

  (a) bonuses the amount of which falls to be determined by reference to service or performance within a single financial year;
  (b) compensation for loss of office, payments for breach of contract and other termination payments; and
  (c) retirement benefits.

Meaning of "shares" and "share option" and related expressions

9 In this Schedule–

(a) "**shares**" means shares (whether allotted or not) in the company, or any undertaking which is a group undertaking in relation to the company, and includes a share warrant as defined by section 779(1) of the 2006 Act; and

(b) "**share option**" means a right to acquire shares.

Meaning of "pension scheme" and related expressions

10(1) In this Schedule–

"pension scheme" means a retirement benefits scheme as defined by section 611 of the Income and Corporation Taxes Act 1988; and "retirement benefits" has the meaning given by section 612(1) of that Act.

10(2) In this Schedule, "**company contributions**", in relation to a pension scheme and a director, means any payments (including insurance premiums) made, or treated as made, to the scheme in respect of the director by a person other than the director.

10(3) In this Schedule, in relation to a director–

"**defined benefits**" means retirement benefits payable under a pension scheme that are not money purchase benefits;
"**defined benefit scheme**" means a pension scheme that is not a money purchase scheme;
"money purchase benefits" means retirement benefits payable under a pension scheme the rate or amount of which is calculated by reference to payments made, or treated as made, by the director or by any other person in respect of the director and which are not average salary benefits; and "money purchase scheme" means a pension scheme under which all of the benefits that may become payable to or in respect of the director are money purchase benefits.

10(4) Where a pension scheme provides for any benefits that may become payable to or in respect of any director to be whichever are the greater of–

(a) money purchase benefits as determined by or under the scheme; and

(b) defined benefits as so determined, the company may assume for the purposes of this paragraph that those benefits will be money purchase benefits, or defined benefits, according to whichever appears more likely at the end of the financial year.

10(5) For the purpose of determining whether a pension scheme is a money purchase or defined benefit scheme, any death in service benefits provided for by the scheme are to be disregarded.

References to subsidiary undertakings

11(1) Any reference in this Schedule to a subsidiary undertaking of the company, in relation to a person who is or was, while a director of the company, a director also, by virtue of the company's nomination (direct or indirect) of any other undertaking, includes that undertaking, whether or not it is or was in fact a subsidiary undertaking of the company.

11(2) Any reference to a subsidiary undertaking of the company–

(a) for the purposes of paragraph 1 (remuneration etc.) is to an undertaking which is a subsidiary undertaking at the time the services were rendered, and

(b) for the purposes of paragraph 2 (compensation for loss of office) is to a subsidiary undertaking immediately before the loss of office as director.

Other minor definitions

12(1) In this Schedule–

"**net value**", in relation to any assets received or receivable by a director, means value after deducting any money paid or other value given by the director in respect of those assets; "**qualifying services**", in relation to any person, means his services as a director of the company, and his services while director of the company–

(a) as director of any of its subsidiary undertakings; or
(b) otherwise in connection with the management of the affairs of the company or any of its subsidiary undertakings.

12(2) For the purposes of this Schedule, remuneration paid or receivable or share options granted in respect of a person's accepting office as a director are treated as emoluments paid or receivable or share options granted in respect of his services as a director.

SCHEDULE 4   Regulation 6(1)

COMPANIES ACT ABBREVIATED ACCOUNTS FOR DELIVERY TO REGISTRAR OF COMPANIES

History – Sch. 4 omitted by SI 2015/980, reg. 21, with effect in relation to–

(a) financial years beginning on or after 1 January 2016, and
(b) a financial year of a company beginning on or after 1 January 2015, but before 1 January 2016, if the directors of the company so decide.

Former Sch. 4 read as follows:

SCHEDULE 4   Regulation 6(1)

COMPANIES ACT ABBREVIATED ACCOUNTS FOR DELIVERY TO REGISTRAR OF COMPANIES

PART 1 – THE REQUIRED BALANCE SHEET FORMATS

1(1) A company may deliver to the registrar a copy of the balance sheet showing the items listed in either of the balance sheet formats set out below, in the order and under the headings and sub-headings given in the format adopted, but in other respects corresponding to the full balance sheet.

1(2) The copy balance sheet must contain in a prominent position a statement that it has been prepared in accordance with the provisions applicable to companies subject to the small companies regime.

Balance sheet formats – Format 1

A. Called up share capital not paid

B. Fixed assets

    I. Intangible assets
    II. Tangible assets
    III. Investments

C. Current assets

    I.   Stocks
    II.   Debtors *(1)*
    III. Investments
    IV. Cash at bank and in hand

D. Prepayments and accrued income

E. Creditors: amounts falling due within one year

F. Net current assets (liabilities)

G. Total assets less current liabilities

H. Creditors: amounts falling due after more than one year

I. Provisions for liabilities

J. Accruals and deferred income

K. Capital and reserves

    I.   Called up share capital
    II.   Share premium account
    III. Revaluation reserve
    IV. Other reserves
    V.   Profit and loss account

Balance sheet formats – Format 2

ASSETS

A. Called up share capital not paid

B. Fixed assets

    I.   Intangible assets
    II.   Tangible assets
    III. Investments

C. Current assets

    I.   Stocks
    II.   Debtors *(1)*
    III. Investments
    IV. Cash at bank and in hand

D. Prepayments and accrued income

LIABILITIES

A. Capital and reserves

    I.   Called up share capital
    II.   Share premium account
    III. Revaluation reserve
    IV. Other reserves
    V.   Profit and loss account

B.   Provisions for liabilities

C.   Creditors *(2)*

D.   Accruals and deferred income

Notes on the balance sheet formats

(1) *Debtors*

(Formats 1 and 2, items C.II.)
The aggregate amount of debtors falling due after more than one year must be shown separately, unless it is disclosed in the notes to the accounts.

(2) *Creditors*

(Format 2, Liabilities item C.)
The aggregate amount of creditors falling due within one year and of creditors falling due after more than one year must be shown separately, unless it is disclosed in the notes to the accounts.

PART 2 – NOTES TO THE ACCOUNTS

Preliminary

2 Any information required in the case of any company by the following provisions of this Part of this Schedule must (if not given in the company's accounts) be given by way of a note to those accounts.

Disclosure of accounting policies

3 The accounting policies adopted by the company in determining the amounts to be included in respect of items shown in the balance sheet and in determining the profit or loss of the company must be stated (including such policies with respect to the depreciation and diminution in value of assets).

Information supplementing the balance sheet

Share capital and debentures

4(1) Where shares of more than one class have been allotted, the number and aggregate nominal value of shares of each class allotted must be given.

4(2) In the case of any part of the allotted share capital that consists of redeemable shares, the following information must be given–

(a)   the earliest and latest dates on which the company has power to redeem those shares,
(b)   whether those shares must be redeemed in any event or are liable to be redeemed at the option of the company or of the shareholder, and
(c)   whether any (and, if so, what) premium is payable on redemption.

5 If the company has allotted any shares during the financial year, the following information must be given–

(a)   the classes of shares allotted, and
(b)   as respects each class of shares, the number allotted, their aggregate nominal value, and the consideration received by the company for the allotment.

Fixed assets

6(1) In respect of each item to which a letter or Roman number is assigned under the general item "fixed assets" in the company's balance sheet the following information must be given–

- (a) the appropriate amounts in respect of that item as at the date of the beginning of the financial year and as at the balance sheet date respectively,
- (b) the effect on any amount shown in the balance sheet in respect of that item of–

    - (i) any revision of the amount in respect of any assets included under that item made during that year on any basis mentioned in paragraph 32 of Schedule 1 to these Regulations,
    - (ii) acquisitions during that year of any assets,
    - (iii) disposals during that year of any assets, and
    - (iv) any transfers of assets of the company to and from that item during that year.

6(2) The reference in sub-paragraph (1)(a) to the appropriate amounts in respect of any item as at any date there mentioned is a reference to amounts representing the aggregate amounts determined, as at that date, in respect of assets falling to be included under that item on either of the following bases, that is to say–

- (a) on the basis of purchase price or production cost (determined in accordance with paragraphs 27 and 28 of Schedule 1 to these Regulations), or
- (b) on any basis mentioned in paragraph 32 of that Schedule, (leaving out of account in either case any provisions for depreciation or diminution in value).

6(3) In respect of each item within sub-paragraph (1) there must also be stated–

- (a) the cumulative amount of provisions for depreciation or diminution in value of assets included under that item as at each date mentioned in sub-paragraph (1)(a),
- (b) the amount of any such provisions made in respect of the financial year,
- (c) the amount of any adjustments made in respect of any such provisions during that year in consequence of the disposal of any assets, and
- (d) the amount of any other adjustments made in respect of any such provisions during that year.

Financial fixed assets

7(1) This paragraph applies if–

- (a) the company has financial fixed assets that could be included at fair value by virtue of paragraph 36 of Schedule 1 to these Regulations,
- (b) the amount at which those items are included under any item in the company's accounts is in excess of their fair value, and
- (c) the company has not made provision for diminution in value of those assets in accordance with paragraph 19(1) of that Schedule.

7(2) There must be stated–

- (a) the amount at which either the individual assets or appropriate groupings of those individual assets are included in the company's accounts,
- (b) the fair value of those assets or groupings, and
- (c) the reasons for not making a provision for diminution in value of those assets, including the nature of the evidence that provides the basis for the belief that the amount at which they are stated in the accounts will be recovered.

Details of indebtedness

8(1) For the aggregate of all items shown under "creditors" in the company's balance sheet there must be stated the aggregate of the following amounts–

    (a) the amount of any debts included under "creditors" which are payable or repayable otherwise than by instalments and fall due for payment or repayment after the end of the period of five years beginning with the day next following the end of the financial year, and

    (b) in the case of any debts so included which are payable or repayable by instalments, the amount of any instalments which fall due for payment after the end of that period.

8(2) In respect of each item shown under "creditors" in the company's balance sheet there must be stated the aggregate amount of any debts included under that item in respect of which any security has been given by the company.

Sums denominated in foreign currencies

9 Where sums originally denominated in foreign currencies have been brought into account under any items shown in the balance sheet or profit and loss account, the basis on which those sums have been translated into sterling (or the currency in which the accounts are drawn up) must be stated.

DORMANT COMPANIES ACTING AS AGENTS

10 Where the directors of a company take advantage of the exemption conferred by section 480 of the 2006 Act (dormant companies: exemption from audit), and the company has during the financial year in question acted as an agent for any person, the fact that it has so acted must be stated.

SCHEDULE 5

Regulation 7

MATTERS TO BE DEALT WITH IN DIRECTORS' REPORT

Introduction

1 In addition to the information required by section 416 of the 2006 Act, the directors' report must contain the following information.

Political donations and expenditure

2(1) If–

    (a) the company (not being the wholly-owned subsidiary of a company incorporated in the United Kingdom) has in the financial year–

        (i)   made any political donation to any political party or other political organisation,
        (ii) made any political donation to any independent election candidate, or
        (iii) incurred any political expenditure, and

    (b) the amount of the donation or expenditure, or (as the case may be) the aggregate amount of all donations and expenditure falling within paragraph (a), exceeded £2000, the directors' report for the year must contain the following particulars.

2(2) Those particulars are–

(a) as respects donations falling within sub-paragraph (1)(a)(i) or (ii) –

  (i) the name of each political party, other political organisation or independent election candidate to whom any such donation has been made, and

  (ii) the total amount given to that party, organisation or candidate by way of such donations in the financial year; and

(b) as respects expenditure falling within sub-paragraph (1)(a)(iii), the total amount incurred by way of such expenditure in the financial year.

2(3) If–

(a) at the end of the financial year the company has subsidiaries which have, in that year, made any donations or incurred any such expenditure as is mentioned in sub-paragraph (1)(a), and

(b) it is not itself the wholly-owned subsidiary of a company incorporated in the United Kingdom, the directors' report for the year is not, by virtue of sub-paragraph (1), required to contain the particulars specified in sub-paragraph (2).

But, if the total amount of any such donations or expenditure (or both) made or incurred in that year by the company and the subsidiaries between them exceeds £2000, the directors' report for the year must contain those particulars in relation to each body by whom any such donation or expenditure has been made or incurred.

2(4) Any expression used in this paragraph which is also used in Part 14 of the 2006 Act (control of political donations and expenditure) has the same meaning as in that Part.

3(1) If the company (not being the wholly-owned subsidiary of a company incorporated in the United Kingdom) has in the financial year made any contribution to a non-EU political party, the directors' report for the year must contain–

(a) a statement of the amount of the contribution, or

(b) (if it has made two or more such contributions in the year) a statement of the total amount of the contributions.

3(2) If–

(a) at the end of the financial year the company has subsidiaries which have, in that year, made any such contributions as are mentioned in sub-paragraph (1), and

(b) it is not itself the wholly-owned subsidiary of a company incorporated in the United Kingdom, the directors' report for the year is not, by virtue of sub-paragraph (1), required to contain any such statement as is there mentioned, but it must instead contain a statement of the total amount of the contributions made in the year by the company and the subsidiaries between them.

3(3) In this paragraph, "contribution", in relation to an organisation, means–

(a) any gift of money to the organisation (whether made directly or indirectly);

(b) any subscription or other fee paid for affiliation to, or membership of, the organisation; or

(c) any money spent (otherwise than by the organisation or a person acting on its behalf) in paying any expenses incurred directly or indirectly by the organisation.

3(4) In this paragraph, "non-EU political party" means any political party which carries on, or proposes to carry on, its activities wholly outside the member States.

Charitable donations

4 Repealed.

History – Para. 4 repealed by SI 2013/1970, reg. 8(1) and (2), with effect from 1 October 2013 in respect of financial years ending on or after 30 September 2013. Prior to repeal, para. 4 read as follows:

4(1) If–

   (a) the company (not being the wholly-owned subsidiary of a company incorporated in the United Kingdom) has in the financial year given money for charitable purposes, and

   (b) the money given exceeded £2000 in amount, the directors' report for the year must contain, in the case of each of the purposes for which money has been given, a statement of the amount of money given for that purpose.

4(2) If–

   (a) at the end of the financial year the company has subsidiaries which have, in that year, given money for charitable purposes, and

   (b) it is not itself the wholly owned subsidiary of a company incorporated in the United Kingdom, sub-paragraph (1) does not apply to the company. But, if the amount given in that year for charitable purposes by the company and the subsidiaries between them exceeds £2000, the directors' report for the year must contain, in the case of each of the purposes for which money has been given by the company and the subsidiaries between them, a statement of the amount of money given for that purpose.

4(3) Money given for charitable purposes to a person who, when it was given, was ordinarily resident outside the United Kingdom is to be left out of account for the purposes of this paragraph.

4(4) For the purposes of this paragraph, "charitable purposes" means purposes which are exclusively charitable, and as respects Scotland a purpose is charitable if it is listed in section 7(2) of the Charities and Trustee Investment (Scotland) Act 2005.

Disclosure concerning employment etc. of disabled persons

5(1) This paragraph applies to the directors' report where the average number of persons employed by the company in each week during the financial year exceeded 250.

5(2) That average number is the quotient derived by dividing, by the number of weeks in the financial year, the number derived by ascertaining, in relation to each of those weeks, the number of persons who, under contracts of service, were employed in the week (whether throughout it or not) by the company, and adding up the numbers ascertained.

5(3) The directors' report must in that case contain a statement describing such policy as the company has applied during the financial year–

   (a) for giving full and fair consideration to applications for employment by the company made by disabled persons, having regard to their particular aptitudes and abilities,

   (b) for continuing the employment of, and for arranging appropriate training for, employees of the company who have become disabled persons during the period when they were employed by the company, and

   (c) otherwise for the training, career development and promotion of disabled persons employed by the company.

5(4) In this paragraph–

(a) "**employment**" means employment other than employment to work wholly or mainly outside the United Kingdom, and "employed" and "employee" are to be construed accordingly; and

(b) "**disabled person**" means the same as in the *Disability Discrimination Act* 1995.

Disclosure required by company acquiring its own shares etc.

6 Repealed.

History – Para. 6 repealed by SI 2013/1970, reg. 8(1) and (3), with effect from 1 October 2013 in respect of financial years ending on or after 30 September 2013. Prior to repeal, para. 6 read as follows:

6(1) This paragraph applies where shares in a company–

(a) are purchased by the company or are acquired by it by forfeiture or surrender in lieu of forfeiture, or in pursuance of any of the following provisions (acquisition of own shares by company limited by shares)–

(i) section 143(3) of the Companies Act 1985,
(ii) Article 153(3) of the Companies (Northern Ireland) Order 1986, or
(iii) section 659 of the 2006 Act, or

(b) are acquired by another person in circumstances where paragraph (c) or (d) of any of the following provisions applies (acquisition by company's nominee, or by another with company financial assistance, the company having a beneficial interest)–

(i) section 146(1) of the Companies Act 1985,
(ii) Article 156(1) of the Companies (Northern Ireland) Order 1986, or
(iii) section 662(1) of the 2006 Act, or

(c) are made subject to a lien or other charge taken (whether expressly or otherwise) by the company and permitted by any of the following provisions (exceptions from general rule against a company having a lien or charge on its own shares)–

(i) section 150(2) or (4) of the Companies Act 1985,
(ii) Article 160(2) or (4) of the Companies (Northern Ireland) Order 1986, or
(iii) section 670(2) or (4) of the 2006 Act.

6(2) The directors' report for a financial year must state–

(a) the number and nominal value of the shares so purchased, the aggregate amount of the consideration paid by the company for such shares and the reasons for their purchase;

(b) the number and nominal value of the shares so acquired by the company, acquired by another person in such circumstances and so charged respectively during the financial year;

(c) the maximum number and nominal value of shares which, having been so acquired by the company, acquired by another person in such circumstances or so charged (whether or not during that year) are held at any time by the company or that other person during that year;

(d) the number and nominal value of the shares so acquired by the company, acquired by another person in such circumstances or so charged (whether or not during that year) which are disposed of by the company or that other person or cancelled by the company during that year;

(e) where the number and nominal value of the shares of any particular description are stated in pursuance of any of the preceding sub-paragraphs, the percentage of the called-up share capital which shares of that description represent;

(f) where any of the shares have been so charged the amount of the charge in each case; and

(g) where any of the shares have been disposed of by the company or the person who acquired them in such circumstances for money or money's worth the amount or value of the consideration in each case.

SCHEDULE 6   Regulations 8(1) and 10

GROUP ACCOUNTS

PART 1 – FORM AND CONTENT OF COMPANIES ACT GROUP ACCOUNTS

General rules

1(1) Subject to the following provisions of this Schedule, group accounts must comply so far as practicable with the provisions of Schedule 1 to these Regulations (Companies Act individual accounts) as if the undertakings included in the consolidation ("the group") were a single company.

1(1A) Paragraph 1A of Schedule 1 to these Regulations does not apply to group accounts.

1(2) For item B.III in each balance sheet format set out in Section B of Part 1 of that Schedule substitute–

B.

   III. Investments

      1. Shares in group undertakings
      2. Interests in associated undertakings
      3. Other participating interests
      4. Loans to group undertakings and undertakings in which a participating interest is held
      5. Other investments other than loans
      6. Others.

1(3) In the profit and loss account formats in Section B of Part 1 of that Schedule replace the items headed "Income from participating interests", that is–

(a) in Format 1, item 8, and
(b) in Format 2, item 10,
(c) omitted,
(d) omitted.

History – In para. 1(1), the words "the following provisions of this Schedule" substituted for the words "sub-paragraphs (1) and (2)" by SI 2015/980, reg. 22(2), with effect in relation to–

(a) financial years beginning on or after 1 January 2016, and
(b) a financial year of a company beginning on or after 1 January 2015, but before 1 January 2016, if the directors of the company so decide.

Para. 1(1A) inserted by SI 2015/980, reg. 22(3), with effect in relation to–

(a) financial years beginning on or after 1 January 2016, and

(b) a financial year of a company beginning on or after 1 January 2015, but before 1 January 2016, if the directors of the company so decide.

In para. 1(2), "Section B of Part 1 of" inserted and in para. 1(3), "in Section B of Part 1 of that Schedule" inserted by SI 2013/3008, reg. 12(a), with effect from 1 December 2013 in respect of (a) financial years ending on or after 30 September 2013; and (b) companies, which deliver the accounts required by s. 444 to the registrar on or after 1 December 2013.

Para. 1(3)(c) and (d) omitted; and the word "and" in para. (a) inserted by SI 2015/980, reg. 22(4), with effect in relation to–

(a) financial years beginning on or after 1 January 2016, and
(b) a financial year of a company beginning on or after 1 January 2015, but before 1 January 2016, if the directors of the company so decide.

2(1) The consolidated balance sheet and profit and loss account must incorporate in full the information contained in the individual accounts of the undertakings included in the consolidation, subject to the adjustments authorised or required by the following provisions of this Schedule and to such other adjustments (if any) as may be appropriate in accordance with generally accepted accounting principles or practice.

2(1A) Group accounts must be drawn up as at the same date as the accounts of the parent company.

2(2) If the financial year of a subsidiary undertaking included in the consolidation does not end with that of the parent company, the group accounts must be made up–

(a) from the accounts of the subsidiary undertaking for its financial year last ending before the end of the parent company's financial year, provided that year ended no more than three months before that of the parent company, or
(b) from interim accounts prepared by the subsidiary undertaking as at the end of the parent company's financial year.

History – Para. 2(1A) inserted by SI 2015/980, reg. 22(5), with effect in relation to–

(a) financial years beginning on or after 1 January 2016, and
(b) a financial year of a company beginning on or after 1 January 2015, but before 1 January 2016, if the directors of the company so decide.

3(1) Where assets and liabilities to be included in the group accounts have been valued or otherwise determined by undertakings according to accounting rules differing from those used for the group accounts, the values or amounts must be adjusted so as to accord with the rules used for the group accounts.

3(2) If it appears to the directors of the parent company that there are special reasons for departing from sub-paragraph (1) they may do so, but particulars of any such departure, the reasons for it and its effect must be given in a note to the accounts.

3(3) The adjustments referred to in this paragraph need not be made if they are not material for the purpose of giving a true and fair view.

4 Any differences of accounting rules as between a parent company's individual accounts for a financial year and its group accounts must be disclosed in a note to the latter accounts and the reasons for the difference given.

5 Amounts that in the particular context of any provision of this Schedule are not material may be disregarded for the purposes of that provision.

Elimination of group transactions

6(1) Debts and claims between undertakings included in the consolidation, and income and expenditure relating to transactions between such undertakings, must be eliminated in preparing the group accounts.

6(2) Where profits and losses resulting from transactions between undertakings included in the consolidation are included in the book value of assets, they must be eliminated in preparing the group accounts.

6(3) The elimination required by sub-paragraph (2) may be effected in proportion to the group's interest in the shares of the undertakings.

6(4) Sub-paragraphs (1) and (2) need not be complied with if the amounts concerned are not material for the purpose of giving a true and fair view.

Acquisition and merger accounting

7(1) The following provisions apply where an undertaking becomes a subsidiary undertaking of the parent company.

7(2) That event is referred to in those provisions as an "acquisition", and references to the "undertaking acquired" are to be construed accordingly.

8 An acquisition must be accounted for by the acquisition method of accounting unless the conditions for accounting for it as a merger are met and the merger method of accounting is adopted.

9(1) The acquisition method of accounting is as follows.

9(2) The identifiable assets and liabilities of the undertaking acquired must be included in the consolidated balance sheet at their fair values as at the date of acquisition.

9(3) The income and expenditure of the undertaking acquired must be brought into the group accounts only as from the date of the acquisition.

9(4) There must be set off against the acquisition cost of the interest in the shares of the undertaking held by the parent company and its subsidiary undertakings the interest of the parent company and its subsidiary undertakings in the adjusted capital and reserves of the undertaking acquired.

9(5) The resulting amount if positive must be treated as goodwill, and if negative as a negative consolidation difference.

9(6) Negative goodwill may be transferred to the consolidated profit and loss account where such a treatment is in accordance with the principles and rules of Part 2 of Schedule 1 to these Regulations.

History – Para. 9(6) inserted by SI 2015/980, reg. 22(6), with effect in relation to–

(a) financial years beginning on or after 1 January 2016, and
(b) a financial year of a company beginning on or after 1 January 2015, but before 1 January 2016, if the directors of the company so decide.

10 The conditions for accounting for an acquisition as a merger are–

(a) that the undertaking whose shares are acquired is ultimately controlled by the same party both before and after the acquisition,

(b) that the control referred to in paragraph (a) is not transitory, and

(c) that adoption of the merger method accords with generally accepted accounting principles or practice.

History – Para. 10 substituted by SI 2015/980, reg. 22(7), with effect in relation to–

(a) financial years beginning on or after 1 January 2016, and

(b) a financial year of a company beginning on or after 1 January 2015, but before 1 January 2016, if the directors of the company so decide.

Former para. 10 read as follows:

10(1) The conditions for accounting for an acquisition as a merger are–

(a) that at least 90% of the nominal value of the relevant shares in the undertaking acquired (excluding any shares in the undertaking held as treasury shares) is held by or on behalf of the parent company and its subsidiary undertakings,

(b) that the proportion referred to in paragraph

(a) was attained pursuant to an arrangement providing for the issue of equity shares by the parent company or one or more of its subsidiary undertakings,

(c) that the fair value of any consideration other than the issue of equity shares given pursuant to the arrangement by the parent company and its subsidiary undertakings did not exceed 10% of the nominal value of the equity shares issued, and

(d) that adoption of the merger method of accounting accords with generally accepted accounting principles or practice.

10(2) The reference in sub-paragraph (1)(a) to the "relevant shares" in an undertaking acquired is to those carrying unrestricted rights to participate both in distributions and in the assets of the undertaking upon liquidation.

11(1) The merger method of accounting is as follows.

11(2) The assets and liabilities of the undertaking acquired must be brought into the group accounts at the figures at which they stand in the undertaking's accounts, subject to any adjustment authorised or required by this Schedule.

11(3) The income and expenditure of the undertaking acquired must be included in the group accounts for the entire financial year, including the period before the acquisition.

11(4) The group accounts must show corresponding amounts relating to the previous financial year as if the undertaking acquired had been included in the consolidation throughout that year.

11(5) There must be set off against the aggregate of–

(a) the appropriate amount in respect of qualifying shares issued by the parent company or its subsidiary undertakings in consideration for the acquisition of shares in the undertaking acquired, and

(b) the fair value of any other consideration for the acquisition of shares in the undertaking acquired, determined as at the date when those shares were acquired, the nominal value of the issued share capital of the undertaking acquired held by the parent company and its subsidiary undertakings.

11(6) The resulting amount must be shown as an adjustment to the consolidated reserves.

11(7) In sub-paragraph (5)(a) "qualifying shares" means–

(a) shares in relation to which any of the following provisions applies (merger relief), and in respect of which the appropriate amount is the nominal value–

(i)   section 131 of the Companies Act 1985,
(ii) Article 141 of the Companies (Northern Ireland) Order 1986, or
(iii) section 612 of the 2006 Act, or

(b)   shares in relation to which any of the following provisions applies (group reconstruction relief), and in respect of which the appropriate amount is the nominal value together with any minimum premium value within the meaning of that section–

(i)   section 132 of the Companies Act 1985,
(ii) Article 142 of the Companies (Northern Ireland) Order 1986, or
(iii) section 611 of the 2006 Act.

12(1) Where a group is acquired, paragraphs 9 to 11 apply with the following adaptations.

12(2) References to shares of the undertaking acquired are to be construed as references to shares of the parent undertaking of the group.

12(3) Other references to the undertaking acquired are to be construed as references to the group; and references to the assets and liabilities, income and expenditure and capital and reserves of the undertaking acquired must be construed as references to the assets and liabilities, income and expenditure and capital and reserves of the group after making the set-offs and other adjustments required by this Schedule in the case of group accounts.

13(1) The following information with respect to acquisitions taking place in the financial year must be given in a note to the accounts.

13(2) There must be stated–

(a)   the name of the undertaking acquired or, where a group was acquired, the name of the parent undertaking of that group, and
(b)   whether the acquisition has been accounted for by the acquisition or the merger method of accounting; and in relation to an acquisition which significantly affects the figures shown in the group accounts, the following further information must be given.

13(3) The composition and fair value of the consideration for the acquisition given by the parent company and its subsidiary undertakings must be stated.

13(4) Where the acquisition method of accounting has been adopted, the book values immediately prior to the acquisition, and the fair values at the date of acquisition, of each class of assets and liabilities of the undertaking or group acquired must be stated in tabular form, including a statement of the amount of any goodwill or negative consolidation difference arising on the acquisition, together with an explanation of any significant adjustments made.

13(5) In ascertaining for the purposes of sub-paragraph (4) the profit or loss of a group, the book values and fair values of assets and liabilities of a group or the amount of the assets and liabilities of a group, the set-offs and other adjustments required by this Schedule in the case of group accounts must be made.

14(1) There must also be stated in a note to the accounts the cumulative amount of goodwill resulting from acquisitions in that and earlier financial years which has been written off otherwise than in the consolidated profit and loss account for that or any earlier financial year.

14(2) That figure must be shown net of any goodwill attributable to subsidiary undertakings or businesses disposed of prior to the balance sheet date.

15 Where during the financial year there has been a disposal of an undertaking or group which significantly affects the figure shown in the group accounts, there must be stated in a note to the accounts–

  (a) the name of that undertaking or, as the case may be, of the parent undertaking of that group, and
  (b) the extent to which the profit or loss shown in the group accounts is attributable to profit or loss of that undertaking or group.

16 The information required by paragraph 13, 14 or 15 need not be disclosed with respect to an undertaking which–

  (a) is established under the law of a country outside the United Kingdom, or
  (b) carries on business outside the United Kingdom, if in the opinion of the directors of the parent company the disclosure would be seriously prejudicial to the business of that undertaking or to the business of the parent company or any of its subsidiary undertakings and the Secretary of State agrees that the information should not be disclosed.

16A Where an acquisition has taken place in the financial year and the merger method of accounting has been adopted, the notes to the accounts must also disclose–

  (a) the address of the registered office of the undertaking acquired (whether in or outside the United Kingdom),
  (b) the name of the party referred to in paragraph 10(a),
  (c) the address of the registered office of that party (whether in or outside the United Kingdom), and
  (d) the information referred to in paragraph 11(6).

History – Para. 16A inserted by SI 2015/980, reg. 22(8), with effect in relation to–

  (a) financial years beginning on or after 1 January 2016, and
  (b) a financial year of a company beginning on or after 1 January 2015, but before 1 January 2016, if the directors of the company so decide.

Non-controlling interests

  17(1) The formats set out in Section B of Part 1 of Schedule 1 to these Regulations have effect in relation to group accounts with the following additions.

  17(2) In the Balance Sheet Formats there must be shown, as a separate item and under the heading "non-controlling interests", the amount of capital and reserves attributable to shares in subsidiary undertakings included in the consolidation held by or on behalf of persons other than the parent company and its subsidiary undertakings.

  17(3) In the Profit and Loss Account Formats there must be shown, as a separate item and under the heading "non-controlling interests", the amount of any profit or loss attributable to shares in subsidiary undertakings included in the consolidation held by or on behalf of persons other than the parent company and its subsidiary undertakings.

  17(4) For the purposes of paragraph (4) of Schedule 1 (power to adapt or combine items)–

  (a) the additional item required by sub-paragraph (2) above is treated as one to which a letter is assigned, and
  (b) the additional item required by sub-paragraph (3) above is treated as one to which an Arabic number is assigned.

History – Para. 17 and the heading preceding it substituted by SI 2015/980, reg. 22(9), with effect in relation to–

  (a) financial years beginning on or after 1 January 2016, and
  (b) a financial year of a company beginning on or after 1 January 2015, but before 1 January 2016, if the directors of the company so decide.

Former para. 17 read as follows:

Minority interests

17(1) The formats set out in Section B of Part 1 of Schedule 1 to these Regulations have effect in relation to group accounts with the following additions.

17(2) In the Balance Sheet Formats there must be shown, as a separate item and under an appropriate heading, the amount of capital and reserves attributable to shares in subsidiary undertakings included in the consolidation held by or on behalf of persons other than the parent company and its subsidiary undertakings.

17(3) In the Profit and Loss Account Formats there must be shown, as a separate item and under an appropriate heading–

(a) the amount of any profit or loss on ordinary activities, and
(b) the amount of any profit or loss on extraordinary activities, attributable to shares in subsidiary undertakings included in the consolidation held by or on behalf of persons other than the parent company and its subsidiary undertakings.

17(4) For the purposes of paragraph 4 of Schedule 1 (power to adapt or combine items)–

(a) the additional item required by sub-paragraph (2) is treated as one to which a letter is assigned, and
(b) the additional items required by sub-paragraph (3)(a) and
(c) are treated as ones to which an Arabic number is assigned.

History – In para. 17(1), "Section B of Part 1 of" inserted by SI 2013/3008, reg. 12(b), with effect from 1 December 2013 in respect of (a) financial years ending on or after 30 September 2013; and (b) companies, which deliver the accounts required by section 444 to the registrar on or after 1 December 2013.

Joint ventures

18(1) Where an undertaking included in the consolidation manages another undertaking jointly with one or more undertakings not included in the consolidation, that other undertaking ("the joint venture") may, if it is not–

(a) a body corporate, or
(b) a subsidiary undertaking of the parent company, be dealt with in the group accounts by the method of proportional consolidation.

18(2) The provisions of this Schedule relating to the preparation of consolidated accounts and sections 402 and 405 of the 2006 Act apply, with any necessary modifications, to proportional consolidation under this paragraph.

18(3) In addition to the disclosure of the average number of employees employed during the financial year (see section 411(7) of the 2006 Act), there must be a separate disclosure in the notes to the accounts of the average number of employees employed by undertakings that are proportionately consolidated.

History – In para. 18(2), the words "and sections 402 and 405 of the 2006 Act" inserted by SI 2015/980, reg. 22(10), with effect in relation to–

(a) financial years beginning on or after 1 January 2016, and
(b) a financial year of a company beginning on or after 1 January 2015, but before 1 January 2016, if the directors of the company so decide.

Para. 18(3) inserted by SI 2015/980, reg. 22(11), with effect in relation to–

(a) financial years beginning on or after 1 January 2016, and
(b) a financial year of a company beginning on or after 1 January 2015, but before 1 January 2016, if the directors of the company so decide.

Associated undertakings

19(1) An "associated undertaking" means an undertaking in which an undertaking included in the consolidation has a participating interest and over whose operating and financial policy it exercises a significant influence, and which is not–

(a) a subsidiary undertaking of the parent company, or
(b) a joint venture dealt with in accordance with paragraph 18.

19(2) Where an undertaking holds 20% or more of the voting rights in another undertaking, it is presumed to exercise such an influence over it unless the contrary is shown.

19(3) The voting rights in an undertaking means the rights conferred on shareholders in respect of their shares or, in the case of an undertaking not having a share capital, on members, to vote at general meetings of the undertaking on all, or substantially all, matters.

19(4) The provisions of paragraphs 5 to 11 of Schedule 7 to the 2006 Act (parent and subsidiary undertakings: rights to be taken into account and attribution of rights) apply in determining for the purposes of this paragraph whether an undertaking holds 20% or more of the voting rights in another undertaking.

20(1) The interest of an undertaking in an associated undertaking, and the amount of profit or loss attributable to such an interest, must be shown by the equity method of accounting (including dealing with any goodwill arising in accordance with paragraphs 17 to 20 and 22 of Schedule 1 to these Regulations).

20(2) Where the associated undertaking is itself a parent undertaking, the net assets and profits or losses to be taken into account are those of the parent and its subsidiary undertakings (after making any consolidation adjustments).

20(3) The equity method of accounting need not be applied if the amounts in question are not material for the purpose of giving a true and fair view.

Deferred tax balances

20A Deferred tax balances must be recognised on consolidation where it is probable that a charge to tax will arise within the foreseeable future for one of the undertakings included in the consolidation.

History – Para. 20A and the heading preceding it inserted by SI 2015/980, reg. 22(12), with effect in relation to–

(a) financial years beginning on or after 1 January 2016, and
(b) a financial year of a company beginning on or after 1 January 2015, but before 1 January 2016, if the directors of the company so decide.

Related party transactions

20B Paragraph 66 of Schedule 1 to these Regulations applies to transactions which the parent company, or other undertakings included in the consolidation, have entered into with related parties, unless they are intra-group transactions.

History – Para. 20B and the heading preceding it inserted by SI 2015/980, reg. 22(12), with effect in relation to–

   (a) financial years beginning on or after 1 January 2016, and
   (b) a financial year of a company beginning on or after 1 January 2015, but before 1 January 2016, if the directors of the company so decide.

PART 2 – INFORMATION ABOUT RELATED UNDERTAKINGS WHERE COMPANY PREPARING GROUP ACCOUNTS (COMPANIES ACT OR IAS GROUP ACCOUNTS)

Introduction and interpretation

21 In this Part of this Schedule "the group" means the group consisting of the parent company and its subsidiary undertakings.

Subsidiary undertakings

22(1) The following information must be given with respect to the undertakings that are subsidiary undertakings of the parent company at the end of the financial year.

22(2) The name of each undertaking must be stated.

22(3) There must be stated–

   (a) the address of the undertaking's registered office (whether in or outside the United Kingdom),
   (b) if it is unincorporated, the address of its principal place of business.

22(4) It must also be stated whether the subsidiary undertaking is included in the consolidation and, if it is not, the reasons for excluding it from consolidation must be given.

22(5) It must be stated with respect to each subsidiary undertaking by virtue of which of the conditions specified in section 1162(2) or (4) of the 2006 Act it is a subsidiary undertaking of its immediate parent undertaking.

That information need not be given if the relevant condition is that specified in subsection (2)(a) of that section (holding of a majority of the voting rights) and the immediate parent undertaking holds the same proportion of the shares in the undertaking as it holds voting rights.

History – Para. 22(3)(a) substituted by SI 2015/980, reg. 23(2), with effect in relation to–

   (a) financial years beginning on or after 1 January 2016, and
   (b) a financial year of a company beginning on or after 1 January 2015, but before 1 January 2016, if the directors of the company so decide.

Holdings in subsidiary undertakings

23(1) The following information must be given with respect to the shares of a subsidiary undertaking held–

   (a) by the parent company, and
   (b) by the group, and the information under paragraphs (a) and (b) must (if different) be shown separately.

23(2) There must be stated–

    (a)   the identity of each class of shares held, and

    (b)   the proportion of the nominal value of the shares of that class represented by those shares.

Financial information about subsidiary undertakings not included in the consolidation

24(1) There must be shown with respect to each subsidiary undertaking not included in the consolidation–

    (a)   the aggregate amount of its capital and reserves as at the end of its relevant financial year, and

    (b)   its profit or loss for that year.

24(2) That information need not be given if the group's investment in the undertaking is included in the accounts by way of the equity method of valuation or if–

    (a)   the undertaking is not required by any provision of the 2006 Act to deliver a copy of its balance sheet for its relevant financial year and does not otherwise publish that balance sheet in the United Kingdom or elsewhere, and

    (b)   the holding of the group is less than 50% of the nominal value of the shares in the undertaking.

24(3) Information otherwise required by this paragraph need not be given if it is not material.

24(4) For the purposes of this paragraph the "relevant financial year" of a subsidiary undertaking is–

    (a)   if its financial year ends with that of the company, that year, and

    (b)   if not, its financial year ending last before the end of the company's financial year.

Shares of company held by subsidiary undertakings

25(1) The number, description and amount of the shares in the company held by or on behalf of its subsidiary undertakings must be disclosed.

25(2) Sub-paragraph (1) does not apply in relation to shares in the case of which the subsidiary undertaking is concerned as personal representative or, subject as follows, as trustee.

25(3) The exception for shares in relation to which the subsidiary undertaking is concerned as trustee does not apply if the company or any of its subsidiary undertakings is beneficially interested under the trust, otherwise than by way of security only for the purposes of a transaction entered into by it in the ordinary course of a business which includes the lending of money.

25(4) Part 2 of Schedule 2 to these Regulations has effect for the interpretation of the reference in sub-paragraph (3) to a beneficial interest under a trust.

Joint ventures

26(1) The following information must be given where an undertaking is dealt with in the consolidated accounts by the method of proportional consolidation in accordance with paragraph 18 of this Schedule (joint ventures)–

    (a)   the name of the undertaking,

    (b)   the address of the undertaking's registered office (whether in or outside the United Kingdom),

(c) the factors on which joint management of the undertaking is based, and
(d) the proportion of the capital of the undertaking held by or on behalf of undertakings included in the consolidation.

26(2) Where the financial year of the undertaking did not end with that of the company, there must be stated the date on which a financial year of the undertaking last ended before that date.

History – Para. 26(1)(b) substituted by SI 2015/980, reg. 23(3), with effect in relation to–

(a) financial years beginning on or after 1 January 2016, and
(b) a financial year of a company beginning on or after 1 January 2015, but before 1 January 2016, if the directors of the company so decide.

In para. 26(1)(d), the words "or on behalf of" inserted by SI 2015/980, reg. 23(4), with effect in relation to–

(a) financial years beginning on or after 1 January 2016, and
(b) a financial year of a company beginning on or after 1 January 2015, but before 1 January 2016, if the directors of the company so decide.

Associated undertakings

27(1) The following information must be given where an undertaking included in the consolidation has an interest in an associated undertaking.

27(2) The name of the associated undertaking must be stated.

27(3) There must be stated–

(a) the address of the undertaking's registered office (whether in or outside the United Kingdom),
(b) if it is unincorporated, the address of its principal place of business.

27(4) The following information must be given with respect to the shares of the undertaking held–

(a) by the parent company, and
(b) by the group, and the information under paragraphs (a) and (b) must be shown separately.

27(5) There must be stated–

(a) the identity of each class of shares held, and
(b) the proportion of the nominal value of the shares of that class represented by those shares.

27(6) In this paragraph "associated undertaking" has the meaning given by paragraph 19 of this Schedule; and the information required by this paragraph must be given notwithstanding that paragraph 20(3) of this Schedule (materiality) applies in relation to the accounts themselves.

History – Para. 27(3)(a) substituted by SI 2015/980, reg. 23(5), with effect in relation to–

(a) financial years beginning on or after 1 January 2016, and
(b) a financial year of a company beginning on or after 1 January 2015, but before 1 January 2016, if the directors of the company so decide.

Other significant holdings of parent company or group

28(1) The information required by paragraphs 29 and 30 must be given where at the end of the financial year the parent company has a significant holding in an undertaking which is not one of its subsidiary undertakings and does not fall within paragraph 26 (joint ventures) or paragraph 27 (associated undertakings).

28(2) A holding is significant for this purpose if–

(a) it amounts to 20% or more of the nominal value of any class of shares in the undertaking, or
(b) the amount of the holding (as stated or included in the company's individual accounts) exceeds 20% of the amount of its assets (as so stated).

29(1) The name of the undertaking must be stated.

29(2) There must be stated–

(a) the address of the undertaking's registered office (whether in or outside the United Kingdom),
(b) if it is unincorporated, the address of its principal place of business.

29(3) The following information must be given with respect to the shares of the undertaking held by the parent company.

29(4) There must be stated–

(a) the identity of each class of shares held, and
(b) the proportion of the nominal value of the shares of that class represented by those shares.

History – Para. 29(2)(a) substituted by SI 2015/980, reg. 23(6), with effect in relation to–

(a) financial years beginning on or after 1 January 2016, and
(b) a financial year of a company beginning on or after 1 January 2015, but before 1 January 2016, if the directors of the company so decide.

30(1) There must also be stated–

(a) the aggregate amount of the capital and reserves of the undertaking as at the end of its relevant financial year, and
(b) its profit or loss for that year.

30(2) That information need not be given in respect of an undertaking if–

(a) the undertaking is not required by any provision of the 2006 Act to deliver a copy of its balance sheet for its relevant financial year and does not otherwise publish that balance sheet in the United Kingdom or elsewhere, and
(b) the company's holding is less than 50% of the nominal value of the shares in the undertaking.

30(3) Information otherwise required by this paragraph need not be given if it is not material.

30(4) For the purposes of this paragraph the "relevant financial year" of an undertaking is–

(a) if its financial year ends with that of the company, that year, and
(b) if not, its financial year ending last before the end of the company's financial year.

31(1) The information required by paragraphs 32 and 33 must be given where at the end of the financial year the group has a significant holding in an undertaking which is not a subsidiary undertaking of the parent company and does not fall within paragraph 26 (joint ventures) or paragraph 27 (associated undertakings).

31(2) A holding is significant for this purpose if–

    (a)   it amounts to 20% or more of the nominal value of any class of shares in the undertaking, or

    (b)   the amount of the holding (as stated or included in the group accounts) exceeds 20% of the amount of the group's assets (as so stated).

32(1) The name of the undertaking must be stated.

32(2) There must be stated–

    (a)   the address of the undertaking's registered office (whether in or outside the United Kingdom),

    (b)   if it is unincorporated, the address of its principal place of business.

32(3) The following information must be given with respect to the shares of the undertaking held by the group.

32(4) There must be stated–

    (a)   the identity of each class of shares held, and

    (b)   the proportion of the nominal value of the shares of that class represented by those shares.

History – Para. 32(2)(a) substituted by SI 2015/980, reg. 23(7), with effect in relation to–

    (a)   financial years beginning on or after 1 January 2016, and

    (b)   a financial year of a company beginning on or after 1 January 2015, but before 1 January 2016, if the directors of the company so decide.

33(1) There must also be stated–

    (a)   the aggregate amount of the capital and reserves of the undertaking as at the end of its relevant financial year, and

    (b)   its profit or loss for that year.

33(2) That information need not be given if–

    (a)   the undertaking is not required by any provision of the 2006 Act to deliver a copy of its balance sheet for its relevant financial year and does not otherwise publish that balance sheet in the United Kingdom or elsewhere, and

    (b)   the holding of the group is less than 50% of the nominal value of the shares in the undertaking.

33(3) Information otherwise required by this paragraph need not be given if it is not material.

33(4) For the purposes of this paragraph the "relevant financial year" of an outside undertaking is–

    (a)   if its financial year ends with that of the parent company, that year, and

    (b)   if not, its financial year ending last before the end of the parent company's financial year.

Parent company's or group's membership of certain undertakings

34(1) The information required by this paragraph must be given where at the end of the financial year the parent company or group is a member of a qualifying undertaking.

34(2) There must be stated–

(a) the name and legal form of the undertaking, and
(b) the address of the undertaking's registered office (whether in or outside the United (Kingdom) or, if it does not have such an office, its head office (whether in or outside the United Kingdom).

34(3) Where the undertaking is a qualifying partnership there must also be stated either–

(a) that a copy of the latest accounts of the undertaking has been or is to be appended to the copy of the company's accounts sent to the registrar under section 444 of the 2006 Act, or
(b) the name of at least one body corporate (which may be the company) in whose group accounts the undertaking has been or is to be dealt with on a consolidated basis.

34(4) Information otherwise required by sub-paragraph (2) need not be given if it is not material.

34(5) Information otherwise required by sub-paragraph (3)(b) need not be given if the notes to the company's accounts disclose that advantage has been taken of the exemption conferred by regulation 7 of the Partnerships (Accounts) Regulations 2008.

34(6) In sub-paragraph (1) "member", in relation to a qualifying undertaking which is a qualifying partnership, has the same meaning as in the Partnerships (Accounts) Regulations 2008.

34(7) In this paragraph–

"dealt with on a consolidated basis" and **"qualifying partnership"** have the same meanings as in the Partnerships (Accounts) Regulations 2008;
"qualifying undertaking" means–

(a) a qualifying partnership, or
(b) an unlimited company each of whose members is–

(i) a limited company,
(ii) another unlimited company each of whose members is a limited company,
(iii) a Scottish partnership which is not a limited partnership, each of whose members is a limited company, or
(iv) a Scottish partnership which is a limited partnership, each of whose general partners is a limited company.

34(8) In sub-paragraph (7) the references to a limited company, another unlimited company, a Scottish partnership which is not a limited partnership or a Scottish partnership which is a limited partnership include a comparable undertaking incorporated in or formed under the law of a country or territory outside the United Kingdom.

34(9) In sub-paragraph (7) "general partner" means–

(a) in relation to a Scottish partnership which is a limited partnership, a person who is a general partner within the meaning of the Limited Partnerships Act 1907, and
(b) in relation to an undertaking incorporated in or formed under the law of any country or territory outside the United Kingdom and which is comparable to a Scottish partnership which is a limited partnership, a person comparable to such a general partner.

34(10) In sub-paragraphs (7), (8) and (9) "limited partnership" means a partnership registered under the Limited Partnerships Act 1907.

History – Para. 34(5), "Partnerships (Accounts) Regulations 2008" substituted for "Partnerships and Unlimited Companies (Accounts) Regulations 1993" by SI 2008/569, reg. 17(1)(b), with effect from 6 April 2008.

Para. 34(6) substituted and 34(7)–(10) inserted by SI 2013/2005, reg. 5, with effect from 1 September 2013 applying in relation to a financial year of a company beginning on or after 1 October 2013. The version of para. 34 applying to financial years beginning before 1 October 2013 read as follows:

34(1) The information required by this paragraph must be given where at the end of the financial year the parent company or group is a member of a qualifying undertaking.

34(2) There must be stated–

(a) the name and legal form of the undertaking, and
(b) the address of the undertaking's registered office (whether in or outside the United (Kingdom) or, if it does not have such an office, its head office (whether in or outside the United Kingdom).

34(3) Where the undertaking is a qualifying partnership there must also be stated either–

(a) that a copy of the latest accounts of the undertaking has been or is to be appended to the copy of the company's accounts sent to the registrar under section 444 of the 2006 Act, or
(b) the name of at least one body corporate (which may be the company) in whose group accounts the undertaking has been or is to be dealt with on a consolidated basis.

34(4) Information otherwise required by sub-paragraph (2) need not be given if it is not material.

34(5) Information otherwise required by sub-paragraph (3)(b) need not be given if the notes to the company's accounts disclose that advantage has been taken of the exemption conferred by regulation 7 of the Partnerships (Accounts) Regulations 2008.

34(6) In this paragraph–

"dealt with on a consolidated basis", "member" and **"qualifying partnership"** have the same meanings as in the Partnerships (Accounts) Regulations 2008;

"qualifying undertaking" means–

(a) a qualifying partnership, or
(b) an unlimited company each of whose members is–

(i) a limited company,
(ii) another unlimited company each of whose members is a limited company, or
(iii) a Scottish partnership each of whose members is a limited company, and references in this paragraph to a limited company, another unlimited company or a Scottish partnership include a comparable undertaking incorporated in or formed under the law of a country or territory outside the United Kingdom.

Parent undertaking drawing up accounts for larger group

35(1) Where the parent company is itself a subsidiary undertaking, the following information must be given with respect to that parent undertaking of the company which heads–

(a) the largest group of undertakings for which group accounts are drawn up and of which that company is a member, and
(b) the smallest such group of undertakings.

35(2) The name of the parent undertaking must be stated.

35(3) There must be stated–

    (a) if the undertaking is incorporated outside the United Kingdom, the country in which it is incorporated,

    (b) if it is unincorporated, the address of its principal place of business.

35(4) If copies of the group accounts referred to in sub-paragraph (1) are available to the public, there must also be stated the addresses from which copies of the accounts can be obtained.

Identification of ultimate parent company

36(1) Where the parent company is itself a subsidiary undertaking, the following information must be given with respect to the company (if any) regarded by the directors as being that company's ultimate parent company.

36(2) The name of that company must be stated.

36(3) If that company is incorporated outside the United Kingdom, the country in which it is incorporated must be stated (if known to the directors).

36(4) In this paragraph "company" includes any body corporate.

Construction of references to shares held by parent company or group

37(1) References in this Part of this Schedule to shares held by the parent company or the group are to be construed as follows.

37(2) For the purposes of paragraphs 23, 27(4) and (5) and 28 to 30 (information about holdings in subsidiary and other undertakings)–

    (a) there must be attributed to the parent company shares held on its behalf by any person; but

    (b) there must be treated as not held by the parent company shares held on behalf of a person other than the company.

37(3) References to shares held by the group are to any shares held by or on behalf of the parent company or any of its subsidiary undertakings; but any shares held on behalf of a person other than the parent company or any of its subsidiary undertakings are not to be treated as held by the group.

37(4) Shares held by way of security must be treated as held by the person providing the security–

    (a) where apart from the right to exercise them for the purpose of preserving the value of the security, or of realising it, the rights attached to the shares are exercisable only in accordance with his instructions, and

    (b) where the shares are held in connection with the granting of loans as part of normal business activities and apart from the right to exercise them for the purpose of preserving the value of the security, or of realising it, the rights attached to the shares are exercisable only in his interests.

SCHEDULE 7   Regulation 12

INTERPRETATION OF TERM "PROVISIONS"

PART 1 – MEANING FOR PURPOSES OF THESE REGULATIONS

Definition of "provisions"

1(1) In these Regulations, references to provisions for depreciation or diminution in value of assets are to any amount written off by way of providing for depreciation or diminution in value of assets.

1(2) Any reference in the profit and loss account formats set out in Part 1 of Schedule 1 to these Regulations to the depreciation of, or amounts written off, assets of any description is to any provision for depreciation or diminution in value of assets of that description.

2 References in these Regulations to provisions for liabilities are to any amount retained as reasonably necessary for the purpose of providing for any liability the nature of which is clearly defined and which is either likely to be incurred, or certain to be incurred but uncertain as to amount or as to the date on which it will arise.

2A At the balance sheet date, a provision must represent the best estimate of the expenses likely to be incurred or, in the case of a liability, of the amount required to meet that liability.

History – Para. 2A inserted by SI 2015/980, reg. 24, with effect in relation to–

    (a) financial years beginning on or after 1 January 2016, and
    (b) a financial year of a company beginning on or after 1 January 2015, but before 1 January 2016, if the directors of the company so decide.

2B Provisions must not be used to adjust the values of assets.

History – Para. 2B inserted by SI 2015/980, reg. 24, with effect in relation to–

    (a) financial years beginning on or after 1 January 2016, and
    (b) a financial year of a company beginning on or after 1 January 2015, but before 1 January 2016, if the directors of the company so decide.

PART 2 – MEANING FOR PURPOSES OF PARTS 18 AND 23 OF THE 2006 ACT

Financial assistance for purchase of own shares

3 The specified provisions for the purposes of section 677(3)(a) of the 2006 Act (Companies Act accounts: relevant provisions for purposes of financial assistance) are provisions for liabilities within paragraph 2 of this Schedule.

Redemption or purchase by private company out of capital

4 The specified provisions for the purposes of section 712(2)(b)(i) of the 2006 Act (Companies Act accounts: relevant provisions to determine available profits for redemption or purchase out of capital) are provisions of any of the kinds mentioned in paragraphs 1 and 2 of this Schedule.

Justification of distribution by references to accounts

5 The specified provisions for the purposes of section 836(1)(b)(i) of the 2006 Act (Companies Act accounts: relevant provisions for distribution purposes) are provisions of any of the kinds mentioned in paragraphs 1 and 2 of this Schedule.

Realised losses

6 The specified provisions for the purposes of section 841(2)(a) of the 2006 Act (Companies Act accounts: treatment of provisions as realised losses) are provisions of any of the kinds mentioned in paragraphs 1 and 2 of this Schedule.

Notes – Paragraph 6 inserted by SI 2009/1581 reg 11(1) and (3): 27 June 2009 applying in relation to financial years beginning on or after 6 April 2008 which have not ended before 27 June 2009

SCHEDULE 8   Regulation 13

GENERAL INTERPRETATION

Financial instruments

1 References to "**derivatives**" include commodity-based contracts that give either contracting party the right to settle in cash or in some other financial instrument, except where such contracts–

  (a) were entered into for the purpose of, and continue to meet, the company's expected purchase, sale or usage requirements,
  (b) were designated for such purpose at their inception, and
  (c) are expected to be settled by delivery of the commodity.

2(1)   The expressions listed in sub-paragraph (2) have the same meaning as they have in Directive 2013/34/EU of the European Parliament and of the Council of 26 June 2013 on the annual financial statements etc of certain types of undertakings.

2(2) Those expressions are "available for sale financial asset", "business combination", "commodity-based contracts", "derivative", "equity instrument", "exchange difference", "fair value hedge accounting system", "financial fixed asset", "financial instrument", "foreign entity", "hedge accounting", "hedge accounting system", "hedged items", "hedging instrument", "held for trading purposes", "held to maturity", "monetary item", "receivables", "reliable market" and "trading portfolio".

History – Para. 2(1) substituted by SI 2015/980, reg. 25(2), with effect in relation to–

  (a) financial years beginning on or after 1 January 2016, and
  (b) a financial year of a company beginning on or after 1 January 2015, but before 1 January 2016, if the directors of the company so decide.

Former para. 2(1) read as follows:

2(1) The expressions listed in sub-paragraph (2) have the same meaning as they have in Council Directive 78/660/EEC on the annual accounts of certain types of companies.

Fixed and current assets

3 "**Fixed assets**" means assets of a company which are intended for use on a continuing basis in the company's activities, and "current assets" means assets not intended for such use.

Historical cost accounting rules

4 References to the historical cost accounting rules are to be read in accordance with paragraph 30 of Schedule 1 to these Regulations.

Listed investments

5(1) "Listed investment" means an investment as respects which there has been granted a listing on–

(a)   a recognised investment exchange other than an overseas investment exchange, or
(b)   a stock exchange of repute outside the United Kingdom.

5(2) "Recognised investment exchange" and "overseas investment exchange" have the meaning given in Part 18 of the Financial Services and Markets Act 2000.

Loans

6   A loan is treated as falling due for repayment, and an instalment of a loan is treated as falling due for payment, on the earliest date on which the lender could require repayment or (as the case may be) payment, if he exercised all options and rights available to him.

Materiality

7 Amounts which in the particular context of any provision of Schedule 1 to these Regulations are not material may be disregarded for the purposes of that provision.

Participating interests

8(1)   A "participating interest" means an interest held by an undertaking in the shares of another undertaking which it holds on a long-term basis for the purpose of securing a contribution to its activities by the exercise of control or influence arising from or related to that interest.

8(2)   A holding of 20% or more of the shares of the undertaking is to be presumed to be a participating interest unless the contrary is shown.

8(3)   The reference in sub-paragraph (1) to an interest in shares includes–

(a)   an interest which is convertible into an interest in shares, and
(b)   an option to acquire shares or any such interest, and an interest or option falls within paragraph (a) or (b) notwithstanding that the shares to which it relates are, until the conversion or the exercise of the option, unissued.

8(4)   For the purposes of this paragraph an interest held on behalf of an undertaking is to be treated as held by it.

8(5)   In the balance sheet and profit and loss formats set out in Section B of Part 1 of Schedule 1 to these Regulations, "participating interest" does not include an interest in a group undertaking.

8(6)   For the purpose of this paragraph as it applies in relation to the expression "participating interest"–

(a)   in those formats as they apply in relation to group accounts, and
(b)   in paragraph 19 of Schedule 6 (group accounts: undertakings to be accounted for as associated undertakings), the references in sub-paragraphs (1) to (4) to the interest held by, and the purposes and activities of, the undertaking concerned are to be construed as

references to the interest held by, and the purposes and activities of, the group (within the meaning of paragraph 1 of that Schedule).

History – In para. 8(5), "Section B of" inserted by SI 2013/3008, reg. 13(1) and (2), with effect from 1 December 2013 in respect of (a) financial years ending on or after 30 September 2013; and (b) companies, which deliver the accounts required by s. 444 to the registrar on or after 1 December 2013.

In para. 8(5), the words "and Part 1 of Schedule 4" omitted by SI 2015/980, reg. 25(3), with effect in relation to–

(a) financial years beginning on or after 1 January 2016, and
(b) a financial year of a company beginning on or after 1 January 2015, but before 1 January 2016, if the directors of the company so decide.

Purchase price

9 "Purchase price", in relation to an asset of a company or any raw materials or consumables used in the production of such an asset, includes any consideration (whether in cash or otherwise) given by the company in respect of that asset or those materials or consumables, as the case may be.

Realised profits and losses

10 "Realised profits" and "realised losses" have the same meaning as in section 853(4) and (5) of the 2006 Act.

Staff costs

11(1) "Social security costs" means any contributions by the company to any state social security or pension scheme, fund or arrangement.

11(2) "Pension costs" includes–

(a) any costs incurred by the company in respect of any pension scheme established for the purpose of providing pensions for persons currently or formerly employed by the company,
(b) any sums set aside for the future payment of pensions directly by the company to current or former employees, and
(c) any pensions paid directly to such persons without having first been set aside.

11(3) Any amount stated in respect of the item "social security costs" or in respect of the item "wages and salaries" in the profit and loss account Format 2 in Section B of Part 1 of Schedule 1 must be determined by reference to payments made or costs incurred in respect of all persons employed by the company during the financial year under contracts of service.

History – In para. 11(3), "the profit and loss account Formats 2 and 4 in Section B of Part 1 of Schedule 1" substituted for "the company's profit and loss account" by SI 2013/3008, reg. 13(1) and (3), with effect from 1 December 2013 in respect of (a) financial years ending on or after 30 September 2013; and (b) companies, which deliver the accounts required by s. 444 to the registrar on or after 1 December 2013.

In para. 11(3), the words "Format 2" substituted for the words "Formats 2 and 4" by SI 2015/980, reg. 25(4), with effect in relation to–

(a) financial years beginning on or after 1 January 2016, and
(b) a financial year of a company beginning on or after 1 January 2015, but before 1 January 2016, if the directors of the company so decide.

Appendix C　Model accounts

Example set of micro-entity financial statements prepared in accordance with FRS 105
The Financial Reporting Standard applicable to the Micro-entity regime

The example financial statements illustrate the disclosures and formats that are expected for a company that:

(a)　qualifies as a micro-entity as defined in CA 2006, s. 393(1A); and

(b)　chooses to apply the micro-entity regime.

FRS 105 uses the same terminology as FRS 102 and so refers to the primary statements as an 'Income Statement' and a 'Statement of Financial Position'. FRS 105 allows other titles for these statements to be used as long as they are not misleading. It is, therefore, expected that most micro-entities will continue to refer to these statements as the profit and loss account and balance sheet and this terminology has been used in these example financial statements.

An alternative presentation of the balance sheet (using format 2) is also shown.

These example financial statements illustrate the content as prepared for the members of the company. The company can omit the profit and loss account when the financial statements are delivered to the Registrar of Companies.

Company's Registered Number [   ]

MICRO TRADING LIMITED

Report and unaudited financial statements for the year ended

31 December 2016

MICRO TRADING LIMITED

DIRECTORS AND ADVISERS *

Directors

Registered office

Company's registered number

although it is common practice to give the above information, there is no requirement to do so, and this page may be omitted.

Appendix C

MICRO TRADING LIMITED

CONTENTS	PAGE

MICRO TRADING LIMITED

PROFIT AND LOSS ACCOUNT for the year ended 31 DECEMBER 2016

	2016 £	2015 £
Turnover	X	X
Other income	X	X
Cost of raw material and consumables	(X)	(X)
Staff costs	(X)	(X)
Depreciation and other amounts written off assets	(X)	(X)
Other charges	(X)	(X)
Tax	(X)	(X)
Profit/(loss) for the year	X/(X)	X/(X)

Appendix C

MICRO TRADING LIMITED

BALANCE SHEET as at 31 DECEMBER 201x

		201x £		201x £
Called up share capital not paid		X		X
Fixed assets		X		X
Current assets	X		X	X
Prepayments and accrued income	X		X	
Creditors: amounts falling due within one year	(X)		(X)	
Net current assets/(liabilities)		X/(X)		X/(X)
Total assets less current liabilities		X		X
Creditors: amounts falling due after more than one year		(X)		(X)
Provisions for liabilities		(X)		(X)
Accruals and deferred income		(X)		(X)
Net assets				
Capital and reserves				

Notes

(1) Director's benefit: advances, credits and guarantees

During the year, the company advanced £xxx (2015: £xxx) to a director of the company. During the year, amounts of £xxx (2015: £xxx) were repaid to the company. The maximum outstanding during the year was £xxx. The total outstanding at year end was £xxx (2015: £xxx).

(2) Guarantees and other financial commitments

The bank loans totalling £xxx (2015: £xxx) are secured by a fixed and floating charge over the assets of the company.

These accounts have been prepared in accordance with the micro-entity provisions in the *Companies Act* 2006, Pt. 15 and FRS 105 the Financial Reporting Standard applicable to the Micro-entities Regime.

For the financial year ended 31 December 2016, the company was entitled to exemption from audit under the *Companies Act* 2006, s. 477; and no notice has been deposited under s. 476.

The directors acknowledge their responsibilities for complying with the requirements of the *Companies Act* 2006 with respect to accounting records and the preparation of accounts.

The financial statements were approved and authorised for issue by the Board of Directors on .... and were signed on its behalf by:

A Director

Director

Company Registered Number: [   ]

224

ALTERNATIVE (FORMAT 2) PRESENTATION OF THE BALANCE SHEET

	2016	2015
	£	£
Assets		
Called up share capital not paid	X	X
Fixed assets	X	X
Current assets	X	X
Prepayments and accrued income	X	X
	X	X
Capital, Reserves and Liabilities		
Capital and reserves	X	X
Provisions for liabilities	X	X
Creditors		
Amounts falling due within one year	X	X
Amounts falling due after one year	X	X
Accruals and deferred income	X	X
	X	X

(Notes and other statements as above)

Index